LIVE
JUSTLY.
LOVE
ABUNDANTLY.
WALK
HUMBLY.

GOODNESS

WISING UP ANTHOLOGIES

ILLNESS & GRACE: TERROR & TRANSFORMATION

FAMILIES: *The Frontline of Pluralism*

LOVE AFTER 70

DOUBLE LIVES, REINVENTION & THOSE WE LEAVE BEHIND

VIEW FROM THE BED: VIEW FROM THE BEDSIDE

SHIFTING BALANCE SHEETS:
Women's Stories of Naturalized Citizenship & Cultural Attachment

COMPLEX ALLEGIANCES:
Constellations of Immigration, Citizenship, & Belonging

DARING TO REPAIR: *What Is It, Who Does It & Why?*

CONNECTED: *What Remains As We All Change*

CREATIVITY & CONSTRAINT

SIBLINGS: *Our First Macrocosm*

THE KINDNESS OF STRANGERS

SURPRISED BY JOY

CROSSING CLASS: *The Invisible Wall*

RE-CREATING OUR COMMON CHORD

GOODNESS

A Wising Up Anthology

Charles D. Brockett & Heather Tosteson
Editors

Wising Up Press

Wising Up Press
P.O. Box 2122
Decatur, GA 30031-2122
www.universaltable.org

Catalogue-in-Publication data is on file with the Library of Congress.
LCCN: 2020948848

Wising Up ISBN: 978-1-7324514-7-6

To All of Us:
Past, Present, Future

TABLE OF CONTENTS

III. COMMUNITY

IV. FAMILY

V. ILLNESS/CARE

VI. WHOLE OF LIFE

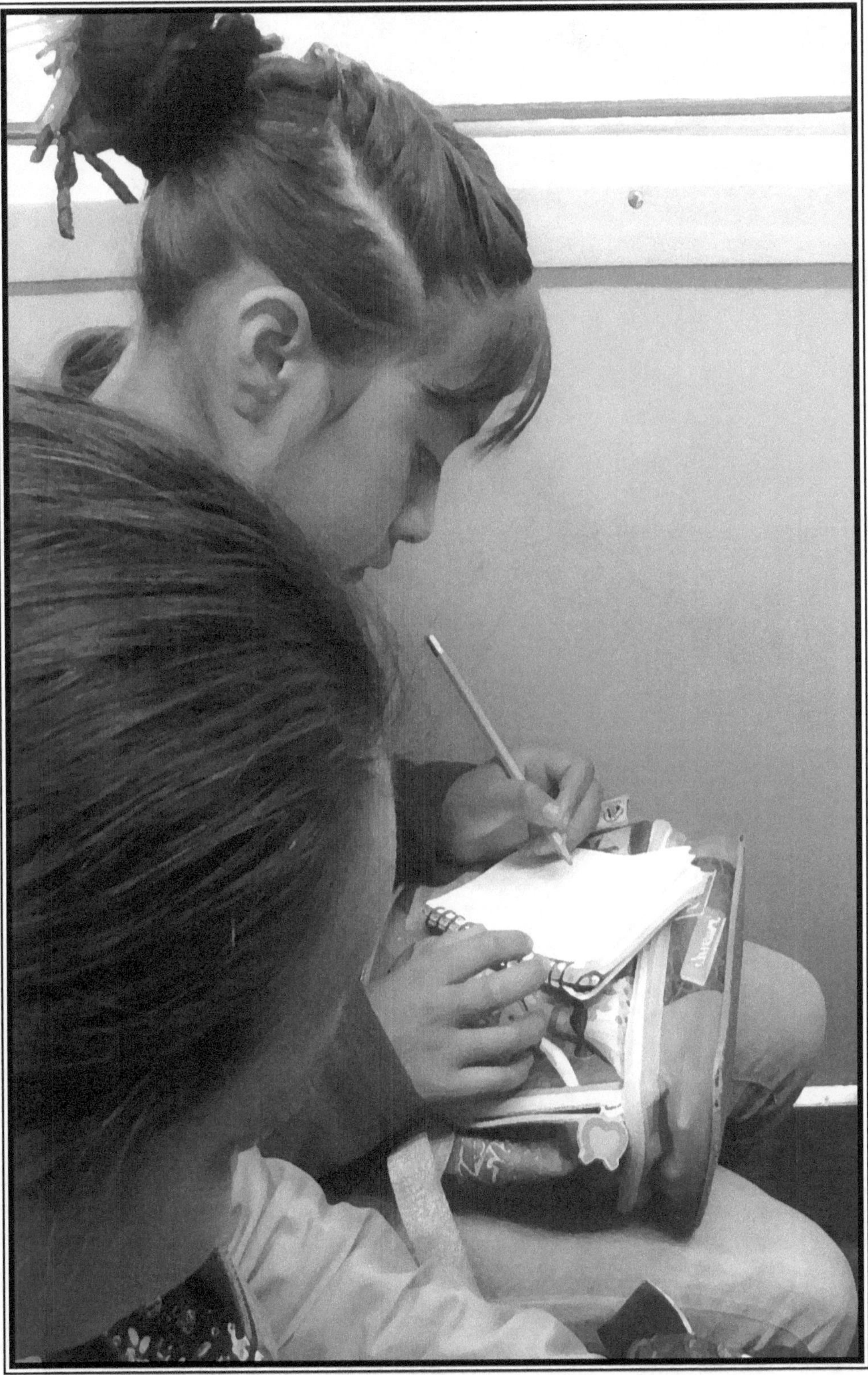

TMNT

HEATHER TOSTESON

GOODNESS: We Know It When We See It

Goodness is hard to define, but we know it when we see it. In action or inaction, that pause that isn't uncertain, that is more like a deep, steady breath, an existential embrace. It is easier to see goodness in others than in ourselves. But do we experience it as a choice or part of their essential nature? If a choice, what is the nature of the choice? What other adjectives constellate around it? Strong? Independent? Loving? Astute? Generous? Sui generis? Trusting? Confident? Firm? Unequivocal? Kind?

Where have you seen goodness in play? How has it changed your own life, the actual choices you make or how you evaluate your choices? Is there a cascade effect? Or is it, in its specificity, always a one-off? What happens to us when we think about it, try to describe it, share our experiences of it with others?

Our Wising Up anthology calls are invitations to others to join us in feeling and thinking our way deeper into an idea or experience that is of active interest to us personally. Sometimes that personal dimension has abated somewhat by the time we receive submissions. Sometimes the subject isn't of interest to others, so we go on to explore it in more private ways. But it feels that contemplating goodness—what it is, where we've experienced it in our own lives, how it affects our relationships with others and the world at large—is, if anything, of more interest to ourselves and to others now than when we first proposed the idea for the anthology.

My original interest was simply a reaction to the tenor of our society now, how quick we are to find and expand on the negative in each other. I am tired of it. *Really* tired of it. And frightened of it as well because I feel there is a tipping point in a society when too many people engage in this kind of polarizing negativity, a point where we become addicted to seeing the worst in each other and the world around us, and I do *not* want to reach it. My interest in finding ways to reset this balance has only grown more acute as we face a deeply contentious election, the aftermath of mass protests and counter protests, and a pandemic. Our responses to each of these reveals how profound and entrenched the polarization in our society has become, how almost nothing in our lives, even our responses to deadly viruses, is untouched by it.

Just thinking about goodness, raising it up as a live and potent term and inviting others to join us in thinking of it, is one way of weighting the scales in the favor of a common good. We each have that power however this election plays out—and however this election plays out, that power will be needed because the toxic habits of division have become so entrenched in us all. Media, with its twenty-four-hour-a-day focus on the negative, heightens this—as does social media, with its encouragement of herd thinking that emphasizes an us/them, in/out mentality without the constraints of real-life reminders that we are *all* flesh and blood, that we are *all* valuable, needy, giving, vulnerable, that what we say matters as much as what we do, *that we each have the power to do well by each other.*

So, with that said, I turn with relief to goodness—as a concept and, most importantly, as an experience. As we said in our submission call, goodness is something that we may find hard to define but that we can readily recognize. *Recognition* is itself an important dimension of the experience of goodness. There is something essentially retrospective about goodness. It isn't an emotion or sensation, it is a cognition, a thought, a thought about a fundamentally positive emotional experience, one that shapes that experience retrospectively and gives it standing in our conceptual world.

This has long precedent: Take, for example, the first chapter of Genesis. For six days running, God was busy making light, seas, earth, plants, day and night, whales, cattle, man, and, at the end of each day, after taking a long look, *saw that it was good.* In other words, God was in conversation with something larger than consciousness that defined the experience positively. God was pleasantly surprised. What would have happened if that assessment were more equivocal?

I may have been primed for my own interest in the alternate because as a strong-willed little girl with messy blond curls, I was often greeted with this rhyme:

There was a little girl
with a little curl
right in the middle of her forehead.

And when she was good,
she was very very good,
and when she was bad
she was horrid.

It feels when we think about goodness, there are two quite different experiences involved. One begins with an abstract concept we strive to realize. The way a child taunted with a poem like this might react by trying to understand what acts she needed to perform to "be" good. This idea of good has in it an essential devaluation of who and what we are now in favor of what we might be if brought into alignment with an inherited, often poorly described, abstract ideal. Just who is setting the terms of that ideal, though, is confusing. Someone raised to emulate saints might see self-mortification as an essential—perhaps *the* essential quality—of goodness. What seems a common characteristic of this conception of goodness is that it is something that requires ceaseless, and perhaps unrequited, self-abnegating striving. It isn't essential to our nature, must be reached for, modeled, imitated.

There is another way of looking at, *experiencing*, goodness that is common to creation of all kinds: that moment when we pause and *recognize*, with surprise and delight and edification, that what we have created is good. Good in this sense is a visceral as well as mental response. It is about finding a name for something profoundly positive. It *redefines* our experience. That redefinition involves a kind of knowing that is greater than immediate experience, receptive. Modest. It is what D.H. Lawrence refers to when he talks about "not me but the wind that moves through me."

This awareness is not limited to artistic creation. An even better example is what parents feel when they look at their newborn infant who is both their creation and also so far beyond their capacities to imagine, let alone consciously create, that they are filled with awe, gratitude, and a deep sense of responsibility. They want to align and care for that living and breathing good before them, which they recognize is more, so much more, than they are but that is also inextricably of them too.

Often when writing or talking or thinking about goodness, people tended to focus back another generation to experiences with their grandparents. In part this may be because as children we experienced a more benign appreciation from our grandparents than was possible in the more intense relationships we had with our parents. It may also be that children are more global in their perceptions—so are more open to a pervasiveness of atmosphere and body state that when it finds a home in a word, like goodness, can be reactivated as something that is both ideal *and* experientially located. In other words, these redefinitions of experiences from just that-which-is to goodness mean that goodness is possible in the here and now.

The power of being seen as good has lasting impact—and also may be part of why people when they try to describe goodness return to very early experiences of acceptance. Two of the people who had the greatest impact on me as a child, my paternal grandmother and the nanny who cared for me my first eighteen months, delighted in me. I think that experience was foundational, and continuously transforming—it was not just that they were loving to me but they saw good in me, and I could feel that. This created a resilient and relational ground of being that I have been able to draw on repeatedly, even in moments of despair. I experienced love from them and for them as a resonant body state. I understood at a level before thought: We can *make* good together. That knowledge was deeply empowering.

I once remarked that I didn't have any problem having all my friends in the same room because I was the same with all of them—and also because I had a taste for goodness, a quality that I recognized in all my friends and, I believed, they would recognize that quality in each other however different their beliefs, temperaments, or life experiences. My experience has been that that is true, although how any one of them would define that quality in another—or if they would recognize it in themselves—is not so clear.

But I've returned to that observation as we've been reading through the poems, stories and essays that make up this book because I believe there are some qualities that are common to those whom we experience as good. They are interested in other people, see other people in a way that is clear-eyed and also faithful. They *experience* our value and show us that they do in their actions and words. Resilient and idealistic realists, they *know* we are capable of goodwill and good faith and invite us back to that place repeatedly by example.

One of the people who most embodied these qualities for me was my father-in-law. Ed was a member of the greatest generation, serving on a warship in the Pacific when he was seventeen. He helped raise six children with a wife who at times was hospitalized for postpartum psychosis. Even so, he and his wife, Joyce, herself a very kind and caring person, maintained a relationship of striking respect and equality, in part because Ed never lost sight of her strengths, the light in her, or allowed her to do so either. One of his nieces, who he took in as an adopted daughter, described how he, finding her in an alcoholic stupor, scooped her up in his arms and said without any judgment, "You're going to be all right." His care and his confidence helped her turn her life around. At his death, all his children and grandchildren laughingly joked about how they each were sure all their lives that they were the favored one.

Another person who embodied the qualities I associate most with goodness was Alicia, a woman I met in Antigua, Guatemala, when she came to my house asking if she could clean it as she had done for its prior inhabitant. She soon became my Spanish tutor instead because her Spanish was so clear. She thought this was amusing since she had been working since she was five in the coffee plantations so had never gone to school. Alicia was illiterate but had made sure her children went to school. Her son taught Spanish with the Peace Corps. She was an extremely small woman with a very large heart. She invited us to the substantial concrete house that she and her husband had built over the years, showing us how they had moved up brick by brick from a house built of *palos,* sticks, to this sturdy, hospitable one. We walked with her up the steep path to the fields where her husband worked, a path she would often climb daily to bring him lunch, a child on her back and one on either side. She was my indefatigable guide to all the processions of Holy Week. Alicia had a confidence and generosity and inner force that still resonate for me. I remember her spending several days with me wandering through neighboring villages trying to find a carpenter who I had heard made wooden hands. She never asked me why I wanted these, certainly not why I wanted them so urgently, just treated the desire as a soul hunger. That simple and profound acceptance, the generosity of it, is what I keep returning to when I think of her. She knew she had something valuable to give and did so freely.

One surprising place my experience of the nature of goodness has been fostered and enriched in the last five years, one that has important social implications, has been our listening project on reentry. We listened extensively and intensively to people throughout the criminal justice system here in Georgia, to ex-offenders, their families, community supervision officers, lawyers, chaplains, legislators, and commissioners of corrections—with only one important precondition for ourselves: *We were committed to listening in good faith.*

That commitment to good faith opened to us a very different way of understanding and responding to one of the most complex and painful dimensions of our society—a way that didn't allow us to disregard any person's perspective as false or without value. It also introduced us to many many good people throughout the system—generous, caring, clear-eyed, responsible, and committed people, who were faithful in a way that filled us with hope and admiration. At times this good faith commitment definitely required we release some closely held preconceptions and prejudices, or made us see ourselves in ways that did not feel comfortable, but the result has been a grounded optimism and a willingness to engage in more nuanced ways, that *don't* assume ill intent, that listen for what someone else understands as good and *why* they feel that way.

Something happens to us when we choose to see others, especially those whose vision of the world differs from ours, as having the same complexity of motives, the same nuance, the same experience of good in them that we give to those who see the world as we do. Something happens to how we understand ourselves when we commit to putting faith back into all the individuals who make up such a complex system. I continue to believe that consistently acting that way and inviting others to do the same will also change our systems—for good.

This brings me to an important dimension of goodness: it is active. What my grandmother and my nana did, what my "good" friends do, what the good people we met throughout the criminal justice system, from people who served several life sentences to supervision officers who worked an equal number of years helping people transition back, is use their power to bless. They see and respond to the good in others, thereby potentiating it further, giving it traction in the world. Most of them would not describe this as being good or doing good—just treating others the way they would like to be treated themselves.

In the stories, poems, and essays we include here, we have people exploring what goodness means in many different contexts: social justice, community, families, illness, age. A writer offers hospitality to a homeless man for a year and possibly learns more about himself than about his guest. A woman follows her "little brother" in and out of the criminal justice system, broadening her own ideas of what it means to keep faith with his promise. Men and women returning from prison try to make that transition easier for others. Neighbors quietly befriend each other, seeing beyond querulousness to profound grief; boys develop a lifetime bond absorbing the impact of a tragic accident. Families that didn't understand themselves as cohesive come together in response to the illness of one of their members and in the process change their understanding of themselves as families. People looking back at their lives begin to see them afresh, redefining an arc that often felt painful and confusing, as fundamentally good.

What all these stories share is a sense that the presence of goodness—and our participation in it it—shapes us even more profoundly than its absence. To live that difference is, repeatedly, a choice we do have control over. We *do* have the power to say yes to the best in ourselves and in each other, to bless.

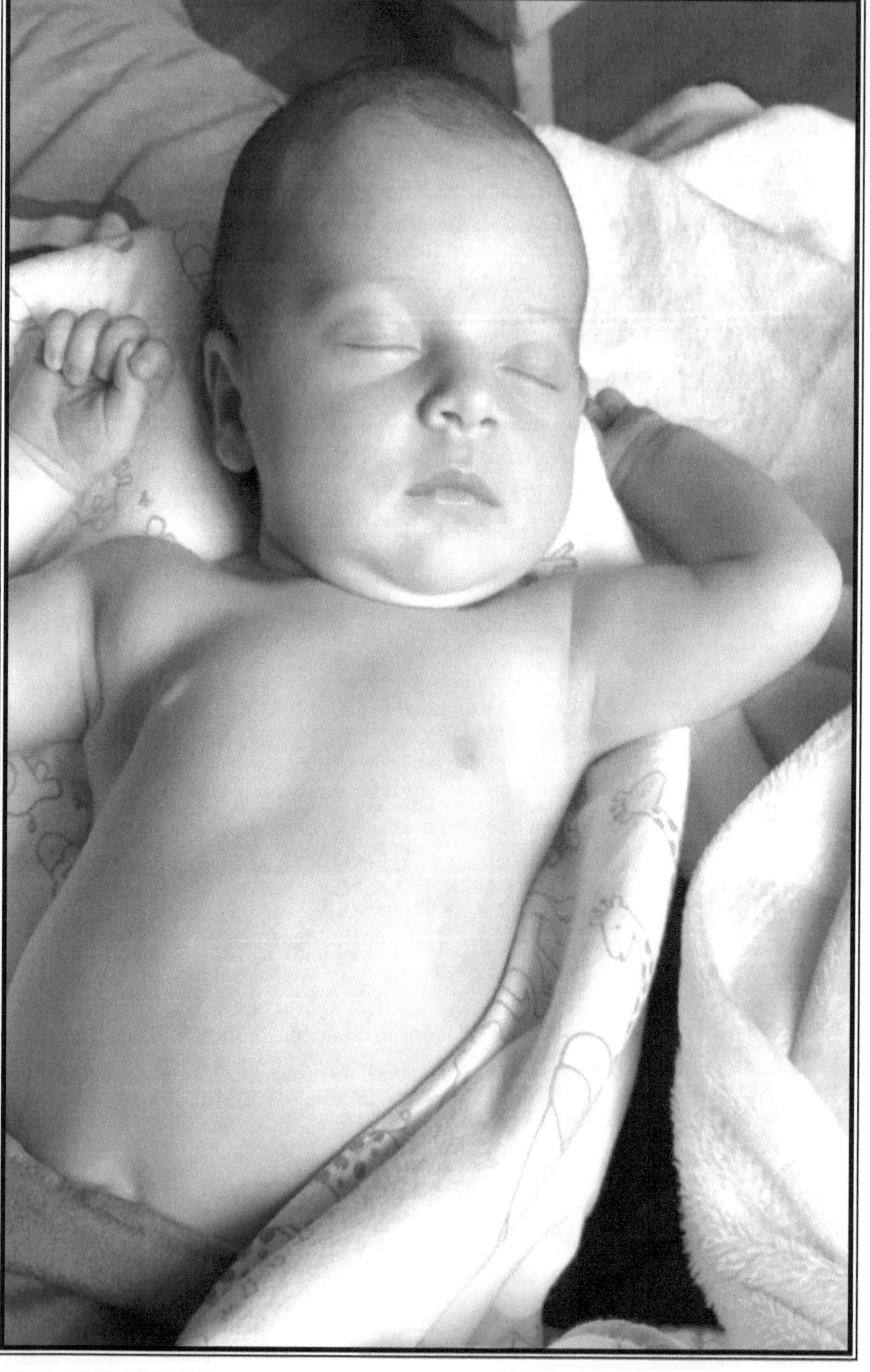

I.
THE IDEA OF GOODNESS

LEE GAITAN

GOODNESS AT 3 A.M.

If goodness were a smell, surely it would be the intoxicating scent of a baby's head. With a little tomato rice soup on the side and a splash of my husband's cologne. Through some magical process that defies scientific principles, the molecules of these smells enter directly into my soul and cause it to vibrate at the same frequency as goodness. Or maybe that's bliss. Or even its more carnal cousin, pleasure. My sensate explanation reveals how earthbound my relationship with goodness remains despite seeking a higher, more impressively evolved understanding.

Even turning the word *goodness* over in my mind, trying to define it as an abstract philosophical concept, produces an involuntary rush of feel-good hormones. Presumably owing to that flood of endorphins, I interpret goodness as a sensation, one that feels overwhelmingly rich, deep, full, and pure, and is the progenitor of compassion, generosity, and kindness, my most deeply prized values. Thinking about goodness didn't always produce such dreamy, puppy-love feelings in me. There was too long a time when contemplating goodness made me anxious and conjured up feelings of being judged as unworthy, as not making the mark. That tendency still rises from the ashes at times, most notably around 3 a.m. when even seven graham crackers and an old episode of *Mannix* have failed to bring sleep. Tonight is one of those nights. I'm plumbing the dark depths of my soul, questioning my every move and motive, calibrating my spiritual growth, seeking comfort and assurance that I'm good (enough).

As a Catholic schoolgirl growing up in the 1960s, I was aware that goodness was not my natural state, my infant soul having entered this world marked with the stain of original sin. That stain, though theoretically washed away at baptism, left the ghost of an outline that if not regularly scrubbed into submission by goodness, would stubbornly reappear. Goodness was necessary to commune with a god who could abide nothing less. No good, no god. So, I dedicated myself to being good, hoping to earn a few minutes in the back of the Almighty's throne room. In my young, pragmatic mind, being good implied not a state of being, but rather the action of doing, of *be*-having. I determined to be the best *behaver* ever, which as a girl translated to compliant, obedient, and deferential, all helpful qualities when following public safety laws on the interstate, but not so much as a metaphorical roadmap for life's journey. Over my lifetime, I have perfected the art (sometimes act?) of being a good daughter, student, patient, employee, wife, ex-wife, and mother by doing the good and right things expected of those roles.

Not that there's anything wrong with doing the good and right things. Would that everyone strove to do so, but what's good and right is open to interpretation and can be so easily manipulated by family, religious, societal, and other forces. Growing up when and where I did, good and right was generally about being nice, that is, following the rules and not making waves. That role was an easy fit for me because as it happens, I am not naturally defiant. I'm someone who sincerely enjoys making others happy, who recoils from confrontation, and who is a skilled consensus builder. Even for me, however, goodness governed by the dictates of niceness was often stifling and worked to my detriment. I kept my boundaries too fluid and put myself last too many times, clearly not a unique story among women my age.

The ability to sacrifice and put others' needs ahead of our own is an admirable trait, but when that practice becomes overburdened with expectations of *should*, it usually breeds resentment, even bitterness, and begs questions such as: 1) Is unnecessarily self-sacrificing, muttering martyrdom actually goodness? 2) Do conflicted motives taint the goodness of the outcome? 3) Does a supposed act of goodness serve the proverbial greater good?

Good actions can even be weaponized to make others feel artificially less than. Are good deeds that come from a place of shame or guilt or that are (even unconsciously) designed to elicit those feelings in others really good? Does the desire to be recognized, to be *known for*, always doing the good and right things overshadow the goodness of those actions?

Judging the relative goodness of an action is a tricky business, and extending that judgment to the wholeness of a person is monumentally so. Since we don't have windows into people's souls, we look to their actions to reveal their natures, which poses another dilemma. Are all actions of equal weight, or are some to be counted and others discounted? Is personal goodness an all-or-nothing proposition? Is someone who robs a bank, but saves the life of a drowning child good or not? For me, the quintessential example of this moral conundrum is Oskar Shindler. Shindler, with the oft-downplayed help of his wife Emilie, saved 1,200 Jews from Nazi death camps, but was also a lying, cheating, hard-drinking cad. Emilie, whom he deserted, was quoted near the end of her life as saying he was a hero to those he saved, but not to her personally.

Shindler is an extreme example, but surely perfection cannot be required for someone to be judged as good. By that yardstick, we are none of us good, as we are none of us perfect. Given the inherent imperfection of humanity, perhaps goodness of character needs to be determined by a preponderance of the evidence, rather than beyond a reasonable doubt.

That thought helps quiet the furious swirling of the 3 a.m. imponderables. If my goodness is evaluated on a preponderance of the evidence, I think I'll make the grade. Kindness, compassion, generosity, understanding, forgiveness—these come fairly naturally to me, and I try to hold myself to these standards even in situations where they don't come as naturally. I acknowledge that I am also naturally given to fear, indecision, over-sensitivity, frustration, a touch of laziness, and immutable and loudly expressed impatience with malfunctioning technology. And cards on the table, while I'm proficient at forgiving, I'm less so at forgetting, which makes me grateful for that *preponderance* provision.

3:30 a.m., old demons subdued, I turn my focus back to the richness of the word *goodness*, and that cascade of comforting sensations washes over me. A final flip on my side puts the profile of my sleeping husband directly in my sightline, and those ooey-gooey feelings overflow. He is, to me, the essence of goodness, someone who has suffered tremendous loss at the hands of life's unfairness, yet remains the most earnest, guileless person I've ever known. He shows his goodness to me in grand gestures like buying me a new car and mundane, but just as meaningful ones, like letting me sleep in while he cleans that car, stem to stern.

Eyelids finally heavy, I accept that my reflections fall several levels below profound. Having failed to soar to lofty intellectual heights, my thoughts have now landed back in the prosaic sensate realm with a thud. And that's okay. Even minus the baby and soup, an elixir composed of equal parts kindness and consideration, topped off with a splash of cologne, makes a powerful soporific. Maybe I will bottle it and sell it. And I'll call it—what else?—*Oh My Goodness.*

ANDY ORAM

BECAUSE THERE IS LIGHT

Why did God create light?

We could have found our way around by sense of smell,
gliding through scrub-brush like wolves,
absorbing the world's murk through the flare of our nostrils,
drilling or drifting, dancing instinctively with outbreaks of
texture and sensation,
acting only through our amygdala, adopting creature ways,
embedded, infused, and intoxicated by the immediacy of existence.

The fruit from the Tree of Knowledge could not have opened our eyes.
We would not go whoring after our eyes.
No one could do what was right in his eyes.
Lot's wife would not have gazed back toward Sodom,
And David could not have spied a woman bathing.

We would respond to each encounter in turn,
Alerted but unassessing, using neither schemes nor schemas,
mingling the sacred and profane.

But if we could not view our surroundings in their discrete elements,
We could not mark the ground on which we stood.
We would not say, this I do and no other.
There would be no antithesis and no dialog.
No wrongs could be called out.
No one would rise to challenge God,
and to disappoint God, and to ask for favor in God's eyes.
And therefore all God's goodness would not pass before our faces.

JANET McCANN

REFLECTION WITH AND WITHOUT MIRROR

The nun said our tongues
would turn black if we lied.
I told her a lie, stuck out
my pink, innocent tongue.

And when were you last astounded,
stricken with awareness?
Awareness of truth. Its simple, classic beauty.

Richard Wilbur is dead now
and with him the precision
of metaphysics in poetry.
Let's send each other copies of
"Love Calls Us to the Things
of This World." Though it seems
sometimes it is the things of this world
that call us to love.

I hang my ugly wash out back
like the Italians do—the clean but ratty
slips, sheets, a blouse flapping against
the sky. Things call us, Love calls us.
No. I knew I was being rude, but I
was six, I wanted to know if my tongue
would turn black. Never tell lies
easily disproved.

In the mirror now my tongue is mostly gray.

VIGILANTES

You read about them, perfect arbiters
of justice, seeing beyond us
into the depths of evil, cutting it out.
You want a ten-foot tall man or woman
to look into hearts, see what is there.
But they can't be human, because
they might make mistakes. And then
there are always the gray fields, where evil
is not bad enough to smite, but it is there,
corroding. And do they think about
the source of evil, those avengers,
over generations? Or is it just
the black spot, to be cauterized
so the good, even the tepidly good,
can breathe? Who are the good
anyway? Why is ordinary justice
such a lumbering, bumbling machine?
And we still want the avengers we find in books.
And now it is 4 a.m., past the point
of no return on sleep. Thrones
and dominions, principalities and powers.
The infinite pounding of God
on the stone of my heart.

WENDY JONES NAKANISHI

THE GOODNESS OF GOODNESS

In Greek the word for goodness—*agathosune*—connotes an uprightness of heart and life. Plato claimed that the "Good" is the highest of all the forms that make up the natural world and that all objects aspire to be "good." In the Bible, goodness is a manifestation of the work of the Holy Spirit: "the fruit of the Spirit is love, joy, peace, forbearance, kindness, goodness, faithfulness, gentleness and self-control. Against such things there is no law" (Galatians 5:22-23).

In the Greek and the Biblical interpretations of the term, there is an emphasis on goodness as an ideal. Plato's "Good" also bears a close relationship to the notion of "God" developed in the Middle Ages: "God" and "the Good" are more perfect than anything else and responsible for all virtue and rationality in the world.

This is a cursory outline of the historical significance of the concept, but what is goodness in the twenty-first century?

Although, nowadays, Plato is little studied and even less understood and despite our inhabiting a "post-Christian world," the quality of being moral, of displaying what is considered virtuous behavior, continues to be extolled in the present day. Modern children are exhorted by their parents and teachers to be "good," just as they have been for centuries. Goodness is the condition we are supposed to aspire to. We are urged to curb or change our sinful natures and become better people.

When I was a small child, my parents insisted I kneel by my bed every night and recite the following prayer:

Now I lay me down to sleep,
I pray the Lord my soul to keep.

If I should die before I wake,
I pray the Lord my soul to take.

It was only after my father left us, when I was seven, that this familiar routine came to an abrupt halt. And it was only at that time that I gave any thought to the prayer I'd been accustomed to mumble as quickly as I could, impatient to crawl into my comfortable warm bed. It was a shock to realize the prayer asked me to contemplate my own death. As a child I believed I would live forever.

Dad's departure also meant my brother and sisters and I were no longer required to attend the church just across a field from our house where he had served as the choir director. Mom began to rise late, as if reluctant to leave the bed she no longer shared with her husband, and we gave up religion at the same time as any pretensions to constituting a happy "normal" family. We lived in a tiny community in the rural northwest of Indiana, and it had long been common knowledge in our town that my parents' marriage was in serious trouble. We children got used to being pointed at and gossiped about.

I lost my faith in God and, for a time, in human goodness.

When I left my hometown to enter the wider world, I encountered a far greater variety of people than I had been used to. I noticed that many, from large cities, were more "street smart" and worldly-wise than me—and that they considered me provincial and ignorant. Once I recovered from a consequent crippling sense of inferiority—when I was no longer stricken by shyness and fear and could interact with my new friends frankly and freely—I found some of them were religious and others proudly acclaimed themselves atheists, some were so kind I immediately thought of them as "good" while others exhibited a selfishness that repelled me.

I never regained my faith, but I became increasingly interested in "goodness" and especially in how I might live a "good" life.

At university I began reading the Anglo-Irish novelist and philosopher Iris Murdoch (1919-1999). Most of her twenty-six novels are explorations of how we can be good and how we can find goodness in the contemporary secularized world.

Murdoch drew some of her ideas from Plato. She argued for the replacement of the modern notion of a rational will by other ideas, such as notions of "love" and the "Good." Unlike Plato, however, for Murdoch the "Good" was not a metaphysical concept but a psychological and moral one.

Murdoch believed we can make ourselves better by paying attention to the "Good." For Murdoch, the "Good" is a concept that has characteristics formerly attributed to God, but she described it as "a single perfect transcendent non-representable and necessarily real object of attention."(1) The act of attention itself is a way of cultivating virtue: moral improvement is equated to improvement of vision. The individual must undergo a process of "unselfing," abandoning his egocentric view of the world. He needs to try to look at others and objects and events without subjective or personal bias clouding his vision.

In my twenties I considered myself a seeker after truth. I wanted to find some meaning to existence. In addition to Murdoch, I read Rollo May's *Love and Will*, drawn to his idea that an awareness of death is essential to an appreciation of life, as well as M. Scott Peck's *The Road Less Traveled* in which Peck outlined the attributes and actions he believed necessary for individual fulfillment.

I wasn't content to seek salvation in reading alone. When I took up residence in Edinburgh in my mid-twenties to begin a doctorate in English, I enrolled in a meditation group guided by a Scottish writer who was a disciple of the Indian spiritual leader Sri Chimnoy. I used to don a green sari twice a month and hurry up the road from my flat to the meditation center, often struggling through the gale force winds off the Firth of Forth that tugged and pulled at the flimsy fabric of my dress. Sometimes the journey seemed a metaphor for the difficult path to enlightenment.

I often wore a heavy duffel coat over my sari because even summer in Scotland can be brisk approaching the wintry. I attracted curious stares. Ten or eleven of us would meet in a small room to discuss Sri Chimnoy's teachings and spend half an hour sitting cross-legged on cushions on the floor, focusing on a candle flame. I'd tried meditation before. For me, the challenge of meditation was to be "present in the moment." It was a great effort to concentrate, to suppress idle thoughts, to "unself" myself, as Iris Murdoch would have put it.

I also took yoga classes each week at the university. I found the stretches, the training in controlled breathing, the focus on physical and mental concentration, beneficial to achieving a kind of calm and a sense of wellbeing. I would sometimes recall how my favorite word as a child was "serenity." As a nervous, anxious, shy child, it was what I longed for and, even now, in my sixties, the state I still desire, that sometimes seems just beyond my grasp.

❦ ❦ ❦

In my late twenties, having completed my doctoral thesis on the eighteenth century English poet Alexander Pope, I got a job at a university in the west of Japan. I was a "Guest Professor" teaching English: the literature and the language. I'd intended to spend only a year or two. I wanted to return to the UK, which I'd found very congenial. In the event, I met a Japanese farmer; we married and had three sons; I got a tenured position at my university.

I spent thirty-six years in Japan, juggling my duties as a wife and mother with my full-time employment. I was on Shikoku, the smallest and most rural of Japan's four main islands. It had its inconveniences: there were few foreigners, the stores offered little by way of international foods, and scarcely any of my neighbors could speak English. But I liked it. I'd been raised in a tiny town and, like my husband, would describe myself as someone who preferred the country to the city.

In retrospect, I believe it was a stroke of good fortune that I was able to spend so much of my life in Japan. The Japanese are rigorously trained in the art of self-discipline from an early age. Unlike the West, which places an emphasis on individual fulfillment, Japan (like most Asian countries) inculcates its citizens in the necessity to conform and contribute to the "group." For the Japanese, there are many "groups" an individual will belong to in the course of his life. As the child grows into adulthood, his circle of groups expands, from his family to his neighbors, from his schoolmates to his fellow employees. Even nationality is a kind of group. Japan has, perhaps, the most homogeneous population of any country in the modern world. With nearly ninety-eight percent of its population Japanese, being born and bred Japanese is like belonging to an extended tribe.

Selfishness is considered a regrettable vice in Japan. It is also reprehensible to lose one's temper. Arguments are rare. The Japanese are always anxious to preserve peace and order. In public they rarely express their own views frankly. In meetings, they search for consensus. At their jobs they are conscientious employees who routinely work overtime with no extra pay. Physical courage and the stoic endurance of pain and suffering are highly prized.

I found it difficult to adapt, to relinquish the individualistic Western values that, for the first three decades of my life, I'd unconsciously assumed were universal. Before arriving in Japan at the age of twenty-nine, I'd already lived in the UK for six years, in France for one, and in Holland for six months. None of those other cultures proved anything like as challenging and ultimately "foreign" as Japan. I fought against being forced to change. Eventually, I succumbed and accepted it was necessary and even wise. Learning to master my desires and to question my own assumptions and to alter my thoughts and behavior was a painful process but one that was ultimately rewarding.

Less than one percent of Japanese profess to be Christian, and Japanese routinely describe themselves as people who have no religion. However, the tenets of Buddhism and Shintoism heavily influence Japanese society. Buddhist rituals are observed in funerals and Shinto rites at weddings. The Shinto notion of the sacredness of nature pervades day-to-day life in Japan. Before any meal, for example, the Japanese invariably observe the ritual of clapping their hands together and bowing their heads while intoning thanks for the food they are about to eat. After the meal, they again express gratitude.

Despite their not adhering to any organized religion—which, at one time, I would have thought a prerequisite to or conducive to the development of human goodness—the Japanese are the kindest and most honest people I have ever encountered. We ex-pats in Japan often traded anecdotes of how we'd left a wallet or camera somewhere but could—nearly always—retrieve it from the nearest police box, where some law-abiding Japanese had turned it in. I once left a considerable sum of cash on the top of an ATM at a bank, only realizing what I'd done an hour later, when I was trying to pay for my groceries at a supermarket. On returning to the bank, I found the money had been handed in and I could collect it without needing even fill out any forms.

The Japanese are also very polite and thoughtful. They are modest to the point of self-deprecation. Their avoidance of egotistical behavior means that while most Japanese inhabit densely populated cities, they can interact efficiently but, above all, harmoniously. They cultivate rich private lives, but the face they show to the outside world is the "public" one, and they act in unison to ensure the smooth working of society.

The Japanese would dismiss the idea that they are "good," just as they reject the idea that they are "religious". But these are conclusions that we ex-pats resident in Japan often found inescapable. Of course, there are selfish and "bad" Japanese, but the workings of Japanese society are designed to instill "good" virtues in its citizens.

❦ ❦ ❦

Having retired after working full-time for thirty-six years in Japanese academia, I've recently set up home back in the UK. I love Britain but, altered by my long residence in Japan, I find myself deploring the phenomenon of "virtue signaling" I sometimes find here, inspired in part by the stresses and strains imposed by the recent coronavirus pandemic. I think the anonymity afforded by social networking sites such as Facebook and Twitter feed the frenzy, eliciting, inviting and encouraging outbursts of indignation and outrage. It is mostly confected, I believe: an egotistical bid for attention.

They say we despise in others the bad qualities we know ourselves to possess. I'm appalled now by how judgmental I was in my twenties, thirties and forties. I wonder if it was because I had found being considered a country bumpkin when I first went to college so painful that I went on to judge others with such relish. I used to wallow in the pleasure of self-righteousness. When others offended me, I loved tearing them to bits with friends similarly disposed to fault finding.

This means I now dislike self-righteousness while fully recognizing its attractions. It is tempting to put myself above others, to believe they are wrong and I am right. Censoriousness is like a guilty pleasure. But having had my sense of values shaken and reshaped by life in Japan, I'm much less willing now to place myself in judgment over others.

Similarly, I have come to believe goodness should be done by stealth. As the Bible advises, "Take heed that ye do not your alms before men, to be seen of them: otherwise ye have no reward of your Father which is in heaven" (Matthew 6:1). Those who insist on advertising their virtue are bores. A "goody two shoes" inspires annoyance rather than admiration.

Roger Scruton (1944-2020), the British writer and philosopher, has identified the enduring problem in life as "How to live in right relation with others, even if there is no God." His answer is included in his final book, about Wagner's final opera: "Whether or not there is a God, there is this hallowed path towards a kind of salvation, the path that Wagner described as "godliness," the path taken by Parsifal, and it is a path open to us all."(2)

In her review of Scruton's book, Sue Prideaux observes that both Wagner's opera and Scruton's book are intended to be taken as "Last Words: testaments of belief at the end of a long spiritual journey."(3).

"The unexamined life is not worth living" is a famous dictum attributed to Socrates at his trial for impiety and the corruption of youth for which he was condemned to death. It naturally follows that the examined life is a noble one. "Know thyself" is an ancient Greek aphorism, and it is a topic often explored by Plato in his Socratic dialogues. Many of Iris Murdoch's novels similarly concern the comic mistakes and misunderstandings of characters who know themselves little and others even less.

For Murdoch, we can achieve a kind of goodness by learning to live without egotism. This means we must recognize others exist as well as ourselves and respect all living creatures. Murdoch was influenced by Simone Weil, the French philosopher, mystic, and social activist, who once said "*Attention,* taken to its highest degree, is the same thing as prayer. It presupposes faith and love. Absolutely unmixed *attention* is prayer." Weil also said that "Attention is the rarest and purest form of generosity."

The question "What is goodness?" is related to another: "How can we live well?" To live well, we need to have some understanding of our own nature. For centuries, meditation and yoga have been practiced by those intent on achieving enlightenment. Self-knowledge can help us to behave wisely and avoid harming ourselves and others. We can learn to treat our fellow men with kindness and compassion. We can become "good."

Like so many of the old proverbs, "Virtue is its own reward" has a deep, abiding wisdom. Recent studies have shown that we are flooded with positive emotions when we help others and that having many friends is linked to good health. The Greek idea of goodness as an "uprightness of heart and life" reflects a belief that exercising self-discipline over our mind and body results in self-fulfillment. In being virtuous—or, as the Bible advises, in being wise and kind, non-judgmental and gentle—we fill ourselves and those about us with love and joy. When we can act as clear-sighted individuals freed from selfish concerns and egotistical desires, we can taste the sweet fruit of goodness.

(1). Floora Ruokonen, "Good, Self, and Unselfing— Reflections on Iris Murdoch's Moral Philosophy," Web.
(2). Sue Prideaux, 'Swan Song,' a review of Ruger Scruton's *Wagner's Parsifal: The Music of Redemption*, printed in *The Spectator*, 9 May 2020, page 32.
(3). Ibid.

KEVIN STUART BRODIE

THE KING IS DEAD

The old Honda roars
into the Mobil station,
screeches to a halt.
I whirl around from the pump,
just in time to see him leap out:
Fortyish, unkempt beard, olive skin,
Middle Eastern.

All of us in the station
fix our gazes.
We say nothing.
His eyes widen in excitement,
he reaches into his coat pocket
withdraws a long, black cylinder.
We remain silent,
exchange anxious looks.
He squeezes the cylinder,
at the end of it emerges
a tiny Egyptian flag.

The man raises his arms
in triumph and shouts:
EGYPT!
EGYPT IS FREE!
He races through the gas bays,
waving his flag,
Leaping and skipping
like a third grader
on the last day of school.
EGYPT!

NO MORE MUBARAK!
EGYPT IS FREE!

He darts into the convenience store,
charges through the tiny aisles.
I can't hear him anymore,
But can plainly read the word
EGYPT on his lips.

The door flies open,
and he's back outside with us,
face overcome with joy,
body quivering with giddy laughter.

Suddenly I envy him—
I have never lived
without the privilege
of taking my freedom
for granted.
I wonder how it must feel
to wrestle it away
from a tyrant.

Maybe that's why
when he darts past me again,
I smile, almost give him
a thumbs up, then remember
he's Egyptian.
He stops suddenly, squints,
as if he's trying to decide
how well he sees me.

He then jerks me
into a sudden embrace,
screams NO MORE MUBARAK!
into my ear.
I'd return the hug,

but my arms
are pinned under his.

I notice the other patrons,
quietly climbing back
into their cars,
fearful they may be next.

He releases me.
For several moments,
we laugh together,
like old friends remembering
an inside joke
no one else understands.

One more shout of EGYPT!
and he squeezes my shoulders.
He plants a kiss on one cheek,
then the other,
grabs my hands
and thrusts them to the sky.
EGYPT IS FREE!
This time we shout it together.

He lets go of my hands,
jumps back into his car.
He peels out onto the road
honking feverishly,
as the faint cry of EGYPT
disappears into the night.

MARY KAY RUMMEL

THE SPINNING UNIVERSE: KONYA, TURKEY

I. The Dance

Love waited in every doorway for Rumi.
It sent him whirling,
I am so small I can barely be seen.
How can this great love be inside me?
a dance he taught his teacher,
Shams of Tabriz,
and all the dervishes.
Look at your eyes. They are small,
But they see enormous things.

The dance doesn't speak
in any known tongue.
Rumi taught Shams to spin, to let stars
take over the field of his mind.

This day dervishes whirl
outside the dark room where Rumi
dreamed the ecstatic dance.

Tulip shaped saffron colored gowns
shade the light of their bodies.
I don't know if they belong to the earth
or to the air.

With them I rise toward the clouds,
deep blue—flowing into the future.
With them I see how prayer might live in us
if we would let it.
How time circles in us.
What it means to be ecstatic in love.

II. The Women

Through a market place
of burka clad women,
my friend and I follow
a golden spire
to the poet's emerald tiled tomb
where more women
chant and bow.

We bend to enter the dark cell where he
slept on a cot, prayed and wrote—
Qur'an, parchment with stylus—
his sandals upon the 800 year old floor.

My Turkish friend despairs:

Ten years ago women in this city
were all dressed like you and me.
Now look at them—pressured to be covered.
In black we are going backward.
I have a plan to get my daughter out, if I need to.

III The Prayer

Rumi, teach us to see
our path of light, of love
while history and governments
whirl away like planetary dust.

JOHNNY TOWNSEND

WHAT WOULD ANNE FRANK DO?

When faced with a moral decision, Christians often ask themselves, "What would Jesus do?" Atheists sometimes pose the same question by quoting Christ's actual words when they feel the secular answer is more "Christian" than the mainstream religious response. The problem is that some people think Jesus would rip children away from their parents and imprison them. Others think Jesus would make sure everyone was fed, with no effort to shame the hungry or make them jump through hoops in the process. Some feel that Jesus would bomb civilians. Others don't believe Jesus would be the strongest supporter of waterboarding. It's clear there are far too many answers to this question for it to be useful as a tool in guiding our behavior.

So I decided to ask myself a different one.

As a Mormon, I considered, "What would Joseph Smith do?" But even the most basic awareness of the history behind the mythology steered me away from that litmus test pretty quickly. I *didn't* want to have sex with the family babysitter in the barn.

I next considered, "What would Gandhi do?" but that possibility was ruined as well when a former bank manager told me, "We should all be like Gandhi and help people get loans."

Perhaps then it's impossible to pose the question using any historical or religious figure. But I still felt the need for a moral template and decided to give "What would Anne Frank do?" a try.

Well, Anne Frank would record everything she witnessed, wouldn't she? She'd think, she'd revise to improve the accuracy and readability of her account, she'd make the best of a bad situation and try to see the good in people.

Still, Anne Frank could be a bit of a brat, to judge by her own writings.

Martin Luther King, Jr. had lots of extramarital sex.

Laura Ingalls Wilder was biased against Native Americans.

I began wondering if perhaps we should all become "cafeteria" admirers and simply pick and choose which behaviors we wanted to emulate in others. But what kind of evaluation technique could I use to help me answer that?

"What would Jesus pick and choose?"

Dagnabbit!

We've been told it isn't good to meet our heroes, that the reality always falls short of the ideal. But there's no reason we can't appreciate the good in people and follow their positive examples without condoning their sins and failures. We can ask, "What would my mother do in this situation? What would Maria's grandfather do, Levi's high school English teacher, my neighbor Cathy's ex?" and take the best examples from everyone we know when making our own decisions on difficult matters.

One evening many years ago, while walking through the French Quarter, a friend and I heard the sound of scuffling from the block ahead, and a young woman's voice calling out desperately. "Help us! Help!"

My walking companion turned the corner and headed away from the mugging. And I followed, leaving the young couple to their fate.

Far too often, we follow the *worst* aspects of other people's behavior.

Still, if I wasn't brave enough to offer assistance on my own, why didn't I at least run into a bar and call the police?

If we find ourselves more flawed than Maya Angelou, or Rabbi Akiva, or Sarah Winnemucca, we need a Plan B.

Before the pandemic, my husband Gary went door to door once a month talking to people about socialism. My friend Robert volunteered to teach English to immigrant adults. My friend Donna volunteered at a public garden. Those are all great things, but I know myself well enough to understand I simply won't do them, even if things ever "return to normal." Yet there's no value beating myself up over it. I did manage to volunteer through Jewish Family Services to play pool regularly with an elderly shut-in. I volunteered as a proofreader for a progressive Mormon magazine and a socialist newspaper. I volunteered to help prepare meals for people with HIV. I volunteered a year and a half of my time researching the Upstairs Lounge fire. I volunteered as a slush pile reader for a science fiction magazine.

And I volunteer now by writing op-eds, taking part in a community effort to find solutions to our country's most pressing problems.

We can ask what our heroes, our mentors, our friends and family, would do in any given situation, but even if *they* would make an especially good decision regarding the question at hand, it's still not necessarily what *we* should do. Or even *can* do. I'm *not* going to call prospective voters on the phone even to support causes or candidates I believe in deeply. It's not that calling folks wouldn't be the right thing, it's simply that I won't do it, so I have to find something good I *will* do.

I get so tired of seeing successful CEOs or other people in prominent positions dismiss the needs of others with, "If I can do it, so can they." No, not everyone can be a CEO. And how, exactly, would society even function in this lift-yourself-up-by-your-bootstraps scenario? All CEOs and no workers? All management and no inventors or delivery drivers or physicians or plumbers?

We can't all perform the exact same high-paying—or low-paying—job. And we can't all make the exact same decisions when faced with a moral dilemma. What we can do, though, is choose a morally appropriate response out of the several possibilities before us.

I do a decent job of listening when someone wants to tell me what they're going through. I may not have anything useful to say in response, but sometimes the help is in not saying anything at all. I can't donate $10,000 to a good cause, but I can donate $15. I may never be the world's best author, but I can say a few things in a way that's meaningful to at least some people. I can keep my mind open to other opportunities that utilize my strengths. I can choose which weaknesses to work on and when.

There's no reason we can't consider what Theodora would do in our place, what the Buddha would do, what the Gaon of Vilna would do.

These are all fair questions and could very well provide useful guidance. Reflecting on the best course of action is almost always a good idea. Ultimately, though, the only question any of us can realistically ask ourselves is this: "What will *I* look back on—the last day of my life, with my life flashing before my eyes—and wish *I* had done?"

II.
SOCIAL JUSTICE

MICHAEL KONIK

THE PORCH WATCHER

We're huddled behind the Nerdmelt, waiting for the Monday night open mic to commence. Someone is telling a story about a comedian who used his precious three minutes of stage time to slowly, wordlessly remove all his clothing—except one sock.

"Remember that other crazy dude that used to come here?" Kyle, the host, interjects. "With the Selena Gomez stories?"

"Mike," I say, nodding. "My man, Fisher King Mike."

"Yeah. Him. So, I'm walking down Sunset, on my way here, and I see Mike at the bus bench over there by Chipotle. And, I swear, no shit, he's wearing an *alligator costume*, like, a furry felt alligator, like, a mascot, and he's got a big smile on his face, just, like, oblivious."

"Maybe he'll come to the mic like that," I say. "Gator comedy is very alt."

Kyle laughs. "Fisher King Mike is all about the alt, you know what I mean?"

We nod and chuckle and add tags onto what's been said before, a subtle current of one-upmanship rippling beneath the jokes. You can detect strenuousness behind our brand of funny, the effort to find laughs. Guys like Fisher King Mike don't have to try.

"So when's the last time you saw him?" I ask.

"Like, literally ten minutes ago."

"Yeah? I haven't seen him in a while. When's the last time he did the mic?"

"Seems like forever," one young comedian says. "Months?"

Kyle takes a deep drag from an omnipresent cigarette. "Yeah, I wanna say, like, it's been about three months since he did a set here."

"All that time I haven't seen him once," I say. "He used to do 'Revolutionary Words' over at Elderberries. Religiously. Never missed it."

"Didn't you have to ban him here once?" another guy asks Kyle.

"It wasn't, like, an outright ban. I just had to remind him about some of the ground rules. Like, the light. You gotta respect the light."

Murmurs of solemn assent. "No doubt." "Fo sho." "You *gotta.*"

I'm about to mention logorrhea, compulsive talkativeness, but I know in this crowd such a word will only lead to discussions of watery stool, so I keep it to myself.

Fisher King Mike can't stop once he starts. He seems to have the same desires and compulsions as all the talented, striving young comedians grinding their way through the dues-paying mill of Los Angeles. All of us performers crave an audience. We all want someone—or a whole bunch of someones—to listen and laugh, as though what we have to offer the world is necessary and unmissable, when, in reality, it's often of interest only to the guy on stage. Fisher King Mike, unlike Hollywood aspirants who own cars and live in apartments, has no self-editing function, no superego mode to impart shame and insecurity. *Of course,* he runs the light. And of course, he's wearing an alligator costume today. Why wouldn't he?

Mike and I once went back-to-back at one long-forgotten show. To my initial alarm and eventual delight, he used most of his set—and some of the next person's—to offer a detailed commentary on what he'd just watched before he was called to the stage: *my* set. It wasn't a review or a critique, really, and it wasn't a reiteration, either. My set served as a kind of jumping off point for Mike's digressions, a starting line with no finish in sight. The mystery and surprise of where his disjointed rant might lead was kind of funny and sort of mesmerizing, and, in the end, utterly inscrutable. If it weren't a schizophrenic homeless man delivering the performance, people would call it boundary-breaking, genre-smashing, comedy genius.

Delivering an entire stand-up set dressed as a cartoon alligator—and never referencing the outfit—would be something I'd like to see. Alas, Mike doesn't show up for the Nerdmelt event that night. Or the following one, or the one after that.

But the next week, when I amble into the parking lot on a mild Monday night, Fisher King Mike is there, standing by himself, off to the side, looking very much as he did when I last saw him three or four months earlier strolling on the sidewalk outside our front garden.

He's wearing dark sunglasses and his Hollywood hat, which seems to have been inscribed with bible verses on most of the available fabric. Mike's outer coat is also covered with hand-written messages, some of them Jesus quotations, some of them incomprehensible. "Mr. Punky," he says as I approach.

"Mr. Mike," I reply. "Good to see you. How you been?"

"No, no, it's not that. Had some family complications. My wife. My kids. You know how it is."

I nod. But, I have no idea, actually, how it is when you're able to hear obscure messages emanating from distant corners of consensus reality.

We go inside together and put our names in the bucket, on crinkled slips of paper. They choose twenty-five (from about 150 entries). Neither Fisher King Mike nor MK Punky gets picked.

"Good to see you again, Mike," I say, slipping out the back door. Five minutes later, I'm home.

"Did you win the lottery?" Charmaine calls to me from her upstairs office.

"No. I've probably already used up my share of luck this time around," I say, flashing Charm a look that indicates she's the big lottery prize in my life. Which is true. I'm loved and I give love, and that's the greatest luck of all. But my partnership with Charmaine isn't the exception in my life; it's closer to the rule. I've been extraordinarily, incomprehensibly *lucky* in this lifetime. Although I could surely catalog all the elements of what I consider my great good fortune, my privilege, let's merely start with the fact that I was born a white male in the United States of America. That's a pretty good break.

So I don't buy lottery tickets, and when I enter a charity raffle it's really charity, because I don't harbor a tiny feeling (or desire) that I might win. I feel like I've already won, that I've already gotten more than my fair share of good breaks and golden opportunities. I've already used up my good luck inventory; better for someone less lucky to enjoy a taste.

Just then, when I'm feeling altogether jolly about my high ideals and blah-blah-blah, I hear knocking at the front door.

"Are you expecting anyone?" Charmaine asks.

"No. Maybe it's a solicitor. I'll check."

"Please don't open the door until you know who it is," she implores.

I assure her I will. A few weeks earlier, on a mild weekday night, Charmaine was robbed at gunpoint in our driveway by two masked assailants. Her calmness served her well. They took Charm's phone and wallet, but, mercifully, they didn't hurt her physically. They never touched her. Emotionally, though, the wounds were deep. The fear lingered.

Now we take extra care with security. We do a full 360-degree scan of the street and sidewalk, like Secret Service agents, before getting in or out of Charmaine's car, and I installed motion-sensor floodlights around the property, bright enough for nighttime tennis. Still, when the sun goes down, Charm sometimes feels a little frightened, a little anxious.

I open the window shutters beside our front door and peer onto the porch, illuminated with LED bulbs. No one's there.

Then I look down the path leading toward the front gate. On one side of the gate is Fisher King Mike; on the other side are all of Fisher King Mike's bags.

"Babe, it's Fisher King Mike," I call out. "I'll go talk to him outside."

"Isn't it a little late?" Charmaine asks.

"Yeah. It is. I just saw him at the open mic. He didn't say anything, didn't say he was coming. Don't worry. I'll be back."

"All right," she says, in a tone that I understand to mean *everything is not all right.* "I'm going to lock the front door. Take your key."

Sure. Whatever makes her feel better about living in the heart of this enormous, sometimes-violent city.

I step outside. "Mike! Everything OK?"

"No, no it's not that. I didn't want to disturb you and your wife—I know how important family is, family is the most important thing there is, nothing comes before your family, and I know you know that, and so I *knocked* on your door but I thought I should wait here, down here, where, you know, I'm not intruding on your space, giving you your space, you see what I'm saying?"

"Thanks for your courtesy," I say, with as much patience as I can muster, which, I confess, is not something I manage with great success. "What's up?"

"No, no, it's not that," he says, shaking his head and making a small dismissive wave of his hand. "I just didn't want to disturb—"

"I got you, brother. And thank you for that. So what's going on?"

Mike looks down at the path, avoiding eye contact. (He's wearing dark sunglasses tonight, anyway.) "Look, I hate to ask you this, and, and if you," he holds up both hands in a *hey-it's-no-big-deal* gesture, "if you can't . . . I just was wondering if you would have a problem with me leaving my bags behind your hedge over there, where it's out of sight, won't be in nobody's way."

He's got two canvas bags, slightly larger than airplane carry-ons but smaller than a traveler's duffel. "Sure," I say nonchalantly. "How long do you want to keep them there?"

"No, no, see, it's not that. I just have to get to the Valley for a couple of days, and, see, what people don't understand is, I have to get back here to do my work, to minister, because I'm a street pastor and there are so many people here who need help, they need help, and no one wants to help them, and so I've got to help them, and, and, if I can leave these bags here for a couple of days—"

"A couple of days," I repeat. Not a question. A statement of fact.

"A couple of days," Fisher King Mike repeats. "While I'm in the Valley. Gotta take care of some business there with my family."

"Right," I say. "So we'll keep your bags here for a couple of days."

"A couple of days. *Puh-shweep.*" He gestures like he's wiping off a counter.

"OK. You got it."

"Thanks. Look, I didn't want to disturb you and your wife, but I gotta take care of some business in the Valley, and, and, you know, what people don't understand is that when you're a minister, a street pastor, you've got a lot of responsibilities."

"Well, thank you for your good works," I say amiably. "We're glad we can help you out." And before he can launch another monologue, I grab his bags and plod toward the front porch, where a six-foot-tall hedge does indeed provide full privacy from street views, and from the neighbors and their children. In my rush to make things all better, I neglect to ask my wife if she's cool with making our front porch a temporary storage facility for a loquacious homeless fellow.

Fisher King Mike follows me, carrying his backpack and a white plastic takeout bag filled with his sundries. "Here," I say, sliding the bags beneath a low square table flanked by wooden chairs. "We can stash them under here."

He nods affirmatively several times, and sighs heavily. Then he shakes his head "no" several times, and sighs heavily. "Hey, look, I just want to say . . ." his voice trails off, and his frail, bony shoulders begin to tremble.

I'm about to make a comment about how rare it is for the great orator to be at a loss for words, when Mike begins to sniffle and dab at his eyes. "Oh, man, it's OK," I tell him. "Everything's going to be OK. We'll take care of your stuff. It's no problem. You didn't disturb anything. Everything's fine, Mike."

Before he trudges off to wherever he's actually going—and maybe, in some alternate universe, it really is his estate next to Kanye West's—Fisher King Mike flashes a knowing smile at me, a comedian's smile, someone who's in on the joke, who gets the irony and absurdity of the humor. A smile that says, *Sir, you are one funny dude. 'Everything's fine. Everything's fine.' Yes, sir, you are hilarious.*

His bags stay on our porch for three days and nights, talismans of Mike, symbols of all he has and doesn't have. And every time I look at them, they seem to flash me the same myth-busting smile.

Never again am I going to tell Fisher King Mike that every- thing's OK, I resolve. I'm going to help him *make* everything OK—even if that "everything" is, in the grand scheme, almost nothing.

Because something is almost always more than nothing.

In the interval, before Mike comes back for his possessions, Charmaine has the opportunity to school me on the importance of making bilateral decisions about the use of our household, particularly when it involves the warehousing of bags that contain *who-knows-what* and have been previously stashed *who-knows-where.*

Noted. Must consult the wife. Got it. Because, and what people don't understand is, there's nothing's more important than family.

Even when that family consists of two people.

We don't have children. We don't own a dog (or a cat or any other creature). After Ella, our white Greyhound-Labrador mutt memorialized in my book *Ella in Europe: An American Dog's International Adventures* and on the Animal Planet show "Ella & Me," died at fifteen and a half, a couple years after we were married, the timing was bad to adopt another pet. We were grieving for a great friend, yes. But we were also traveling all over the globe for Charmaine's concerts, and to the Philippines for family visits. Taking in a puppy from a shelter—no other option works in our canine value system—"rescuing" often means dealing with abandonment issues. We didn't want to be a mom and dad who were seldom there.

These days, we're traveling less. Charmaine's parents, Baldomero, eighty-seven, and Nieves, eighty-two, are both in declining health. Dad is on dialysis every other day. Mom has precancerous internal lesions and mobility issues. Charm doesn't like being away from them for more than a week at a time, and almost every Sunday that she's in town, she visits them at their two-bedroom condo in the valley, nowhere near Kanye's place.

I'm not welcome, having been declared *persona non grata* by Mom Clamor as a result of losing my cool and speaking harshly (loudly) to her—and then immediately apologizing for my momentary lapse of decorum. She determined it was all unforgivable.

They used to live with us, in the retrofitted garage that today serves as Charmaine's private therapy clinic. Now they're forty minutes away and growing more distant by the day. Getting ghosted by Mom, I eventually realize, is a wonderful affirmation of how the most disparate world cultures are often surprisingly similar, that even the most devoutly Christian person can behave exactly like an Orthodox Jew. *You're dead to me! [ripped shirt thrown disdainfully to the floor]*. More proof, to my mind, that *We* Are One. *Namaste.*

When Charmaine hangs with the 'rents, I putter in the garden, read on the back deck, write poetry in my head. On Sundays, I try to disconnect. After posting my Thought of the Week essay on my website and doing a sweep for any urgent emails, I shut down the internet. Since I don't have a smartphone and I don't text, I'm blissfully removed from the constant noise that emptiness makes.

I find that Sundays are some of my happiest days. The more I'm away from a computer screen and the more I'm in the dirt, growing things, the better I feel. The opportunity to muse, to ponder, to cogitate—it seems our modern culture allows fewer and fewer chances to simply *think*. Setting aside an entire day for reflection, a Sabbath, if you will, has made me slightly more centered than I was the month before.

Sometimes, though, after hours alone pulling weeds—alone except for the birds and worms and squirrels—what's missing is a companion, someone to chitter-chatter with. Or be silent with. Someone whose presence affirms that you're not alone in the world.

A friend.

I don't have many. Definitely a quality over quantity situation, which suits the writer's need of solitude. Still . . .

As if on cue, as though I'm able to manifest my wishes through meditation and positive imaging, an exceptionally skinny fellow wearing two coats and a "Hollywood" hat appears at the front gate. When Fisher King

Mike returns for his bags three days after he left them, not quite as promised but close, I'm outside in the garden, planting onion bulbs. "Hey! Mike!" I say, genuinely glad to see him, and even gladder that he's sort of followed through on his pledge. "You're back!"

"Yeah, yeah, I know. I *told* you I was coming back in a few days," he says, astonished that anyone would doubt Mr. Reliable. "Selena is getting ready for a big tour, going away for the whole summer. Europe. And, and, you know how it is."

"I have some idea," I say, noncommittally. "You OK? You hungry?"

"No, no, I've got plenty to eat," he says, holding up a Wendy's bag. "You want some fries?" He tilts the bag toward me. It's filled with wrappers and ketchup packages and a giant soda-filled cup with a straw in it, and possibly some potatoes hiding somewhere.

"No, thank you," I say. "I'm on a celery binge at the moment."

"Yeah, yeah, I know. Hey, look, I was wondering," he says, setting down the carryout bag on our vegetable donation table stationed between the sidewalk and the curb, on what's technically known as "the parkway." Wendy, the pigtailed, freckle-faced mascot who seems super happy that you've purchased such a nutritious meal from her company, smiles magnanimously over our garden, content in the knowledge that the food grown here will never end up in her restaurant. "I was wondering if you could let me stay with the bags tonight."

"On the porch?"

"I need to get my head together. I just need a night to get my head together. See, what people don't understand is, and I tell them this, you know, you can't help all the people that need a street pastor, you can't help them if your stuff is in one place and your family is in another, and, and, I'm having some problems with, you know, holding it, and, and if I could just get my head together." He nods and chews his lips.

"So, you want to sleep on the porch?"

"I just need to get my head together, going back and forth, and, and, the bus stops running after ten, and all my stuff."

"You can leave it here," I assure him. "Your bags are safe."

"No, no, it's not that, I just need to get my head together."

I nod. "As far as I'm concerned, it's OK. You can stay on the porch tonight. But I've gotta ask the wife. I'm sure you know what I mean."

"Yeah, yeah, I know," he says, chuckling wearily. "Check with the boss."

I instruct Mike to make himself comfortable, take a seat, have a rest while I go inside and get official permission from the Executive Committee.

My moral barometer says that if we're able to let strange bags sleep on our porch, we should be able to let a human being do the same. Why wouldn't we?

Instead of philosophical arguments, when I find Charmaine upstairs in her office, singing in Tagalog, I frame the Fisher King Mike pitch as a home-security move. Sure, I tell her, it's unusual to have a homeless person sleeping on our front porch. But, given what Charmaine went through in the robbery, wouldn't having a night watchman on the premises give us an added level of comfort and confidence? Fisher King Mike could be a kind of early-warning system if anyone suspicious walks down the driveway or loiters near our gate—something his bags, fully approved and permitted for porch-sitting, can't do.

"And where exactly is he planning on sleeping?" Charmaine asks.

"I'm not really sure. I think he might have a sleeping bag, or a mat or something. I get the feeling that anything is better than the street."

"Or the shelter?"

I shrug. "From what I'm told, the shelters are notoriously dangerous, so our front porch is a big improvement."

"And the bathroom?"

I tell her, "We didn't really talk about that. I think he goes to the church, on Hollywood, when he needs a toilet. Or the supermarket, the Ralph's on Sunset."

"And it doesn't worry you that he's mentally ill?" Charmaine inquires, a bemused smile curling her lips.

I think about it for a second. "No doubt. He's definitely experiencing a different reality than we are. But he's also totally harmless. All his ravings, I mean, they're weird and strange, but he never talks about hurting anyone, nothing violent. And as far as I know, he doesn't drink. I don't get any threat vibes from him. Do you?"

Charmaine agrees. She doesn't think Mike's dangerous, just unpredictable. "It's hard to make arrangements and agreements with someone like that," she reminds me.

We decide to let him stay for one night. *One night*—boundaries clearly defined. Then Fisher King Mike, Wendy, and all the bags will have to move on, going wherever Mike's ministerial services take him.

I bound downstairs and find Mike on the porch, asleep on one of the wooden deck chairs, his spindly legs thrust outward, his sunken jaw resting on his chest. His mouth—I figure he must have done a lot of meth at some point. He's got that look: desiccated facial muscles, skin like a chicken's after boiling, missing teeth. Plus, he chain-smokes Camels and guzzles Coke—regular, caffeinated, corn-syrup-infused Coke, no effete diet stuff. All that's got to wreak havoc on your dentistry.

I watch him doze. He smells better than the last time he was on this porch.

The sun is beginning to set. I leave Fisher King Mike to his slumber, wondering when he last slept soundly, wondering where he goes to when he disappears into "the Valley," wondering if he really does have a family who worries about him and misses him and counts on him. Not Selena Gomez. But someone.

Before Charmaine and I have (a non-Wendy's) dinner inside our warm, capacious home, I check on Mike, ready to slide him a sandwich and a cup of tea. When I peer through the dining room shutters onto the porch, he's no longer in the chair; he's moved to the concrete, sleeping in the fetal position, a knapsack his pillow. I go back inside and grab a throw pillow from the living room couch and a wool blanket slung over an armchair.

Placing them on the ground beside him, I whisper, "Good night, Mike." He doesn't stir. The city, that mean, cold place just two blocks from here, has gone silent, the sounds of traffic replaced by chirping crickets and Fisher King Mike's shallow, rapid breathing. There's a certain rhythm and harmony to their sounds, a kind of nocturnal music formed in the blending. I add a sigh to the choir and go back inside, where a bed, with a mattress and feathery pillows and a comforting snuggling partner, awaits.

In the morning, I rise early with the sun and go downstairs to check on our porch tenant. He's not there.

His bags are, but Fisher King Mike is gone, only a couple of torn and emptied sugar packets in the ashtray left behind.

Before I return upstairs, I shuffle in my bathrobe to the corner of our driveway, just yards from where Charmaine was robbed. We have a tiny community library there, founded in 2012 and built entirely from found materials, including an old picture window frame that serves as the library's see-through door. In addition to keeping the books organized and the guestbook up-to-date, the library offers poems for the people—"Free! Take One!"—two different poems every day, on each side of one piece of paper. Most of them have been previously published on my website, as part of semi-annual MK Poetry Festivals featuring new material for a week or two, or until I can't come up with anything worth sharing. But one of my resolutions for 2016 is to submit my poetry for publication, whether in magazines and journals or anthologies and collections. (Another resolution is to try to get *Year 14*, a novel my literary agent has found to be unsellable, published somewhere, anywhere.) I have no ambitions or expectations of the poetry world; I'm not sure I even belong there. Sharing the work, as pretentious as it sounds, is reason enough.

The Vista Street Community Library is well-stocked this morning. Someone has left eight books from a cat mystery series, a genre with which I am not familiar but which I'm certain pays better than poetry.

As I'm assessing the Free Poems inventory—I like to keep four to five in stock—I hear the crackle of jacaranda pods on the sidewalk behind me. It's Fisher King Mike, shuffling down the street with what appears to be a *grande* coffee in hand and a white earbud in one of his earholes.

"No, I was just at the church," he announces. "Little breakfast. Doughnuts."

"Was everything OK last night?"

"No, no. Fine." He walks past me to the porch. I follow him.

"So, what's the plan today?"

"Listen, do you think I could leave my bags here while I do my work?"

"You mean, today? During the day?"

"No, no, see, it's not that—"

"Yes," I interrupt him. "Yes, you can. You may." I'm relieved it's only the bags and not their owner occupying our front porch. I imagine, by nightfall, Fisher King Mike will move on to whatever comes next in his improvised adventure.

"Thanks. See—and that's what people don't understand—when you're ministering to the homeless, when you're a street pastor, and you've got a family that counts on you, I just need to get my head together."

"I'm glad we can help," I say, sincerely, silently wishing we could do more, but relieved that, for now, we don't have to do more. "Have a good day, Mike. I'll see you later."

"Yeah, yeah, I know." He checks the pockets on his outermost coat, fishing out a pack of cigarettes, purchased by mysterious means. "Don't worry. I know, I know: no smoking on the porch."

"Or the garden! Charmaine doesn't like it."

"No, no, see, that's what I'm saying." He chuckles and shakes his head. "I'm not gonna do nothing that don't respect the space." He looks at me like I'm nuts. Then he ambles away, his possessions left on the porch.

He's gone all day. Periodically, on breaks from work in my home office, I check out front. Mike's bags are undisturbed, untouched while their owner's on walkabout, doing whatever he does on a hot Los Angeles day. I figure he'll be back by sundown.

Charmaine says not to count on it. "You have to be careful about having any expectations," she warns me over lunch. "You're not dealing with a normal person. He's not really capable of keeping his word, even if he means to. His brain just doesn't work that way."

He came back for his bags, I remind her. "Just like he said he would—you know, a day later."

"Just be careful," she counsels. "I know you want to help, and that's lovely. So kind. But some people are very difficult to help."

As if to demonstrate his reliability—his *normalcy*—Mike knocks on the front door just as the sky is turning dusky. "Hey, sorry to disturb you, I don't mean to cause any problems, it's just that, I was wondering, it's going to be hard to get to the Valley right now, and, and, I was wondering if, you know, I could crash here tonight. With my bags. Stay with my bags. I won't make any noise or nothing."

"You want to sleep on the porch?"

He looks at the ground and nods, chewing his lips.

"Let me ask the boss."

Charmaine doesn't see why not. "Sure," she says when I seek her blessing. "As long as all the boundaries are clear . . ." We agree Fisher King Mike can stay one more night on our front porch, and so can his bags—and that he can have the pillow and blanket, and that we can make his slumber a bit more comfortable with an old exercise mat we'll donate.

Neither of us feels inordinately magnanimous letting a refugee from the streets spend the night on our front porch. If we were to really go above and beyond, we'd offer Fisher King Mike a night in Weed Hollow Cabin.

In the back corner of the backyard, tucked beneath a blood orange tree canopy, and with a tangerine tree outside the front door, we have a one-room redwood cabin, with a proper shingle roof, functioning electricity, and a queen-size bed. There's no plumbing. The previous owner of our house used the cabin to play video games and smoke weed; Charm and I turned it into a quaint hideaway, an adorable bed and breakfast without the breakfast. Over the years, we've hosted dozens of guests: family members, social justice travelers, friends-of-friends, musical collaborators, entitled freeloaders, parents and children, people in need. One friend, between jobs, stayed there for more than two years. Another friend, post-divorce, stayed there for six months.

And once we let a homeless man sleep there. We were trying to be generous. The cabin was unoccupied at the time. We wanted to help.

It didn't go well. Boundaries were not respected. Cleanliness was not maintained.

The wife was not happy.

We agreed that would be the last time a transient would stay in Weed Hollow Cabin—unless, of course, they were of the privileged young backpacker variety, couch-surfing for a few nights between Burning Man and their flight to Cambodia. Weed Hollow isn't meant to be a casual crash pad, not for random crashers or society's crash victims, the denizens of the street.

And nor is Charmaine's backyard clinic, Be Well Therapy. Formerly the in-law apartment, it has a full bathroom with a shower, a working kitchen, and a Murphy bed. But it's also her healing space by day and almost never available to guests. Numerous people with our financial interests at heart have encouraged us to rent Be Well and Weed Hollow on a short-term basis. We've chosen to hold the spaces rent-free, ready and available when there's a need.

It doesn't occur to me that "there's a need" for Fisher King Mike to sleep in Weed Hollow Cabin. Or Be Well, or our empty guest bedroom, which we use as a screening room, or on the couch in the living room, or the couch in my office, or on an auxiliary blow-up mattress we keep in the closet.

He's got our porch, and that's a whole lot better than the bus stop, isn't it?

"The Porch Watcher" is excerpted from Michael Konik's *The Unexpected Guest: How a Homeless Man from the Streets of Los Angeles Redefined Our Home* published by Diversion Books (2020), available wherever books are sold.

University

BONNI CHALKIN

I KNOW YOU EXIST

The other night as I was walking my dog Shanti on the Upper East Side of Manhattan, I heard a man talking in a loud pleading voice. "Doesn't *anybody hear me?*" he spoke. The block was desolate, dimly lit, so I couldn't see him at first. Oh, but I *heard him.* "Doesn't *anybody see me?* All I want is a bag of Cheetos. I *only* want a bag of Cheetos." I had already walked past him, but knew on my way back I was going to stop by the shadow of a man I saw sitting on a wooden flower box. It was then . . . I heard it. I don't think I'll ever forget his words. His words went right to my heart: "Doesn't *anybody even know I exist?*" Upon hearing that I turned around and walked over to the man sitting on the wooden box, looked down into his sad eyes, and reached my hand out for his. Our hands became entwined as if we were old friends. I spoke gently, "I know you exist." Tears streamed down his cheek as he gazed up into my eyes. "Thank you," he said, "thank you." We stayed like that for a bit, and when he slowly released my hand, I reached into my pocket and handed him the only bill that was in there. "Thank you," he said again.

NORITA DITTBERNER-JAX

PEACE HOUSE

The only building left standing on the block next to the freeway. Inside, folding chairs line the room, people already sitting, moving around, getting coffee. On the walls are the rules, what will get you thrown out and for how long. Everything is simple here and unadorned except for a few tired Christmas decorations, but here's light and heat and soon there will be food.

The discussion is about to begin. Martin locks the door so there are no interruptions, unless someone bangs on it, angry at missing the deadline. But for now it's peaceful, no one's drunk or high, one man sleeps, but he's not snoring and the rest seem alert. They all have hats and gloves, gifts of a church organization.

Now the leader asks for news and Noreen says how three people who were lighting their cigarettes in the street at dawn were hit by a truck. Her husband is one of them and she's looking for a ride to the hospital. The leader says he'll give her a lift. Then the topic for discussion, the giving of gifts, the complications of giving and receiving. So many of those gathered have broken and missing teeth, rheumy eyes and bodies older than their years, but they talk about the uneasy transaction of receiving gifts. Suddenly, Stanley starts speaking, his voice ringing out, his mind ablaze. He says that he always knows when the spirit is wrong behind a gift, but he doesn't let that stop him. "I let the Lord turn it around. The Lord turns it around!"

The leader directs the traffic of their voices and they all get heard. It's his birthday, and so they all sing the birthday song that everyone knows. Then Al brings platters of fried chicken, bowls of potatoes and salad, trays of Christmas cookies and sets them on low tables in the middle of the room. After lunch, the door is unlocked and the stragglers come in out of the cold.

J.O. HASELHOEF

THE CROWN ROYAL AFFAIR

June 2014

A spring night. A man in his thirties walks into the parking lot of a convenience store a few blocks from his rented apartment. He picks up a stone and smashes the glass to unlock it. Estimated replacement cost, $500. Inside, he selects a bottle of Crown Royal, retailing for $24.95. The police respond to the alarm and arrest him.

No stranger to the judiciary system, the man has a rap sheet, which includes numerous misdemeanors, starting at age eighteen for walking on a highway. Various driving violations and possession of marijuana follow. Because he is in jail for one of these minor offenses, he can't show up for another of his hearings and is arrested for Failure to Appear and later, Failure to Comply. He is placed on probation again.

A fall night—a few months later. According to the video on a surveillance camera at the same convenience store, the same man picks up a stone and breaks the glass door. He selects a bottle of Crown Royal and a pack of cigarettes. He exits, sits on the curb nearby, lights a cigarette, and drinks the alcohol.

The police, responding to the alarm, take the man into custody. As he is escorted to a squad car, he yells, "Hell yes, I broke into the store. I admit it."

Police records note the defendant, while on probation for the first break in, burglarized the same store a second time. The man pleads guilty, is assigned a public defender, and waives his right to a pre-sentence investigation and report. Had the two been completed, they might have pointed out the peculiarities of his case or his diagnosis of schizophrenia eleven years before.

He agrees to a plea bargain and accepts four years of prison for the two felonies—burglary and criminal damage for breaking the glass. Two other warrants, one for misdemeanor drug possession and the other for public intoxication, are quashed.

Jason enters the state prison system in December of 2014, with the days already spent in jail counting toward his release.

With good behavior, he will be released with supervision July 21, 2016.

❦ ❦ ❦

June, 1990

I read Jason's crimes as a cry for help, but maybe you see it differently. Maybe you have to know him.

We met in Peoria, Illinois, in 1990; he was nine years old and I was thirty-six. We were part of the Heart of Illinois Big Brothers Big Sisters (BBBS) Program of America. My (now) ex-husband, Harry, and I chose to be a Big Couple, selecting Jason from a number of profiles, age eight through twelve. At the time, Harry wondered if our racial differences—Jason, Black; we, white—would be a problem. I argued no, though I remember when the three of us stopped for lunch at a café in a rural, white town, not far from Peoria. I felt uncomfortable for Jason. From then on, we chose the places we visited more carefully.

Edna, Jason's single parent, looked to BBBS for the male influence her son was missing. As Jason grew up, she worked in a daycare, attending to newborns and managing adolescents after school. She was good at what she did and seemed to thrive on it. She surrounded Jason with her large family and their children and took him to church every Sunday. Their rented single-family home in a low-income neighborhood was kept neat and clean; the shades were always drawn.

As a Big Couple with Jason, we hiked, visited friends, went to county fairs, made meals, and just hung out together. The program encouraged "the Bigs" not to be cash cows or Disneyland friends. We weren't. We spent a lot of normal life together, whether we were with Jason alone or with Edna, watching her son play sports. I also tutored him in math, without much success, and thought he might have a learning disability. Bottom line: he was a good kid. He used his manners, followed directions and didn't push boundaries. He was a pleasure to be with as he tried new things and responded excitedly about the results.

Harry and I moved from Peoria when Jason turned fifteen. By the time we returned two years later, he was no longer interested in the BBBS relationship—typical of most kids his age. He dropped out of high school at eighteen.

Edna called during a Christmas holiday. Jason was in jail—for possession of marijuana. She thought the jail time might do him some good, but I could hear her concern and arranged the bail for his release. She also told me that, during an arrest in 2003, Human Services diagnosed him with schizophrenia and prescribed medication.

Jason and I reconnected after my divorce from Harry. Jason and I never talked about jail nor much about the divorce. Jason played me, occasionally, for money—once asking me to pay for an inexpensive computer for which he would reimburse me—but never did. He introduced me as his sister to his new girlfriend, a serious relationship. "Jason's a great guy!" she said. "Funny, friendly, caring." I agreed.

I moved to Wisconsin with my new partner, Mike, and Jason and I kept up on the phone. We never wrote letters. That would change.

❦ ❦ ❦

December, 2014

Edna called to tell me about Jason's felony conviction at the convenience store. Still, I was shocked when I received the Number 10 envelope on which Jason had neatly printed his return address and prison number. His one-page letter in black, ball-point pen on lined paper with hole punches to the left began, "Dear Judy." In his first correspondence, he offered to mentor my twenty-three year-old son, whom he watched grow during the BBBS days. "I've got lots of experience now and know where no one should ever be—here," Jason wrote. "I want him to know that loud and clear."

He also asked if Harry would write him.

Mike, a former juvenile probation officer, helped me search through the state prisoner database on the Internet. The state of Illinois incarcerated Jason for Robbery, Class 2. A felony—but a relatively victimless crime. That last part made me feel better.

During the next two years, Edna and I made three visits to Shawnee Correctional Facility, four hours south of Peoria in Vienna, Illinois. Jason and I continued to write letters. They filled the time between visits and gave him the space to verbalize his frustrations—the inedible soy-based food, the anger of his first cellmate and the twenty-one of twenty-four hours he spent daily in his cell. He went to church and the library and the gym. "I go to anything I can go to," he said, "just so I can get outta my cell."

He said the prisoners did receive good medical care. Staff made sure he took his medicine for what he called anxiety and psychiatrists had labeled schizophrenia. Jason laughed. "They don't want anything to happen if I'm not medicated."

⁕ ⁕ ⁕

July, 2016

Just a few days before his parole, Mike and I received another letter from Jason. We remembered one of his first prison stories—the trip from the prison intake center near Chicago to the medium-security facility downstate. He called it the longest, scariest bus ride he'd ever experienced as he didn't know what was in store for him. This narrative was different. He wasn't scared to start fresh. "My goal is simple no matter where I go," he said. "Job. Money. Apartment. Car."

On the day of Jason's prison release, July 21, Mike and I met Jason at Shawnee to drive him to the northern edge of Illinois and the halfway house he'd parole out to. His release, two years early, carried a few stipulations about counseling, classes in anger management and substance abuse as well as the directions to take his prescribed medication. They eliminated the option for Jason to parole out to a local homeless shelter, which many incarcerated people initially did. He also had the usual requirements—to check in with his parole officer two times a week and find employment.

The bottle of booze Jason stole from the convenience mart seemed expensive, considering the cost of incarceration. It would have made more sense to me to send Jason to the local community college to teach him a trade and let him pay back the $1050 for the two bottles of Crown Royal and the repair of two broken glass doors. Instead, Shawnee Correctional Facility spent around $38,000 each year on their incarcerated men—$105 per day. The United States incarcerated 1,306,300 individuals in 2017. Jason's crime seemed one of those types that could be better sorted out with therapy and other human services.

That anticipated morning of Jason's release, he exited through the bullet-proof glass door at the promised 8:30 a.m. with a huge smile on his face and one cup of coffee in his stomach. He was too excited to eat the prison breakfast. He wore a new, prison-issued white T-shirt, gray sweat pants (despite the ninety degree/seventy percent humidity outside) and black, army boots. He carried a bag, the size and shape of a thirty-pound summer sausage. In it were a variety of "survival" items, including one roll of toilet paper, which I could see through the mesh as it worked its way to the base. The prison also provided him with $10 and four days of medication for his schizophrenia.

Jason came right to the point as he hugged me, "I'm never going back there."

We drove the four hours north to Peoria listening to Drake and Kendrick Lamar. Mike and I dropped Jason to spend a few hours with his mother and two beloved aunts. Edna served him his favorite foods—fried chicken, bar-b-que ribs and potato salad. He showered the prison off and then met us for the other half of the drive north, carrying two duffle bags full of new clothes Edna had purchased for that very moment.

A thunderstorm pelted us with rain as we couldn't find the address of his new home in the night. A man approached us selling drugs in the lightless neighborhood. We arrived, at last, at a rundown tenement building. The night manager for the eight men in residence, all released from prison over the last six months, met us at the door. He shook Jason's hand, welcomed him inside and immediately told him he couldn't leave the premises until he met with his parole officer. Jason, tired from the emotions of the day, said good night to us. When he saw my look of concern, he added, "This is still better than where I was."

Jason arrived at the halfway house with lots of hope and many challenges. A felony arrest stacks the odds for success against you. The conviction stays on your record permanently, leaving a stain many can't shake when getting a job, renting an apartment or buying a car. Many employers have removed from their job application the question, "Have you ever been convicted of a felony?" but many others haven't and continue to use a blanket policy not to hire a felon. Rates for returning to prison are highest in the first two years after an offender's release. An estimated thirty-seven percent of parolees are rearrested while on parole.

Think about what you would do if you had no job, no money and no identification. Jason's first weeks out of prison were difficult even though he had much more personal support than the average parolee. Mike slipped him $50, Harry paid for his first week of groceries, Edna handed him a copy of his birth certificate and I covered the cost of his lodging. He and I visited the Department of Motor Vehicles, where staffers told him he needed a photo

I.D. to get a photo I.D. Jason persevered. He showed me his identification and medical card at the end of his second week out of incarceration.

He had entered prison without many job skills and left that same way. The state of Illinois' stated mission was "providing a rehabilitative foundation for the offender's reintegration into society." We all believed that meant actively helping the offenders during their years of incarceration. Jason didn't get a job as a kitchen helper until his last few months at Shawnee and, though he received a new text book, he never did get a seat in the GED classes. John, the man who founded and owned the halfway house, came through on his promise to direct Jason to a local employment agency that helped parolees find $10/hour factory jobs.

❦ ❦ ❦

Fall and Winter, 2016

John's place, in a neighborhood where Jason often heard sirens and gunshots, provided each man with minimal facilities for $125 per week. Jason slept for his first month on a sofa until another parolee moved out, leaving a vacant bed. It was infested with bedbugs. When Jason had his wallet lifted during his shower and complained, John made it clear, the fault was Jason's for not taking better precautions with his valuables. The halfway house offered Jason one silver lining: The residents bought their own food, which they cooked for themselves in a shared kitchen. Jason loved to cook. He prepared meals for the other men and became not only an integral part of the household community, but also was valued by his fellow parolees.

That November, Jason turned thirty-five. He told me he knew what he'd accomplished in the past year and that he hadn't been alone in his efforts. Not once had his Mom said, "Jason, you've got to get your act together!" He acknowledged her help and said, "She knows how much work it's taken."

He also knew that he could call Mike or Harry or me, that he had the support of those at his new job and the employment placement agency. He worked hard and was dependable. And he had two more things going for him, "One, I know God has a plan for me," he said "and two, I've got a phrase that I tell myself when I come up against a problem: "I CAN do it."

During the holiday season, the halfway house prepared care boxes for some of the state's 50,000 prisoners. Jason helped fill the boxes and stack them for delivery. Organizers encouraged Jason to write a note with his name and prison number. He wrote fifty men incarcerated at Shawnee, telling each he was OK and encouraging them to keep up their spirits.

He spent Christmas with us and announced to Harry, my son, Mike and me over the breakfast he cooked, "2017 will be my pinnacle year." I was full of hope for my little brother. To see him in our kitchen, flipping eggs over-easy, with plenty of his favorite bacon grease—you would have felt the same.

❦ ❦ ❦

Spring, 2017

Halfway-house John had warned me that the Department of Corrections would release Jason with a minimal amount of medication. John encouraged me to pay for a private psychiatrist instead of letting Jason wait six months to see a doctor via the public medical system. I found a doctor and took Jason to his appointment. However, the psychiatrist re-diagnosed Jason as anxiety-prone—not schizophrenic—and prescribed a low-dose of Ambien. When Jason and I ate lunch some weeks later, I watched him nod off to sleep in the middle of his burger. By our next visit, he'd stopped taking the drug.

As the story went, John ran prostitutes before his own incarceration. Not only did he know the system and those who participated in it from first-hand experience, but he had dirt on all the local officials as well. Soon after he exited prison, he founded the parolee resource, putting together the funding for the house and receiving the necessary local official support.

Jason complained that John insisted the parolees miss some of their paid shifts at the factory to do "volunteer work" to support the non-profit designation under which the halfway house was formed or help put money in John's own pocket. There was little recourse for the parolees. John always held the upper hand as he had good connections with the parole officer to whom the men regularly reported.

Seven months after arriving, Jason could take no more of John's house. I felt proud that Jason's self-assurance had grown to the point that he could cut those ties. John's place, as difficult as it was, served as my little brother's first home after prison and gave him some grounding. Jason moved nearby to a homeless men's shelter. A group of churches took in the men, provided them with beds, two meals, and a connection to social service support. In exchange, the administrators required them to attend church and leave the shelter during the day. Jason found the shelter's rules and arrangements easier to navigate than John's.

Some weeks later, the manufacturing company changed his shift to third. Jason had a difficult time getting the necessary sleep and leaving the shelter every day as required. He called Mike and me one day from the psych ward of the local hospital after an episode at the shelter. Instead of arguing or fighting, like before, "I just left and checked myself in," Jason said. He had taken a big step, controlling himself and his issues. He was re-diagnosed with schizophrenia and given new meds.

Jason quit the factory job and picked up work part-time with a landscaper. When Mike and I met him at a Pizza Hut near the shelter, Jason looked good and sounded well. He flirted with our female server as he told us a staff person in social services was helping him set up some life objectives. He appeared on track, hitting his one-year anniversary of parole. He had beaten the odds and stayed out of prison. He remained employed, kept a roof over his head and held onto his good behavior. It seemed pretty close to the "pinnacle year" he foretold in January.

The positive energy flowed forward. A few weeks later, Jason shouted through the phone, "I got my check!" I didn't know what he was talking about. The social worker at the shelter had encouraged him to file for Social Security Supplemental Income, based on his psychiatric disability of schizophrenia. With that secure, though minimal, income, he would head south to live in Bloomington, a city forty-five minutes away from his hometown of Peoria. Bloomington was where the buses ran from Chicago, and employment seemed more certain.

Mike and I were happy for him but concerned. Edna had told us that during his twenties, Jason received supplemental income because of his diagnosis. He had not worked, but lived on the small stipend and housing allowance provided by the government. By his own admission, he had little incentive to do anything and fell in with the wrong crowd. Misdemeanor arrests peppered his life. Now, again, he was on medication, receiving government support, and without any real structure in his life. We didn't think it spoke well for his future. The rate that incarcerated males returning to prison lessened only slightly every year they were out. In 2016, Illinois saw 71,551 new convictions; of those, eighty-nine percent were reoffenders headed back to prison. The chances of Jason returning remained high.

❋ ❋ ❋

October, 2017

Jason and I exchanged only a few text messages or phone calls during the fall. I was uncomfortable but tried to be patient. One day, he called out of the blue. He had gone through with his plans to move to a homeless shelter in Bloomington.

On the one hand, he had taken a big step to make that move on his own and I was proud of him. He had jumped forward on the trajectory he wanted. On the other hand, he was calling to ask for money. I hesitated and then said, "I'm sorry, Jason, I can't right now." I hoped that was the right thing to do.

A few weeks later I texted, asking how he was. He answered, "I'm going this week to see Mom in Peoria. Had permission issues, but been working with DHS." He was still advising the Department of Human Services of his travels as part of his parolee requirements. Jason never arrived at his mom's.

Edna called his mobile repeatedly. I texted him many times, including on his November birthday. Neither Edna nor I received a response.

Numerous times during and after prison, Jason had said he wanted a job, money, a car, an apartment and, on good days, he added in "a girlfriend." But Jason was part of a group, in fact, many groups, each of which often have difficulties achieving those simple goals: He's Black, poor, raised by a single parent, has a disability, and holds a felony record.

It's my nature—isn't it all of our natures?—to point a finger, to find someone to blame, to get the problem fixed by him, or her, or them. I tend to think that a simple obvious, immediate solution can fix a problem when really the issue is too lengthy and complex for a quick fix. In looking back at the small, individual pieces that assembled the whole of Jason's life, I'm fairly certain all participants worked to capacity to help Jason, but the opportunity to place blame pulls at me strongly.

Edna was a hard-working woman who was a loving, responsible mother. Should she have been tougher with him? The Peoria District schools, which Jason attended, manage 36,000 students every year and pride themselves on a ninety-three percent graduation rate. What do they do about the seven percent in which Jason fell? Jason's series of misdemeanors were small infractions for Illinois' departments, programs, and processes tasked with readjusting wayward youth. Should his many nickel-dime arrests have been a bigger red flag to the agencies, his family and friends? The public defender allowed Jason to waive his Pre-Sentence Investigation and Report, eliminating the individual attention that the justice system offered through that document. Didn't his psychiatric diagnoses deserve more attention? And finally, Social Security provided Jason with money to live, accommodating his disability. If the stipend isn't enough money to survive but restricts recipients from earning more, what can we expect them to do legally?

❦ ❦ ❦

December, 2017

November stretched into December that gave way towards Christmas—with no word from Jason.

His mother, Mike and I had spent the last month of the year contacting shelters, social service agencies, hospitals, and finally the sheriff, thinking Jason lay on a slab somewhere as a John Doe. Every few days, I called or texted his mobile with some upbeat "Happy Holidays" or "Hoping to celebrate Christmas with you." No reply. Late afternoon December 28, I texted: "I'm worried. So's your mom. Please call."

Within a minute, I received a text in response, "I was at inpatient for alcohol abuse," he said. "It was getting out of hand, so I got help." He wasn't exactly clear how long he'd been there to get the support he needed—maybe a week, maybe four. Sometimes the details don't really matter, right? I felt so relieved.

Released, Jason returned to a private apartment he shared with a roommate and the part-time job he held. He helped remove and clean out properties where debris or personal possessions were left behind after an eviction. It was one of the types of jobs that felons could get.

I said to Mike that night, "Jason's story never seems to end."

"And it won't." Mike responded. "It's his reality and, like everyone's, his holds a number of twists and turns." Mike pointed out that Jason's life held both bad and good—the full spectrum. He thought the best we all could hope and work for was to increase the number of good over the bad—or at least minimize the depth of both to move Jason closer to the center. "I do think he trusts you—us—and we will keep hearing from him," Mike said. "We didn't always know that."

Jason called again a few months later from the mental ward of another hospital. This time, Mike and I drove south and picked up Edna in neighboring Peoria. We stopped at Walmart. Each of us disappeared in a separate direction into the endless aisles. We met at the checkout counter with the items we thought Jason needed from the thousands available. Edna came with boxer shorts and two T-shirts, hoping size 2XX was right. Mike tossed in a large bag of Skittles, saying if he were in the hospital, he knew what he couldn't live without. And I added to the check-out belt a crossword puzzle workbook and a science magazine—items he liked me to send while in prison.

Visiting hours began at 5 p.m. Mike knocked on the single door at the end of a long quiet hallway. I expected Nurse Ratched from "One Flew Over The Cuckoo's Nest" to answer. Instead, a smiling security guard said nicely, "Come on in. Leave everything, including the stuff in your pockets and those Walmart bags, in those lockers over there."

We entered the hallway of patient rooms. I didn't recognize Jason, who stood almost in front of me. He weighed 25 pounds more than the last time I saw him and wore glasses. He was dressed in green scrubs and I thought he worked for the hospital. But his big smile, the one I knew from when he was a twelve-year old, made me relax and stop thinking about Nurse Ratched.

They had admitted Jason at his own request. He was going to two different hospitals at the same time and was prescribed three medications—at least one of which caused him to hallucinate. The doctors at this facility checked his urine and blood levels often and planned to keep him there for five days. They changed his diagnosis to bipolar disorder with anxiety.

Edna viewed him with motherly concern. "Jason, you're so heavy. You gotta move!" He nodded, but it was probable that his meds caused him the weight gain. He told us he stayed on them as much as he could, but when they gave him diarrhea or hallucinations, he stopped taking them.

Mike and I drove Edna back to Peoria and then headed north to Wisconsin. Both of us were thinking about Jason when Mike broke the silence. "This might be as good as it gets for him." I nodded my understanding in the darkness.

At ten the next morning, my mobile buzzed. I recognized the number from the hospital, and held my breath as I answered. It was Jason wanting to ensure we made it home safely and thank us for the gifts that security gave him after we left. "It was really nice that you came to see me," he said, "and brought my mom too."

❋ ❋ ❋

July, 2018

Jason always talked openly with Mike and me, but I never felt wholly comfortable with the subject of his psychological diagnoses—it seemed too intrusive. He had been diagnosed with anxiety, schizophrenia and bipolar disorder but how did he feel about the accuracy of any of them? He said he didn't hear voices, didn't fly from really happy to really sad nor sit in a corner in a ball. "None of them describes me," he said. "But I guess I spent twenty-one out of every twenty-four hours locked up because of one of those."

How would he analyze himself at that moment? "Probably PTSD. It's the things I've seen, like my friend getting shot," he said. "I haven't told you, but it was pretty bad in Peoria."

I was quiet—dumbfounded. I hadn't heard this before and I wondered if Jason had told any of his psychiatrists. I felt inadequate that I couldn't say anything appropriate yet felt, somehow, a sense of relief. I always thought Jason was a good boy. This one event suggested he was but, shaken from what he'd seen years ago, went bad. OK. It wasn't that simple. Jason had to take some responsibility for the many occurrences and decisions that followed. This story gave me a start date for the difficulties that snowballed out of control.

I said at the beginning that I read Jason's crimes of stealing two bottles of Crown Royal from the same location as a cry for help. Now, do you also see that?

Jason was reaching his goals on his own. Despite the high recidivism rate for those incarcerated, Jason appeared to be the exception. He had learned from his mistakes, righted them, and moved ahead. He knew the family and friends on which he could fall back, and he trusted himself as well. He knew that when his meds were off, life wouldn't go well. And he had learned that he had every reason to strive for personal wins to celebrate.

As with any brother-sister relationship, I've watched Jason go through excitement, joy, heartache, frustration and sadness for twenty-eight years. I've learned I can't live his life, nor can I fully understand the difficulty of his challenges. I do appreciate that he's shared so much with me, for he has enriched my life. I hope I've added to his and look forward to another twenty-eight years as his big sister.

It was a hot, sultry day in the middle of summer. I hadn't seen or heard from Jason for some months. Edna told me he was doing some work at a rib joint in Bloomington and was thinking about moving in with a girlfriend. I still held my breath when I saw Jason identified on my phone as the caller. Today was no different until I remembered it was July 21. I picked it up to hear Jason on the other end.

"I'm off parole!"

CHARLES BROCKETT & HEATHER TOSTESON

TOGETHER FOR THE LONG HAUL

For almost two years we attended monthly support group meetings of the *Persons Impacted by Incarceration Collaborative* (PIIC), a group of formerly incarcerated men and women that was formed with the mentorship of A.J. Sabree, former director of reentry services at the Georgia Department of Corrections (DOC). (Our attendance at these PIIC meetings was central to a listening project culminating in a book on reentry after mass incarceration from which this essay is a revised extract.) Many of these individuals had been incarcerated for very long periods of time, so they had known each other, for years, in a very different context. Several of the PIIC members travelled frequently to various Georgia prisons to talk to people serving long sentences. The monthly support group was open to anyone who wanted to come.

A.J. SABREE: Reentry Begins with You

A.J. Sabree, who we had first heard about through the African-American Muslim community, was very open to speaking with us when we first met him at a large faith-based reentry meeting held down at the DOC headquarters an hour south of Atlanta in Forsyth. He invited us to a PIIC meeting that evening.

PIIC grew out of A.J.'s thirty-year career in DOC, where he served as a prison chaplain, assistant director of chaplaincy, and then, for a decade, as director of an over-arching department of reentry services that included chaplaincy, risk-reduction services, and community reentry. When we met him, he had recently retired from DOC and was serving as a reentry consultant to the Department of Juvenile Justice, helping create reentry centers in their prisons. A.J. was in his early sixties. Since leaving DOC, he had lost a hundred and fifty pounds, but photographs of him during his time in DOC showed a substantial man with a commanding physical presence. It was easy to understand how he could have been a core member of the

Imam W. D. Mohammed's security detail. Many of the members of PIIC had known him when, as a young imam, he came in to some of the worst prisons and helped them effect change. A.J. is slow spoken, with a stutter that precedes and adds gravitas to his thoughtful comments.

A.J. 's relationship with DOC was complex. He knew that his religion had impeded his career, was told this directly more than once. On the other hand, he had been able to rise administratively in the system and was able to make changes that were valuable to him and to those who lived in the prisons. His commitment to reform of the prison system had very personal origins, ones that he shared at PIIC and with us.

As a young man, he had been involved in various illegal activities, primarily selling drugs, but was never convicted. His younger brother, with whom he was very close, followed his example. However, his brother was caught, convicted, and imprisoned for twenty years. Both men are very bright—A.J. mentioned that his brother had tested as having the highest IQ in the prison. They came from a law-abiding family that valued education. A psychologist who was asked to see his brother before the trial told their parents that they should keep A.J. away from his brother because he was a pathological influence on him. "I had become cold," is how A.J. described it. But the psychologist's description of him troubled A.J. so deeply that he began to turn his life around. He became very involved with the Nation of Islam, especially with the rise of the more moderate W. D. Mohammed, and began visiting the prisons. A.J. found Islam attractive "because of its social theology and its discipline—and like Roman Catholicism, it was ritualistic and sacrificial. It helped me cold turkey stop what I was doing."

A.J. had a great sense of guilt about his brother's incarceration and whatever influence he had on him, a guilt he said he had never shared with his brother until after his brother came to one of the PIIC meetings. But A.J. talked often in those meetings about the dangers of becoming cold. A.J. was clearly deferred to in the PIIC meetings, but he usually kept silent until the close, when he would react to what he had heard, summarizing and synthesizing the themes of the evening in a way that was usually both cautionary and motivational. He identified the emotional and social challenges that were intrinsic to reentry, the temptation to fall back on habits that may have worked in prison but did not work in the larger world.

A.J. came into the prisons as a change agent, not necessarily a provocateur, at a time of great turmoil: *From the beginning one of the questions for me was how to impact change without standing on the outside advocating—how to get inside and influence change,* is how A.J. described his intentions. When he first went into Reidsville, it was about to face a federal take-over. There were large numbers of prisoners in open dorms, and knifings were common.

A.J. as a chaplain began to invite the leaders of inmate groups together to start a conversation: *I understood the language and the mindset. I had reformed from the street, so I understood criminal thinking. I could kind of engage, offer them something different. Also, you can't just put the responsibility for change on the staff. The staff run the prison at the pleasure of the population because they're outnumbered.*

A.J. helped the prisoners organize an Inmate Unity Committee. They asked to meet with the administration. At first the warden objected, but eight hundred inmates insisted on meeting with the administration and the dialogue began. Having developed a reputation as someone who could work with both prison groups and the administration, wardens requested A.J.'s presence throughout the prison system.

This work quickly brought him to central headquarters where in 1988 he became the assistant director of the chaplaincy program. He strongly advocated a pluralistic, multi-faith perspective among the 150 full-time clinical chaplains: "Chaplains don't go there to provide services for a particular faith group, but for all offenders." His approach also made him an ideal candidate in the early 2000s to develop a reentry sensibility in the Georgia prison system as attitudes toward reentry nationally began to shift, a project to which he dedicated the last decade of his career at DOC.

> *At that time, no one knew what reentry services were—and they left me alone to chart my way. I could see reentry was going to be the biggest thing in corrections. Reentry begins at the first point you touch the system and continues after release. I knew it couldn't be piecemeal, it affected everything: policy, the culture of corrections, the culture of community supervision, the programs that would contribute and be effective. Risk reduction, vocational education, volunteers, community engagement, they all fell under reentry.*
>
> *I was Commissioner James Donald's person for change. I had to go around and say all that to the program people, tell them, "You can be part of something that will leave a legacy." It took a long time for the leadership to get it. My gift was that I could sell it. I can* <u>*sell*</u> *reentry, make people believe in it. I can approach it from many different perspectives. I'm humble on it. I feel I am receiving*

> *help from something greater than myself. And God is bigger than the challenges.*

A.J.'s dedication to PIIC was both a matter of personal loyalty to the group of men and women in it and a professional commitment to bringing justice full circle: *Martin Luther King used to say the hottest place in hell was saved for those who maintain neutrality in a moral crisis. This is a moral crisis.*

A.J. talked at some length about the particular hopes he had for PIIC:

> *Life is always going to be a process—a process to get where God wants you to be. The people who have done best started the process before they got out. You can be free of prison even if they don't let you out. Once you get to a certain point, the system can't hold you.*
>
> *What are we looking for here? Everyone is at different stages. It takes a lot for me to give up. I want everyone to have another chance. I do know when I hear someone convicted to criminal mindedness. They may have been in for forty years, but they will still commit crime. They'll tell you that. But the majority of people just don't know how to deal with barriers and challenges. They give up and revert. They don't have all the tools they need. Expectations are put on them that are not normal to them. You can't function all the time as a well-organized group if you have no training in group dynamics. In PIIC, I don't try to talk about that, I try to demonstrate it.*

Over his career, A.J. had quietly gathered numerous academic credentials—in clinical chaplaincy, criminal justice, as a paralegal, a real estate agent, often without letting anyone he worked with know. When we last spoke with him he was studying for a PhD in criminal justice. These degrees were a reflection of his intellectual curiosity, his desire for career advancement, and also a crucial counter-balance to the constraints he felt inside the system—they provided him with that inner freedom and self-determination that he was dedicated to helping members of PIIC cultivate. He and his wife also raised eleven children during that time, probably embodying the same message.

REV. HAZEL HORNE: Lift into Life

Another regular member of the support group, Reverend Hazel Horne, had also known most of the core members of PIIC during their time in prison through her prison ministry. Small, elegant, with a soft voice that sometimes verged on the unearthly, Hazel had seen more than most of us, and for longer, and was still charged with hope. Hazel pastors a small, New Thought church in southeastern Atlanta, Jesus Christ Center of Truth, and has had a prison ministry for decades. She often attended meetings with Dorothy Parker, who shared her prison ministry, and with her teenage grandson, Robbie, whose challenges often provided a focus for all the hard won wisdom of the PIIC members.

Our first personal conversation took place at her small white church set in one of those leafy Atlanta suburbs that shift almost instantaneously from large contemporary apartment complexes to vistas that look like a bend in time, as if we were back in the farmland of her challenging, resilient childhood.

Hazel remembered with great warmth her childhood in south Georgia, where her father was a sharecropper. They lived without electricity or running water, but with abundant aspiration. She remembered standing in their front yard and watching FDR drive by on his way to Warm Springs, the hope that his presence engendered in a young black girl in south Georgia, the way her father removed his hat in respect. She also remembered the anger she felt when her father, working in the field, felt obliged to take off his hat to the white man who owned the land. She also remembered the chain gangs that came by once a month to work the roads, how when her father heard them approaching he would send Hazel and her brother out to draw water from the well and gather food from the kitchen. There, with the guards and the guns, they would serve the men. "We would drink out of the same gourd," she said.

Her father had a fifth-grade education, and made educating his children his priority. Hazel and her two siblings all finished high school early. At seventeen she went to Chattanooga to attend a Bible college, working during the week on Lookout Mountain, tending the children of a wealthy couple. There was still a steely anger in her voice at the memory of working for people who could not even care for their own clothes.

Hazel decided early in her life that she was going to care for lost or abandoned children. She had been profoundly shaped by the story of her father's abandonment by his own fifteen-year-old mother. She took him with her on a bus to Atlanta and when a stranger on the bus complimented her on her son, said, "You want him, take him." The man, not knowing what to do, took the child to his boarding house and kept him locked in a closet while he worked. (The boy was ultimately found and raised by one of his maternal aunts.) "I only wanted the children nobody else wants," Hazel explained.

Hazel said she married because she thought she had to if she wanted to foster children. After she and her husband adopted two children, they divorced because he wanted children of his own. When we talked, Hazel's two adopted children had both died quite recently, in their early forties, within eight weeks of each other, the daughter of a chronic illness, the son from complications of an operation. She was clearly still mourning them, especially her daughter who had shared her ministry.

Over her lifetime, Hazel also fostered fifteen children, mostly informally. "I would go out and check my porch to see if anyone had been left there." She found two brothers, abandoned for five or six days, eating out of the garbage and took them in and raised them for twenty years. One of them died of sickle cell, the other was in prison for meth. He had put her on his visitors list saying, "You're the only mother who has been there for me." Hazel also took in the children of several women who were incarcerated. She took in three children of a Nigerian woman who was sentenced to thirty years. The children all finished college. She also took in the two children of a woman who spent several years on death row.

Hazel started a prison ministry in 1978 because her brother "had started going in and out." He had "started taking things." She originally went into a prison with Reverend Barbara King's church group, in part to look for her brother. Although she didn't actually find him, she kept returning. "He was pulling me there. Every week I was showing up. I left my children so alone." Her brother died in 1979, but he had managed to send her some money before he died with the wish that she continue her ministry. She took his wish seriously and began to study and was ordained by King. Hazel began her ministry at the prison near Stone Mountain where her brother had been held, a community at that time known for its intense racism and as the home of the KKK, as she noted. In time, her ministry expanded to other prisons. She was the first woman chaplain to enter notorious Reidsville.

She described in her soft, imperturbable voice how in the prison men would fight over which religious groups could use the chapel. She insisted they see it as a place where God did not encourage divisions. No one had an exclusive claim on God. "God is going to bring the ones here that need to be here," she told them.

She called her ministry *Lift into Life* because she saw that as her mission, to lift up the men she visited. "I told them, what you did yesterday doesn't say anything about where you are today." Hazel didn't say this in a sentimental way, as this story she shared made clear: *A man come to me in the chapel, he was real upset. He told me, "I was raped by five mens last night." I said to him, "Well, that's done. What can I do for you today to help you be the man you want to be?"*

This same ruthless realism and care informed her fostering as well. Mothers might not return for years. Children needed to focus on the here and now.

One story she returned to often was that of the woman who spent time on death row. She had a beautiful voice, was known as "the songbird of the south," and sang in a prison choir that traveled widely. After her sentence was commuted and she was released from prison, she still felt her children, from whom she had been separated for eleven years and who were now nearly grown, were better off with Hazel. However, her son could never accept this, even though Hazel assured him he had a home with her. "Why my mother not want us?" he asked. He thanked Hazel for all she had done for them. At eighteen he died by drowning, and Hazel wondered if it was suicide. She returned to the story because it obviously troubled her. It showed the limit of fostering. He *had* received her love, but she felt it couldn't compensate for his profound sense of abandonment.

With her grandson Robbie, who she brought to PIIC, Hazel faced a similar struggle. She was raising Robbie along with a girl, Tia, about the same age, very bright and resilient, who Hazel had taken in when she was six days old because her mother failed to bond. Robbie also was deeply troubled by the rejection of his mother, who had raised him until the age of five then sent him over to his father to raise. Robbie was as jealous of Tia as he was of the children who lived with his own mother right across the street from him. Grieving the death of his father and fearing the possibility of losing his older brother to prison, Robbie was becoming delinquent, a subject of great, and unifying, concern to PIIC members in the two years we attended meetings.

The last time we spoke with Hazel, she and Robbie were taking refuge in a hotel because a fire caused by faulty wiring in the stove had nearly destroyed her home of sixty years. She described the situation calmly, including as almost an after thought that Robbie's older brother was currently in the hospital with several shots to the abdomen. She thought they were revenge from a spurned boyfriend. He would be fine, she said. They would be too. Her house was insured.

Persons Impacted by Incarceration Collaborative

PIIC

The very first PIIC meeting we attended was one of the most interesting, creating a context in which to understand the ones that followed. The first person we met was an older man who walked around saying to himself and everyone around him, "I don't know anything. I have to be a sponge." He had been incarcerated for forty-six years. He was disoriented physically as well as sociologically. He could not recognize the area he had grown up in or the behaviors of the people he met. He realized that the anger he felt at his own disorientation would be dangerous to him, and was trying to talk himself down with the help of Ariif, a core PIIC member who himself had spent over thirty years in prison on three life sentences.

This meeting took place the evening after the core PIIC group had all gone together with A.J. to one of the first large statewide meetings on reentry during the height of Georgia's criminal justice reform. They had gone to introduce PIIC to a larger audience and were energized by what they had seen.

One of them, Darryl, college-educated and formerly incarcerated twice on drug charges, had developed a career for himself managing halfway houses for those released from prison with mental health issues. When Darryl arrived an hour into the meeting, he was extremely upset. As he was coming over, he had been called by the Sheriff's Department in an adjoining county. A prisoner had been released from prison who was clearly psychotic. They didn't know what to do. He had been left in front of the jail. They couldn't hold him, but they didn't dare release him either. They wondered if Darryl could do anything to help them. He had gone over there and arranged to have the man placed in one of the transitional housing units he used to manage. "All that talk," he said. "That's just what it is. Talk. On the street, psychotic with no meds. Nothing has changed."

A.J., slipping into almost a dream state, began to describe several scenes from his time as a prison chaplain that still haunted him: Having to leave Eloise [another core PIIC member] and other women in a decrepit women's prison ankle deep in water, the guilt of going home to his own dry house at night. Eloise, who had experienced the water lapping around her, seemed unfazed by the memory, but clearly it was a pivotal image that would never leave A.J. Nor would watching a psychotic inmate, who was starving himself to death out of paranoia, being coldly shot to death by prison guards as he, clearly delusional, started climbing a barbed wire fence. That evening these disturbing images were triggered by the very prospect of a more humane approach gaining traction—and the doubt that that traction would hold. The almost sanctimonious optimism of the faith leaders at the conference needed to be balanced against harsh realities that had not yet changed, and possibly never would. In many ways, this was the purpose of A.J.'s closing remarks at the end of each meeting. Too much hope was as distorting as too little.

PIIC members need to give back, and one of the topics that would energize them highly was the idea that young boys might follow in their own footsteps. Hazel would often bring in her troubled grandson, Robbie, who was acting out dangerously. He had at one point lain down in the middle of the street spreading his arms and legs as you would to make a snow angel, claiming he wanted to die. Another time he had set fire to a school bus and was facing charges of arson. At the PIIC support meetings, Robbie was always well-dressed, responsive. He couldn't identify what was driving his aggressive behaviors. His tennis shoe had been scuffed, someone had offended him. But the members of PIIC had a clear concern about where this behavior could lead him and all of them would chime in, providing him with suggestions about how to control his behavior. He relaxed and expanded into the attention, leaving the meetings walking tall, beaming.

Another time, Joe brought in his nephew, who was sixteen. Joe was furious at him. His nephew had waved a gun in front of his mother, Joe's sister, and threatened suicide. His mother had wrestled the gun away. Joe was most angry because his nephew had endangered his own mother. Joe, who had a long history of drug offenses but no violent crimes, was furious at the potential for violence. When A.J. probed Joe's nephew about his ambitions, he said he wanted to be a successful rapper and take care of his mother. A.J. suggested that it was important to always have about a hundred plans for success and routes to them, just in case one or another didn't pan out. It helped reduce frustration. A few months later, his nephew acting up again, Joe again infuriated, insisted that he would like to see the boy incarcerated, only prison would put some sense in him. The support session involved talking Joe down.

In other sessions, conversations turned on the temptation to return to crime when all the ways you were trying to reenter legitimately felt blocked to you: "A person got to eat," the visitor said. Several times men raised concerns about their own sons and the fear that they would follow in their footsteps. Relapse was always a concern. One job loss could send you back to baseline—facing all the prejudice, all the frustration all over again. Having numerous plans was a helpful hedge against frustration, so was never becoming too secure. A.J. mentioned several times how his brother, who had become a successful computer programmer, working for a company for decades, now faced job loss because the company had been bought out and the new company forbid employing anyone with a criminal record. Here today, gone tomorrow. Whatever you do.

Everyone took a protective posture toward Johnny, a large, muscular man in his fifties who had been incarcerated for forty-six years, since he was ten years old. He had gone to prison for murder because he had killed a man who was attacking his mother. In prison, he had been ordered by other prisoners to kill someone, "so I did what I had to do." Hazel, who had known him in prison said he had been beaten up a lot there because he was so young. He kept trying to hang himself, but he told A.J., "I ain't hanging myself to kill myself, just to get attention." Johnny was now married but the marriage was not going well. The wife, according to Hazel, "Marry him, but he can't stay with her. When he has money, she gets under him for the money. A lot of the men get married in prison. Johnny is thinking until death do us part." Childlike in his directness, Johnny was hyper-kinetic and walked for hours every day.

Once, a middle-class professional couple came to try to understand what their son, who had been convicted and was soon to be incarcerated, was going to face in prison. They had read *The New Jim Crow*, wanted to discuss their son's situation in terms of systemic racism. PIIC members saw that as irrelevant to the daily challenges of prison life.

The only other person who explicitly raised racism as a topic was also a middle-class participant of the group who came often in our first year. He too had been inspired by *The New Jim Crow*. He was a deacon at a large Congregational church, home to many of the faculty at the historically black colleges. He had a plan to help formerly incarcerated men build housing for themselves. He asked the group to pray that he would receive millions for this effort. He often would ask people, "Who hurt you?" A question that rarely received an answer.

Since most of the core members had been imprisoned for very long periods and knew A.J. throughout his career in the prison system, they sometimes liked to tease him about his past. Terry liked describing him to newcomers as a firebrand preacher in his youth. Terry himself had been imprisoned for over thirty years on two murder convictions. He is a very bright and charming man, highly literate, now in his sixties. He and Ariif are good friends, but where Ariif had been a proud and resistant convict, Terry was a socially adroit one, learning how to shape the prison context to him as much as he shaped himself to it. In prison he had become a Braille translator. Now that he was out, he had reconnected with his childhood sweetheart, and used his language skills to edit books and develop various movie projects. He particularly enjoyed reading to children at the elementary school his nephew attended.

A lasting image we have of the potential influence of PIIC involved a panel, "My Journey to Freedom," which they presented at the Hillside International Truth Center, Rev. Barbara King's church. Ariif, Eloise, and Terry all shared their thoughts on what was needed for successful reentry.

Terry, whose mother and grandmother had died while he was in prison, described PIIC as his family. He said: *Change has to begin while you are behind walls. People fear the unknown. If you don't have a model of legitimacy, faced with a choice, you will lean toward the familiar. The system is mighty, but God is All-mighty. A lot of people didn't expect me to be standing here today.*

Ariif talked about the social and financial impact of prison on the family, and how he had to move from a systemic understanding of his situation to a personal and spiritual one: *In the military, I faced bigotry. I developed a hard side. I reasoned to myself that the crime I committed was because there was so little tolerance for African Americans. You have to confront yourself in prison, come to terms with yourself. Your preparation for release begins inside. I realized something in life was bigger than me. As I developed my faith, it allowed me to navigate in a more sensible way. When you wake up, you realize you still have your faculties, you return to a sense of right and wrong.*

Eloise shared her insights as well: *I was twenty-seven years in the Georgia prison system. My greatest struggle <u>was</u> Eloise. My greatest struggle <u>is</u> Eloise. I had a dysfunctional upbringing, but my biggest problem was Eloise. There comes a time when you have to take responsibility.*

She also invited the audience to take responsibility: *There are people in prison who have good in them. You have to see how this plight affects you, how recidivism affects you. You need to get the system to understand they need to do their part, like we do our part.*

When an audience member asked how he handled the frustration of being a felon, Terry said, *Go outside and scream as if being scalded, listen to my music, call my friends from PIIC. We are no more or less than anyone else. We're all children of God trying to find our way.*

The Rev. Hazel Horne stood up and introduced herself and said: *When I went into Reidsville, they asked, "What a woman doing here?" I knew I had to go where God sent me. This is what I have to share: Never stop loving. Love is a river. It continues to flow. You can put all kinds of things in a river, but the water will find a way. Never turn your back on them. If you call me at four in the morning, Hazel will find a way.*

MARK TARALLO

MIRRORED EYE

The faces, animated and aflame with alcohol, kept coming at me; it was all I could do to defuse them with polite meaningless words. I suppose I was one of the few unfamiliar faces at the party—most of the others seemed to be members of an extended dysfunctional family—and everyone seemed ravenous for fresh meat.

I was the new neighbor, having moved to Baltimore from DC a few months previous. I barely knew the host; I assumed I was invited as a hedge against a potential noise complaint. But I had nothing going on that night, so I went, and drank gin, hard (for a few reasons, both known and unknown), and this made the women at the party seem even more compelling than usual, yet the things I wanted to focus on visually—cleavage, a sexy mouth, even a forehead mole (silently cheering its pluck for choosing such a prominent location) I felt like I had to avoid out of decorum, so I kept my gaze in check. I started liking the party, yet I didn't quite trust it. I could easily envision anger sweeping through the room like a creedal wave, and the whole affair turning mobbish.

Then again, I might have been projecting. Gin's trouble for me. It usually meant one of two things: accelerated infatuation (which never ended satisfactorily), or, it gets my red flag out, and unburies the aggression I keep deep inside myself. At the time I had been reading *Esquire*—identity-wise, I was very confused—and they had a list, *Fifty Things Every Good Man Should Do Before He Dies*. Sleep Under the Stars for a Week, Have an Affair with a Parisian, etc.

Number Three was Throw One Good Punch. That I had never done, and it was kind of on my mind.

A lull hit around nine. People stopped coming up to me, and I found myself isolated. For about thirty seconds, out of boredom, I imagined myself suddenly becoming a human whirlwind in the crowd—spinning wildly, throwing punches, smashing into the well-fed bodies and plush furniture, flying drinks, cries of confusion.

Smiling, I quietly approached a small group of drinkers already in conversation, but soon realized they were talking about a television crime show I knew nothing about. I sought out others. A guy in a wildly floral shirt was talking to two women in the corner; something about the boring choices rich kids choose. (*That's the thing, they're so incredibly predictable and conservative. Where the kids from poor families, man, they go for it . . .*) It sounded like a buzz kill—the haves and the have nots, etc.—so I moved on. The next group was engrossed in "whatever happened to so-and-so" banter (*Oh God. She moved to California and became like this, Silicon Valley courtesan. She fucked all the digerati. Anything for money.*), but they made no effort to open the conversation to me, so again I moved on. I drifted around the room, alone. The furniture looked smug—an overstuffed earth-tone couch, a leather recliner, two chairs in velvet upholstery, think muffling carpet. Near the far wall an enormous TV screen showed slamming bodies with the sound turned out.

There was a spill.

The crowd parted, tut-tutted. It was a beaut: red wine on the couch. The boy in me still loved spills, and the spiller looked like an elegant woman. The kindly host tried to spin it as a positive, something involving an insurance scheme that would lead to an even better chair. Her pained nervous laugh indicated otherwise.

Then another, not fifteen minutes later, and by the same woman. More kinetic this time: the glass hit the floor and the wine shot up and out, dousing the khakis of the closest bystander and a sizable swath of the rug.

—Oh man! exclaimed the victim. His tense face suggested that was code for, you bitch! I started to realize that the gap between what he said and what he was really saying, between what the host said and how she felt, was everywhere at the party. But I chose action over analysis (the *Esquire* influence), and darted into the kitchen for some napkins.

Soon I was on my hand and knees, next to the elegant spiller.

✵ ✵ ✵

—The weird thing about it, the woman said while we were still on all fours, dousing, is that I haven't even been drinking much, because I'm driving.

The fact that she had spilled twice gave the woman an air of slight daffiness, which perfectly offset her serious-but-lovely looks—firm smooth jawline, high rounded cheekbones, liquid brown eyes brimming with thought. The proximity to her made me nervous, which I channeled into an onslaught of statements.

—Maybe it was just your fingers protesting the inadequacy of the conversation, I said.

Even I could tell this was a stupid thing to say, but she was in such a lowly position—-she was pouring salt on the affected area of the carpet, which almost seemed like an act of biblical recompense—that she went with it.

—What do you mean?

—Well, I was with a group who kept talking about these cop shows.

—Right! *Homicide* and *The Wire*. I'm clueless with that stuff. I don't know any of the references.

—I mean, I lost track after *Hill Street Blues*, I said.

—I can't watch any of them, she said. Too violent. I'd rather watch reruns of *Mary Tyler Moore*.

—Excellent, I said. I could totally see you tossing a beret in the air. Who can turn the world on with her smile.

She smiled.

—Is that your idea of me being progressive? You're dating yourself.

—No, don't knock the seventies. Or, I could see you in one of those "You've Come a Long Way Baby" ads from the 1970s.

—Oh God! she said. Virginia Slims.

—And I mean, certainly more progressive than this young woman here.

I pointed to the girl pictured on the Morton Salt canister she was holding. She turned it in her hand and looked at the Morton Salt Girl.

—What's wrong with her? She looks like someone from a better vanished time.

We kept talking after the clean up. Her name was Cynthia, and she worked for a community development organization that did inner-city work. She was engaging and lively, and the conversation turned and turned, until it formed its own two-person cottage. I told her about my Philosophy of Parties.

—The Torah says the world is a wedding, I said, but I always thought the world is more like a somewhat lame party, where you're stuck with a particular cast of characters for the duration.

—Agreed, she said, conveying with her bright eyes that I might be one of the lame ones.

We both laughed. The second part of my Philosophy of Parties—that if you go to enough of them, sometimes even the most average Joe will be favored by the royal whimsicality of beauty—I kept to myself.

—So, she said, you haven't told me your story yet.

I told her of my recent move to Baltimore, spinning it as an escape from Washington. I started dumping on the typical DC person, the constant spinning, ambition without finitude, the personal emails that read like press releases. Halfway through my schpiel I had the weird feeling that she knew what I was actually doing—cataloguing a certain kind of self-knowledge, much too late acquired. But I soldiered on, and told her what I hated most of all was the restrictive slotting most of all—the way DC people always pegged you based on your place in the food chain. I hated being pegged. But Baltimore—Baltimore would be more real.

She gave me an oh-you-poor-deluded-soul look.

—You think you're going to escape restrictive slotting in *Baltimore*?

—Why not?

—Oh God. The worlds here are completely separate. And never the twain shall meet. It's either this . . .

She fluttered her hand, indicating the well-furnished room and the people inside.

—or the stuff out there.

—What's the . . .

Two people, who seemed to be a couple, came by. Cynthia introduced them to me: Cliff and Madeline. Both seemed pretty buzzed.

—Cyn, Madeline. This party sucks. Can we go to the manse for a drink?

Cynthia hesitated.

—If you promise, she said, not to fuck shit up.

From her mouth, the curses were charming.

—I promise, the woman said.

—I promise too, the guy said.

—We both promise, the woman said. C'mon. Let's go.

Cynthia turned to me.

—Care to join us for a drink at the Manse?

—Sounds good, I said.

She told the host she would return to check on the stain removal progress. I had such a strong sense of, what will happen next? I had no idea, and coming from Washington, where everything seemed planned out in triplicate, that ignorance was rare, and I prized it.

She drove, and her two friends followed us.

—We'll take the scenic route, she said, her eyes a bit cutting.

I didn't know the roads at all, and the changes in landscape were as surreal as the party faces. After a few plush upper-middle-class blocks, the houses became smaller and smaller until we hit a warehouse district area, then we drove under a series of overpasses and rose onto a highway. We exited the highway via a descending clover, then turned onto a dilapidated commercial strip. Turning off the strip, we shot up a hill, then dipped and leveled into an area that looked bombed out.

She slowed the car. Through the sound-muffling car windows, the desolate city streets had an after-the-gunfight feel. She pointed.

—That corner, was legendary in the doowop era, she said. The Flamingoes started here, before they moved to Chicago. They would have sing-offs—the Swallows versus the Orioles. The Clovers versus the Rainbows. The Cardinals versus the Ravens. Some of the older guys in the neighborhood still remember them. And Billie Holiday lived only a few blocks away from here. But the city is too stupid to commemorate her old house.

In the dark, the lopsided rowhouses seemed to stagger against one another. Some were barely shells.

—This section's my favorite, she said. I did a lot of work here. The older woman who lived here was just so lovely, a real generous soul. And the guy who lived next to her was a real dick, but she was incredibly patient.

We stopped at a red light. The next block had no houses on its first half, just weeds, a collapsed fence, concrete blocks veined silver with ore, and a garage wall covered in graffiti. *Remember Me Motherfuckers Remember Me Cocksuckers,* in big white bubble letters, was the only thing I could make out.

She pointed to the far corner.

—The kids who lived in that house were sooooo damn smart. The old guy on the corner was really smart, too, with incredible stories.

—Do none of them live here anymore? I said.

—Some might, but many are gone. Fire is a big problem. The heating systems are constantly breaking down, so people make their own. Some just need them to cook their drugs. For awhile we had fires here every week. And in this neighborhood, the response times can be pathetic.

—How did you like working here?

—I loved the work, but I hated fighting the bureaucracy. As far as the neighborhood, there really is almost as much pretension and identity consciousness as you would find in a middle-class suburb. Just in a different way. But I really miss working with some of them.

There was a flash of light.

—Uh-oh, she said. Cliff is giving me the high-beams. He wants to get the hell out of here.

She waved, then sped up. Soon we were back on the highway, factory neon looming in the distance, mystic messages. It hit me that I had never driven through an inner city neighborhood before with someone who actually knew the neighborhood.

We stayed on the highway a little longer this time. We exited, and got off the long service road, and then we were in an area somehow filled with trees, even a dark meadow, and enormous, lonely looking houses spaced about a quarter-mile apart.

She turned into a driveway.

—Voila, she said. The manse.

The driveway was curved, long and steep, and when the house came into view in the dark she read the "how could a social worker afford . . .?" question on my face.

—House sitting, she said.

—Ah, I said. Nice.

We parked in front of the house, Cliff and Madeline parking next to us. We all got out.

—Where the hell did you take us? Cliff said.

—What was that about? Madeline said.

—Just giving him a tour of my old work neighborhood, Cynthia said.

We all entered. It was like stepping inside a Henry James novel. She took our coats in the anteroom; we followed her into the living room. Except for a small laptop computer in the corner, it was all there: ornate trim, decorated fireplace, the V-patterned hardwood floors, the picture window and old-school portraits of people with that serious, constipated look. The dedication to late nineteenth-century wealth was so manic, it made me a little dizzy. But there was a sense of desperation to it that all the money in the world couldn't erase.

—This is wild, I said, craning my neck to look around. Who is the owner?

—My godmother, she said. The happy widow. She's a traveling curator, in Italy now. Her husband, a much older guy from an old-money family, passed away a few years ago.

—So this place meets her curatorial standards? Impressive, I said.

—Wellllll, she said. I think in some ways it's kind of a joke to her. She's funny. And actually, there's not one truly comfortable chair or couch in the whole place.

She made the three of us drinks. Madeline took hers, a vodka tonic, and quickly left the room. Cliff took a very large scotch and immediately took a large hit. Cynthia held a small amount of red wine in a large goblet. I could tell she wasn't much of a drinker, but it gave her delicate ringed fingers something to hold.

Cliff took another large swig of his scotch and looked at me with unfocused eyes, then looked at Cynthia.

—So what were you guys talking about so intensely at the party?

—Restrictive slotting, Cynthia said. I looked at her and smiled.

Cliff frowned.

—What do you mean? he said. Like tight pussy?

Cynthia made a face, then patted him on the back.

—See what you have to look forward to when you go slumming with the Baltimorons? she said to me.

—Fuck that, Cliff said. I'm not a Baltimoron. I hate fucking Baltimore.

Neither of us responded to this. He took another swig and, a bit unsteadily, walked out of the room.

❋ ❋ ❋

—Where did your friends go? I said.

—They're fans of the king-size bed in the master bedroom, she said. Let me put on some music.

She walked quickly to the laptop, and pressed a few buttons. I went to the picture window.

—This, she said, is the Swallows. Baltimore's finest.

The aching back-harmonies flooded the room.

—Nice, I said.

—Actually, she said, it's great music for dancing.

She held out her arms in invitation. I walked over, held her. Slowly we swayed to the music. In the safety of the enormous house I imagined the Swallows in a warming, fake way: singing counterpoint through little mouth-clouds, dance steps warming freezing feet, a big bottle passed round a dying fire.

We kissed.

After awhile she stopped kissing me and rested her head on my shoulder.

—You're a better kisser than you are a dancer, she said.

—Is that one back-handed compliment, or two? I said.

—Maybe none, she said.

With my finger I lifted her chin and kissed her again. This time I let my hands wander. She stiffened and pulled away.

—Sorry.

—No, it's not you, I'm just . . .

—What?

—I'm kind of . . . estranged from someone, and so I guess he is still on my mind.

I breathed in and out, loudly. The infatuating and infuriating effects of the gin were mixing inside of me.

—An old boyfriend?

—She nodded.

—And are you . . . still kind of involved?

—Well not . . . it's a weird situation. He was badly hurt, and he's recovering now. I'm trying to be supportive, although we're not together anymore.

—Badly hurt, by you?

—No, badly hurt physically.

—What happened?

—It's a long story.

—I got time.

It was an embarrassing, B-movie thing to say. She pointed to the comfortless couch.

❋ ❋ ❋

—We were together for two years. About six months ago, we broke up. He's a programmer with a creative streak. He loves acting, community theater, open mics, that type of thing. Writes poetry and practices monologues by reading poems.

—How did he get hurt?

—He was in a small theater production of *Equus*. The theater is near a rough neighborhood, pretty much an open-air drug market. So one night, he's coming home from rehearsal and he sees several big guys beating the hell out of a little Hispanic guy.

—About what?

He had no idea. When the cops get calls in that area, they tend to make them a very low priority. They just assume it's an internal drug dispute.

—Same thing in DC, I said.

—So Michael stops his car and starts yelling out the window, yelling for them to stop. They just ignored him, and continued the beating. Then he started beeping the horn. Still they ignored him.

I nodded.

—So he got out of the car, she said.

She saw my face change.

—He has a heart of gold, she said. He's the type of guy, I'm sure he didn't even think twice about it.

—So, he goes up to one of the guys, and tells him to stop. The guy starts hitting Michael, who's not much of a fighter. Then, they all start hitting Michael, and stop beating up the Hispanic guy, who was able to crawl away.

—Jesus, I said.

—As I said, that's kind of a no-go zone for cops, so no one intervened.

She took a small sip of wine.

—They left him for dead, she said.

I took a big sip of gin.

✻ ✻ ✻

—Finally, she said, after a few hours someone found him lying on the ground unconscious and called 911. In the emergency room, they went through his wallet, looked up the last name, and called his brother.

—So his brother goes to the intensive care ward, she said. He looks all over the place, but can't find Michael. So he grabs the doctor and says, I was told my brother Michael Totten was here in this ward, but he's not. And the doctor said, that's him on the gurney over there.

—His own brother didn't recognize him, she said, her voice catching ever so slightly.

—Where's the bathroom here? I said.

—Down the hall to the left.

I had a freakout in the bathroom. A visceral, involuntary imagining of what the beating was like came over me: the thunderclaps of the blows, the sears of pain from all over, the burning warmth of blood on my skin, the taste of it in my mouth, my own stupid cries and groans and wretchings, the stomach and chest agonies, the bullets to the face, the craving for an end, for things to go black.

I came back out and asked for another Tanqueray on the rocks.

—How is he now? I said.

✻ ✻ ✻

—They did a really good job with the reconstructive surgery. You can barely tell, actually. He suffers from occasional short-term memory loss, but that's getting better too. But he does seem different, in little ways that are hard to describe. It's just . . . really sad.

—Do you have a picture of him?

I don't know why I said this, it just kind of came out. It seemed to startle her a little.

—I have photos of him, but not here. I only come here when I house sit. I don't carry one with me, no. I do carry a poem he gave me. It was one of his monologue poems.

—Can I see it?

She fished around in her purse and handed me a small piece of folded up paper. I was way too buzzed to read the whole thing, so I read eight or so lines near the end.

We have seen the city; it is a mirrored eye.
All things happen and are resumed within,
but the action has the cold, syrupy flow
of a pageant. But in the mere stillness,
the ease, she sifts the April sunlight
for clues. There are cold pockets
of remembrance, whispers out of time.
Then the ambulance cries after itself
and the sirens fade into a dream . . .

I read the lines without understanding, but still they triggered something.

—Well, for what it's worth—and this is a completely uninformed, unsolicited opinion—but I think you should give him one more shot. He's certainly a much better man than me. I would never have had the guts to get out of the car.

She gave me a hug, briefly.

—I need to get back, she said. I told Jennifer I would check to see if the stain was gone.

—I'll go with you, I said.

—Let me just leave a note for my frolicking friends, and we'll roll, she said.

For the first few minutes of the drive back, we were both silent.

I thought of the crime shows and movies I had watched— taking in the blood-streaked tapestry, happily sanctioning the violence from my living room couch, savoring the adrenaline rush of the shootings, the sadistic pleasures of the beatings and the tortures, the thrill of the revenge killings.

I felt great shame.

I wanted to hear more about Michael but I didn't know what to ask. Finally I said

—Did they ever catch the guys that beat him?

—No. He didn't really pursue it that hard.

—Did he get lot of support, after the . . . tragedy?

—Some. The *Sun* ran a feature story on it—a good-samaritan-almost-dies-doing-a-noble-deed type of thing. But, what really surprised me was that some people, including even some who knew him, had this weird attitude of, well, what he did was so foolhardy, what do you expect?

—No . . . really?

—Yes! Even his friend Jonathan, who was at the party tonight, said to me once after it happened, "I'm sorry, but what an idiot for getting out of the car. How stupid is that?"

I'm not entirely sure why I felt such rage at this. I might have been projecting again, or maybe I wanted to focus on something other than my own cowardice. But it was one thing to be cowardly, and it was something else to be cowardly and deny the courage of others. And then to denigrate that courage—that was beyond the pale. That was despicable.

—Which one was he? I said, as controlled as I could manage.

—He was the guy in the really loud flowered shirt, she said.

For the rest of the ride I was silent, gin-rage simmering. I tried to picture the guy with the floral shirt in my mind.

When we arrived I felt strangely calm and focused.

She parked off the curb in front of the house. I got out of the car, closed the door carefully, looked straight ahead at the front door of the house. I didn't look at Cynthia.

I felt light and hyper-aware when I walked up the driveway, toward the house, feeling the cold and hearing the sound of gravel under my feet. The three little windows on the front door had a warm glow.

I felt a hand on my shoulder. The touch was electric and I tightened, and for the briefest of moments I stepped completely outside of myself, and my first reaction was to spin and drive my fist into the jaw of whoever touched me.

The feeling passed and I didn't, but when I turned round my fist was still clenched. She kissed me with a kind of artful gentleness, soft and slow and deliberate, almost a movie kiss, filled with sensitivity and artifice.

I melted back to my old cowardly self.

When she stopped kissing me, I thought she was going to put her head on my shoulder, but instead she moved her lips near my ear.

—Not that I didn't like that, she said, but honesty requires me to say that I did it more out of distraction than affection.

I looked past her and saw trees, dark sky.

—Understood, I said in her ear. Understood.

NIKE

III.
COMMUNITY

JENNIFER L. FREED

HELP

Because he's so hard of hearing,
my father places the chair exactly
where my mother asked him
not to.

She wants him to move it aside.
He asks why she keeps changing her mind.
She tries not to cry.
He throws his hands in the air.

The aide arrives, feels
the storm hovering,

puts on the tea,
tells my father she's still laughing at that joke
he told yesterday,
rests a palm on my mother's arm,
moves the chair from the path of her walker

and shifts
the air in the room, saving
a small square of the world.

GOLDEN DOOR

Send these, the homeless, tempest-tost to me,
I lift my lamp beside the golden door!
–Emma Lazarus, 'The New Colossus'

Fridays at the Free Library, you navigate
the language that surrounds you here
in your new home.
You've left your bamboo hills,
your missing father, soldiers
cleansing the land
of your people.
You work nights, emptying crates,
filling big-box stores.
You share three rooms
and minimum wage
with mother, sister, her two boys,
your little girl. And today
you urge me to take
the curry noodles you brought
on a foil-covered plate,
and the golden dumplings
your wife fried specially
this morning, for you to give
to me.

ANGEL

The race runs over a mile—
twice around the school, then the lower field, then
along the deep green fringe of fir up on the hill,
and the tiny girl flies
out in front, now body-length, now bus-length ahead, ahead—oh
how her parents glow, oh
how everyone cheers, in awe
as her little legs go, go, go,

and there, too, is the other
girl, round
as a melon, and she, too, pumps, pumps
herself onward, she, too—
but falls body-length, bus-length, field-length behind
the last of all
the rest, and oh

how we cheer—*Go, Angela, go!*—
the boys and the girls, now past the finish line, clap
her on, and the parents, and the teachers,
Go, we shout, in awe
because she is so far away, alone
on the wide green length of grass,
and yet
her legs piston on,
and she, oh she
is the hope of us all.

KEVIN FIDGEON

JOANNE AND ROBERT

I don't believe in God, yet I do believe in goodness, rare though it is. In my seventy-six years, I've experienced it at different times. On those special occasions, goodness grabbed me by the throat and shook my soul. Perhaps I do believe in God.

Twenty-four years old, working as a juvenile probation officer for the DC Family Court system, I interviewed recently arrested juveniles to determine their eligibility for release pending trial. All of them pleaded not guilty, saying, "Tyrone did it." If the police ever arrested Tyrone, the city would be crime free.

Child welfare cases were also managed by the Family Court and on occasion, I would be asked to assist on a case. The assigned social worker had been ill and a court-ordered home visit had not been made. The unit supervisor asked me to do it, advising that it was just a routine, pro forma visit and I could manage it on my way home. She described it as a child-in-need case that had been on the books for years.

The home was easy enough to find, located in a low-income community just inside the Washington beltway and not too far from Andrews Air Force Base. It was a small bungalow surrounded by similar homes that were built most likely in the 1950s.

Greeted at the door by Joanne, she invited me in, seeming genuinely pleased by my visit. "I know you're anxious to see Robert, he's doing very well." Joanne was a sixty-year-old widow, having raised four of her own children, she had sponsored twelve special-needs children over the years. Robert would be her last foster child, she explained as we walked down a short hallway to his room. The walls of the walkway were filled with pictures of smiling children that could have represented the entire world.

Robert laid in a large crib, blind at birth with severe brain damage, a twisted body that would never walk, his speech consisted of cries and moans.

"They asked me to take him until they could place him in an appropriate institution." He had not been expected to live but for a few months. Robert had just turned six years old. Joanne had sung Happy Birthday and gave him a fuzzy blanket to mark the occasion.

His destiny was to live out his life in darkness, fear and pain. Since birth, Joanne had been his caregiver, constant companion and sole source of love. I watched Joanne speak to him and stroke his face. Robert's body relaxed, taking a welcomed breath in response to something Joanne had done thousands of times before.

I had witnessed true goodness in that little bungalow and came to understand the meaning of unconditional love. As I left the home, there was a roar in the sky. Looking up I wondered if that was Air Force One taking off from Andrews Air Force Base. The most powerful person in the world was flying over a tiny bungalow that was filled with goodness.

MARION DEUTSCHE COHEN

MY MOTHER SAID

My mother said She wants a little beauty in her life
about that woman sitting on porch steps
in the kind of neighborhood through which our car was merely passing.
We had not been brought up to believe beauty could be dyed teased hair
or something too dark-red and pasty smeared again and again over rather than on lips.
In our house beauty was van Gogh, Botticelli, Renoir.
So ew, ykk, we had quietly sneered
as our car was escaping that dusty street.
And that's why our mother said
what she said.

MORE ABOUT THE POSITIVE INTEGERS, SMALL AND LARGE

Most math-things number either infinity or one, non-unique usually means infinite, that's why I like polynomials, with their n roots, and the five platonic solids. And the only consecutive perfect powers are eight and nine. Also, there might be a first even number that's not the sum of two primes.

Yes, every number is interesting because the first *un*interesting number would have to be interesting in that way. But what about the *second* uninteresting number, or the third? The truly uninteresting numbers might be something *other* than interesting, something we might need. Yeah, we need at least some uninteresting numbers, in my adolescence I was tired of interesting, I wanted something more relaxing like just-plain beautiful, maybe just-plain loving. I wanted to be loved without having to be interesting, a friend once said to me "Just bring wine to the party. You don't have to always be interesting."

Uninteresting numbers have to still be allowed, they can't be banished from Z+. When Ramanujan said every integer was a personal friend of his in some way, he meant it, he meant even if he came across one that was uninteresting he would still consider it a friend. He never encountered any non-friend, he didn't leave anybody out.

JOHN PIERCE

AN ODE TO D-HALL ASSIGNMENTS

I do not say a word,
but my students' tongues
taste iron in the top of their mouths,
as I reach for the drawer—
THE DRAWER—
where detention slips are stored.

I place the slip
on the podium before us,
and scan the crowd
heads all bowed
before this certain sacrament.

MOTTO

Find the dullest place to be.
Stay there
in a comfortable chair.

The dustiest room.
Draw pictures on furniture.
Look at all that stuff!

Sit down at the bar
of the emptiest diner.
Eat steak
with ketchup.

Visit the old woman
in the nursing home
who whispers to herself in bed.

Take a walk.
Look up at the empty sky,
all of the empty sky.

Find the most useless thing to do.
And do it well.

Find the smallest thing—
the most weak,
the most light,
the most worthless,
the most slight.

Find it
and bow down.

MARY E. KENDIG

GREGORY'S GARDEN

Gregory fears that he's becoming more and more like his Dad.

Gregory's father, John, was a grumpy old salt, a hard-nosed codger who had survived The Great Depression and a stint on a PT boat in the Philippines during World War II. John's wife, Mildred, had died years earlier from a sudden heart attack at age fifty-nine. By the time John got to be sixty-five or so—tolerance be damned—nothing sat well with him. John loved to complain—about everything.

"Jesus, this world is falling apart! We live on one God-forsaken wacky planet!" John used to protest whenever he heard something he didn't like, typically while sitting in his dark-wood-paneled kitchen with the tacky orange-and-yellow floral wallpaper, eating his Swanson's TV dinner and watching *The CBS Evening News with Walter Cronkite* back in the late seventies and early eighties.

John's answer to those daily doses of bad news was to rush to judgment, categorizing the people in question so he could place blame. For instance, when John heard about protestors in front of the White House, he'd judge them as "hippie longhairs" *(a la* the Vietnam-era protestors, who were mostly young male dissenters who—well, okay—happened to wear their hair a bit longer than most folks). Or when reports of riots made the headlines, he'd go off about "those Baptist folk who love to stir things up" *(a la* Martin Luther King, in John's slanted opinion).

John's house was most definitely *not* a judgment-free zone.

I didn't know John, but I know Gregory. John's only son is a rotund man of seventy-two, with a tanned, almost leathery face, a mop of salt-and-pepper hair, and a bushy mustache to match. For shade, he wears his trusty blue baseball cap with the sweat marks on it, along with the same navy-blue pants, navy-blue suspenders, light-blue T-shirt, and black, slip-on boat shoes just about every day. Gregory has been my neighbor for a touch less than ten years and is frequently outside, whether it's to mow his manicured carpet of St. Augustine grass, or trim his hedgerow of ficus bushes, or lay a new coat of cedar mulch around his well-cared-for bougainvillea and crepe myrtle trees of every hue: white, pink, reddish-pink, purple.

To look at his home from the outside, you'd think Gregory a meticulous, detailed lover of organization and beauty. But step inside and you'll see sundry stacks of old mail scattered over a dining room table that hasn't been used in so long it's got a half-inch layer of dust on it, except in the spots where fingerprints and Gregory's cat, Sadie, have interrupted the fuzzy, grayish-white accumulation. The wallpaper in his kitchen is so old that it's curled over in the corners, and the glue stains are coming through in an uneven shade of yellow. His floors haven't been scrubbed, nor his bed made, in probably the better part of a year. His kitchen sink is overflowing with dishes and pots and pans and glasses of every sort. Several piles of old clothing, old shoes, and old socks are strewn about, from the living room trailing into the bedroom.

Gregory lives alone, a widower since 2006 when his wife, Virginia, died from breast cancer. They had no children. Gregory got quite angry when Ginny died, blaming the doctors for missing the spot on her X-ray when she first went to her doctor complaining of a lump under her right armpit. They discovered the cancer when it had metastasized and was at an advanced Stage Four, just one year later. She died five months after that diagnosis.

Sometimes around dinnertime, I see Gregory on his front porch, and I always wave. He is always there, sitting on the pearl-white rocking chair he painted himself. It sits to the left of his front-room window if you're facing his modest ranch-style home, complete with light-green shutters, light-green front door, and light-green soffit trim.

On occasion, time permitting, I make my way to the other pearl-white rocker, on the side closest to Gregory's two-car garage. We sit and talk for a short while as the evening shade turns from orange to red to hues of purple and blue.

Gregory sits on the left side so he can have the best view of Ginny's garden of bushes, trees, and flowers, which encircles a large area on the side of his house. I didn't know Gregory's wife, but he often talks about her: "My Ginny really loved her plants and flowers, always trimmin' and prunin' and diggin' and such." One day, he said to me, "Ginny's the only woman I ever loved and ever will love. I like to be outside tendin' to her garden because I know she can see me from Heaven."

So, with devoted regularity, as each day moves into the late afternoon and early evening, Gregory tends to those plants and flowers fastidiously, in touching tribute to her. Tending to that garden, in fact, has become his mission in life. Tending to the inside of his home, however, is another thing altogether. So periodically, when I can find the time, I have started helping Gregory straighten things up inside the house.

Gregory loves quoting the old sayings and proverbs and always looks for the explanation that will put things in perspective: everything from the importance of his grass and his bushes ("Your hands in the dirt, your head in the sun, your heart with nature"), to the state of our neighborhood ("You reap what you sow," "Good fences make good neighbors"), to the state of our country and the world.

Gregory sometimes talks about his father, John, too. And he fully recognizes that his Dad held many unfounded prejudices. Gregory emphatically does not consider himself to be like his Dad in that particular category—not by a long shot.

"I am *nothin'* like my father, that crazy curmudgeon!"

Gregory wants to make that perfectly clear. He understands that the minute people start to pigeonhole their fellow humans into distinct, broad, and biased categories, the more they can dismiss them as "different" and "not like me" and begin judging them in those narrow-minded contexts. That, in Gregory's opinion, is never a good thing.

John, by the way, left this "wacky planet" in November 1987 at the age of seventy-three, which is, coincidently, the age Gregory will reach on his next birthday. John died alone, ornery, and overcome by the bitterness and contempt he held for so many years.

Gregory does not want to end up like John.

But the older Gregory gets, the more he finds that he agrees with John about the world's general predilection toward absurdity. And the thing is, Gregory feels that—particularly regarding genteel qualities like civility, kindness, and courtesy, "Things have gotten much worse than back when my father was alive."

In particular, he feels that the current uncivil condition of our civil world is caused by the constant drive to "win"—on the need for many to treat their time on this Earth, as he says, "like an all-out competition—like a gall-darned UFC title fight. Folks just don't want to *keep up with* 'The Joneses,' they want to be *better* than them—to *crush* them—and to get instant results."

All of this, Gregory says, has resulted in a severe lack of patience among our populace. "We're all spoiled brats with no manners," in Gregory's view, because we've lost the sense of tolerance we used to have when we were forced to wait for things.

He offers me examples. "I'm talkin' about big things like a raise, or a new car—I remember folks used to order the car they wanted and then sit and wait for Detroit to produce it—maybe waitin' for six or eight months—before they took final delivery. Even little things, like the simple answer to a question, or just gettin' to the front of the line at the grocery store. Nobody is used to waitin' anymore," he reasons.

Similar to his Dad's blame-game strategy, the older Gregory gets, the more he finds himself searching for something to blame these things on. Namely, although Gregory doesn't own a computer but does watch a lot of television (like his Dad used to), he blames our present condition on the growth of, in his words, the "dang-blasted internet." On the internet's enablement of our world to expect to have things immediately, if not sooner. On the all-out war that competing businesses seem to be waging on it. And on its prevalence to expose the public to "kill or be killed" video games, cyber-bullying, and such.

"Oh, there might be some partly redeemin' things about that whole internet nonsense," Gregory acknowledges, like our fingertip accessibility to a plethora of useful data. Or how it helps the elderly or people with disabilities maintain their independence by being able to order things like clothing and food online. But, Gregory fears, this has allowed us to become less *interdependent* on our friends, our neighbors, our families. It has removed opportunities to socialize in person. It has removed the sense of community that people of Gregory's (and John's) generations knew were integral to our humanity and that all of us seemed to count on.

"You just don't see your neighbors face-to-face anymore," he says.

Then there's the lack of filter unfortunately present when some people do speak, or tweet, or post their comments and photos on their social media pages. "America's a great country, because everyone's always had a *right* to their opinion, but that doesn't mean that every opinion is *right*," says Gregory. "Some opinions are best kept to oneself. It's easy to run roughshod over someone on the other end of a computer screen, but it'd be different if you had to face that person and say those things." Of course, that's just Gregory's opinion. Although in fairness, I did ask him for it.

Perhaps nothing has changed at all between John's and Gregory's generations—it's just maybe that things feel like they've gotten more intense, more concentrated, more immediate. When you really think on it, Gregory muses, all the fine qualities that seem to have gone "straight to Hell in a handbasket" as he says—tolerance, patience, gentility, civility, respect, kindness, humility, charity—do and should, as they say, begin at home.

About two months ago, Gregory and I were talking again while we sat in the two pearl-white rockers on his porch. I mentioned some of the stresses of my timeline-driven job and all the emails and other problems I have to wade through each day. When we got around to the part I thought would set Gregory off—the internet—I found, instead, that he turned quieter and more contemplative. He looked at me and said calmly, "Well, maybe people like me should just stop blamin' the internet for every damn thing that's wrong with us." Maybe, he reasoned, we should start to look inward and try to be more like the gentle, civil, kind, positive examples of humankind he's been seeking to find. In other words, the seeds of that perfect role model for a more civil civilization that Gregory's been searching for all this time have been right there all along, within himself and others, too. "Deep down," he said, "I want to believe that we're all good folks, with good intentions. We just have to learn how to cultivate and nurture what's good in us so that those 'good seeds' can grow and blossom. Like the flowers and bushes and trees in this here garden," he said. "My Ginny's garden," he added.

"It's your garden now, Gregory," I said. "It's been yours for years now."

He looked at me wide-eyed, and then sat back in his rocker, contemplating what I'd just said, which seemed to be a revelation for him.

"Hmmh," he said. "I reckon it is." After a still moment or two, he added with a newly minted twinkle in his eye, "You know what? I kinda like it, too. I think my Ginny would be proud."

Just last week, as I walked briskly past my house over to Gregory's for another quick visit, I smelled something incredibly fragrant in the air. Typically, I would've just enjoyed the moment and kept moving, but on that day, I did not. I stopped and looked around, determined to discover where that beautiful scent was emanating from. And I found it, in the form of a lovely juniper bush growing around another neighbor's mailbox. I stood there, taking in the fragrance and looking around, appreciating the quiet and serenity. And then I found myself glancing over toward Gregory's house. I saw him, outside of course, tending to his lovely garden. He had spotted me and was looking my way with a smile.

"It's good to take a minute, ain't it?" he called over to me. I nodded that it was.

When I reached Gregory's house, I told him I'd recently bought a few plants for my own yard. "I'm proud of ya," he added, "startin' your own little garden." I smiled back knowingly, certain that the newfound serenity of my moments with the juniper bush, and the recent purchase of my new plants, were a direct a result of Gregory's presence in my life.

Perhaps we all have some very valuable things to learn from the musings of our neighbors, especially if they're as wise as my gardener friend, Gregory.

PATERNOSTRO

TERRY SANVILLE

A BRIDGE BETWEEN TREES

Whatever Rich had been before, he'd never be again. We all dreaded that. But it took years to figure out as we struggled with the aftermath.

The summer between eighth and ninth grades, Rich, Pete and I decided to build a tree house . . . actually Rich did most of the deciding. Our families lived on Santa Barbara's Calle Poniente where it dead-ended into rolling hills covered with wild oats and spotted with California Live Oaks. Two massive trees stood close together along a ridgeline, silhouetted against the sky.

"That's where we'll build her," Rich said and pointed.

"Ah, come on," Pete whined, "we'll hafta haul everything uphill. We'll be pullin' stickers outta our socks forever."

"He's right," I chimed in.

Rich countered, "We'll be able to see anybody coming. We'll see everything."

"And they'll see us."

"I want them to," Rich said. "This is our place and nobody can take it."

Pete choked back a laugh. "That's funny. Ya sound like you're actin' in some western."

Rich grinned and drawled, "That's right, I'm the Marshal in these here parts."

We all watched *Gunsmoke* on TV every chance we got, lusting after Miss Kitty and making fun of poor Chester. We also knew that Rich was the Marshal and we his deputies. We'd known each other since first grade at Harding School and had tried projects before. The tree house would prove the toughest.

In the late 1950's, Calle Poniente had three mini-fiefdoms: the bottom near Valerio Street belonged to a bunch of little kids; the middle section to John the paper boy, the Mexicans, and pretty Becky; and the upper end to us Three Amigos. We were older than the others by a year or two, a vast difference when you're young.

Rich motioned us into his garage. "Look at this." He rolled open a big sheet of paper across a workbench.

"What am I looking at?" I asked.

"Come on, Chet, your Pop's a draftsman. You've seen blueprints."

"You do this?" Pete asked, eyes wide.

"Yeah. Look, here're the tree trunks, like you're lookin' down from above . . . the first level and the second . . . and the high deck in the other tree." Rich showed us the details laid out in clear lines.

"What's this?" I pointed.

Rich puffed himself up. "That's the bridge between the trees."

"Cool. But how're we gonna get the stuff to build this thing? I've got nothin'."

"Me neither," Pete said.

"There's plenty of scrap lumber at that house project on Marquad."

"Jeez, a frickin' block away." Of the three of us, hulking Pete proved the most adverse to physical exertion.

Rich ignored him. "We'll pick 'em clean . . . take only used stuff . . . they won't care."

"Yeah, but what'll we take?" I asked.

"I know what we need."

Suddenly, our lazy summer of riding bikes down State Street and watching girls bake in the sun on East Beach had been usurped by the tree house challenge, albeit an exciting one.

It took a week just to drag all the materials to our construction site. The most difficult hauls were concrete-stained sheets of plywood. We stored everything under the oaks and covered it with a tarp borrowed from my Dad's woodpile. We did a lot of *borrowing*. We scrounged for nails and screws and used all of our fathers' hand tools. By the second week we'd worn a path up the hill, the annoying stickers no longer a problem.

The tree house took shape slowly. We got fancy: cut up an old red carpet and lined each room; *found* some rolled asphalt roofing and covered our castle; nailed wire over the window openings to keep the squirrels, raccoons and birds out; and built a trapdoor in the first level floor and locked it with a padlock and hasp unscrewed from Pete's father's toolshed.

But the bridge between the trees proved the most difficult. We didn't have long pieces of lumber that could span the twenty-foot distance.

"We'll build it out of two or three planks," Rich said as we stared at his sketch.

"I don' know," Pete said, shaking his head. "I ain't gonna trust that thing."

"What if we build it, ya know, in pieces," I said, "a bunch of boxes nailed together?"

"You mean like some sort of box beam?" Rich asked.

I shrugged. "Yeah, I guess."

It took us a week to bang it together and a full afternoon to lift it with ropes into place. It rested on notches we'd cut into the oaks, maybe ten foot up. The bark proved tough to chop with a hatchet. It looked like gray alligator hide. And a blood-red layer of wood beneath the bark made me regret all the nails we'd driven into those trees.

Less than a foot wide, the bridge rose at a slight angle from one tree to the other. To help keep our balance, we strung waist-high guide ropes on either side—ropes purloined from Mr. Spezack's boat gathering dust in his backyard.

When done, my Dad made me give him a tour of the place, including a stroll across the creaking bridge, and a climb to the high deck in the second tree, our very own crow's nest.

"You boys did a good job nailing this thing together," Pop said. "You be careful up here. When the wind blows this place will really shake."

"Yeah, it'll be cool. Don't worry."

All through August we moved our prized possessions, the things we hid from our parents, into the tree house: dog-eared copies of *Playboy* and *Modern Man*; two packs of Cool cigarettes and a Zippo lighter; a dusty bottle of gin from Pete's father's liquor cabinet; and a pistol with a box of cartridges that Rich found tucked away with his Dad's Korean War stuff.

To get into the tree house Pete and I climbed a ladder, unlocked the trap door and pushed inside the first level room. But Rich usually beat us in by climbing one of the tree's long branches that almost touched the ground. He'd move from limb to limb like a spider monkey, as if he'd been born in the treetops.

We used the enclosed rooms as our smoking/drinking lounges and reading library. But the high deck in the second tree became our favorite spot. From there we could look west into the setting sun and watch soundless waves break along Hendry's Beach and the Hope Ranch Coast. We'd shoot the bull about our dreams of the future: high school, the after-school jobs we'd get, the kind of cars we'd buy, the girls we'd date and which ones might "put out," a term we used with great confidence but with little understanding.

Through all of this Rich would get more and more restless, would break out in laughter, jump up and swing from branch to branch, dancing across the bridge and back as if powered by jet fuel. We'd give him a little sip of gin to calm him down. It didn't help much.

Rich's imagination just wouldn't turn off. He talked about having parties in the tree house and inviting kids from school, about rigging the place with electricity so we could watch TV and stay overnight, about putting a telescope on the high deck to gaze at the stars and do things with girls. Pete and I listened to his wild ideas and let his passion carry us along, trying to believe that anything could be done if we just had the guts to try.

We'd saved the last of that God-awful gin for the final week of summer. Pete and Rich would start ninth grade at La Cumbre Junior High while my parents sent me to the four-year Catholic High School in downtown Santa Barbara. We swore that we'd all do stuff together, stay close and let Rich dream up new adventures.

We sat on the upper deck, legs dangling over its side, and sipped Beefeater from chipped coffee mugs.

"Hey, I know these guys—" Rich began.

"Ah Jeez, here we go," Pete said, snickering.

"Shut up, lard ass. Let 'em finish."

"I know these guys that made their own surf boards. They said they'd show me how."

"Sounds cool," I said. "But nobody I know surfs."

"Yeah, that's why it be cool if *we* did."

Pete shook his head. "Come on, guys. Ya know I sink better than swim."

We stayed quiet for a few minutes. Rich countered with a new plan. "Yeah, well what about us getting after-school jobs and pooling our money. Buy a car and fix it up."

"I can dig that," Pete said. "My Dad can show us how."

Rich started to fidget as his excitement grew. "Yeah . . . we could keep it in our garage and—"

"—work on it on week ends. We've got two years 'til we get our licenses."

"Paint it competition orange," Pete said, "dago the hell out of it, with baby moon hubcaps and blue lights in the wheel wells."

Rich grinned. "And tuck-and-roll inside. My sister's boyfriend had it done in Tijuana, cheap."

Pete and I stared into the sunset. I dreamed about cruising State Street with some bodacious girls in our cool car. Rich couldn't contain himself. He climbed into the treetop and swung from limb to limb. He scooted along a branch that extended toward the opposite tree, and with a shout, dropped to the bridge below. He landed like a gymnast dismounting the high bar to stick the landing.

With a splintering crack, the bridge split in two and Rich fell. He tumbled end over end, arms flailing, and landed with a sickening thud on his back. Pete and I screamed and bolted to our feet. With the bridge gone, there was no easy way to get out of the tree. We shinnied down the trunk, scraping the hell out of our bare arms, and ran to Rich's side.

He lay on top of a huge oak limb that we'd cut off, his eyes rolled back in his head, drool dripping from the side of his open mouth.

"Is . . . is he dead?" Pete whispered.

"No . . . see, he's breathing."

Rich moaned. His eyes seemed to focus on us for a few seconds before closing. But he kept breathing.

"What'll we do?" Pete asked.

"I'll stay here . . . go tell his folks . . . get an ambulance . . . he's . . . he's hurt bad."

Pete tore off down the trail and disappeared into the waning light. I put my hand lightly on Rich's chest, felt it rise and fall. The lower part of his body lay bent at an angle. He didn't move. It seemed like forever before the sound of adult voices engulfed us. Pete gasped for breath and looked ready to faint.

"You didn't move him did you?" Rich's father asked.

"No . . . no sir. He hasn't moved since he fell."

"Okay . . . okay. Why don't you stand back against the tree with Peter. The medics will need room to work."

"Yes, sir."

Rich's mother knelt by his side, tears dripping from her eyes. She leaned forward to touch her son, crying hysterically. But her husband stopped her and they hugged each other, shaking.

I moved into the shadows, feeling scared and somehow guilty that our horseplay had caused this tragedy, as if Pete and I should have kept Rich from doing that stupid stunt. We were his deputies and we let our Marshal get hurt. Pete stood next to me, trembling, his mouth clamped shut.

In the distance, the sound of sirens approached. Every dog in the neighborhood howled. A new Cadillac ambulance arrived with red lights flashing. A patrol car pulled up beside it. The medics hustled a gurney up the trail, struggling in the sandy soil. With help from the cops they carefully lifted Rich onto the wheeled stretcher, strapped him down and headed off. Our friend, our leader didn't make a sound the whole time.

By then, the entire west end of Calle Poniente stood in the street, staring. Pete's and my parents huddled at the edge of the field. They came with the police and us boys to Pete's house. It was after ten o'clock before the cops finished asking questions. Our accounts of the accident jibed, although Pete and I failed to mention the gin.

At home, Mom hugged me. I slipped into my dark bedroom, stripped off my clothes and slid between cold sheets, shivering. The image of Rich tumbling through the air flashed over and over behind my closed eyes. The sky turned gray before sleep and dreams took me away.

❦ ❦ ❦

I slumped on the couch, munched Fritos, and stared blankly at the flickering TV. Mom stood over me, hands on hips.

"He's been home for a week, ya know. You should go see your friend."

"Yeah, yeah, I will."

"Do it now. I won't have you lazin' around here all Saturday."

"Cripes. Okay, I'll go."

Rich had came home the week after Thanksgiving. Pete and I had visited him twice in the hospital. The first time, the drugs slowed him down so much he could hardly speak. The second time, he put on a brave face until the post-surgery pain got too much and the nurses hustled us from his room.

I slammed the front door of our house as I left, mad at Mom for forcing my hand, but knowing she was right, which pissed me off even more. I crossed Calle Poniente and headed toward Rich's house.

"Hey Chet, wait up," Pete called, grinning. "Have you been over to see him?"

"No, have you?"

"Nah. Figured we'd do it together."

"Yeah. Ya know . . . I've been feeling guilty about what happened."

"Why?"

"If we hadn't got Rich all excited, he wouldn't have been messin' around."

"Yeah." Pete went quiet for a moment. "But he got that way all the time. Wasn't our fault."

"I guess."

I tapped on Rich's front door and Mrs. Kirkmeyer answered.

"Come in, come in. Richard is in the rumpus room watching TV. Go on back. He'll be glad to see you."

Her smile seemed pasted on, didn't fit with the dark circles under her eyes and the crow's feet. We passed through their house. Mr. Kirkmeyer looked up from his magazine and nodded but said nothing. I wondered if he too blamed us for the accident, for building that unsafe bridge between the trees.

Rich sat in a wheelchair before a color TV, the actors' faces looking Martian green. A set of small barbells occupied an end table on his right, kept company with pill bottles, a pitcher of water and a glass, Kleenex, and a tiny bell. He looked at us and grinned.

"Hey guys, come on in." He picked up a small box with buttons and pointed it at the TV. With a click, the damn thing shut off.

"Jeez, Rich, that thing's great," Pete said.

"Yeah, I can change channels, make it louder or softer, turn it on and off and not have to get up . . . not that I can."

Pete and I collapsed into chairs on either side of him. His mother came in and laid a plate of chocolate chip cookies on the coffee table. "Thought you boys could use a snack."

"Thanks Mrs. Kirkmeyer," Pete and I said in unison.

"So . . . so how you feelin'," I asked.

The smile faded from Rich's face. He looked pale, with purple patches underneath his eyes. Yellow and green bruises decorated his bare arms. "Ah, ya know. Still gettin' used to the chair and stuff. That's why I have the weights, to build up my muscles."

"Does it hurt?" Pete blurted.

"Can't feel nothin' below my waist. That's why I have the bag." Rich pointed to a plastic sack half full of urine hooked to the side of his chair. "And yeah, I wear diapers."

"Ah jeez, man," I muttered.

"When I get stronger, I'll be able to change myself but I need more muscle ta do that." He tapped a bicep.

"What're the pills for?" Pete asked.

"The pain from where they operated gets bad at night . . . can't sleep. And it sometimes burns when I pee. Take more pills for that."

I felt relieved when Pete changed the subject. "I missed ya at school," he said.

"You're probably flunkin' with me not there to give ya the answers."

"Are . . . are ya comin' back?"

"The doctors say maybe by Easter. Mom's been getting all the books, homework and tests from my teachers . . . so I shouldn't fall too far behind. Besides, schoolwork keeps . . . keeps me from thinkin' about . . . "

The silence grew between us. But ole Rich could still draw us out. "How 'bout you, Chet? You lettin' the priests push you around at Catholic High?"

We talked about teachers, girls in our classes, my new after-school job as a box boy at the A&P, making a whopping $1.25 an hour. None of us mentioned the accident and we wouldn't talk about it until years later. But Rich started right back in with his overactive imagination.

One rainy day sometime after New Year, the three of us sat on Rich's front porch and stared at the tree house on the ridgeline. Other kids from down the street had taken it over even though the bridge lay in pieces where we'd left it. I'd retrieved Rich's father's pistol and put it back in the locker where it came from, Mr. Kirkmeyer none the wiser.

"Remember when we talked about poolin' our money and fixing up a car?" Rich asked.

I nodded. "Do . . . do ya think you can drive?"

"Maybe, maybe not. But I can ride with you guys . . . if we buy the right thing."

Pete and I exchanged glances. "What do ya mean?" Pete asked.

"Look, I'll need something that I can wheel my chair into, tie it down, and be able to see out."

We stared at Rich blankly. "You got some ideas?" I asked, feeling that I'd invited a blizzard of words. I'd missed that.

"Yeah, check this out." Rich opened a newspaper he'd been holding on his lap and pointed to an ad. "This would work great."

Pete and I leaned forward to get a closer look, then broke into laughter. "You wanna . . . wanna buy a milk truck?" I asked.

We laughed so hard that Pete began to choke and I had to pound him on the back to get him to stop.

Rich looked indignant. "Yeah, a milk truck. It's big enough to hold the three of us . . . and can haul a lot of weight." He stared at Pete and dug him in the ribs.

"But a milk truck?" Pete said, still chuckling.

"Think about it. The Live Oak Dairy over on Milpas is always sellin' their old trucks. We could buy one cheap and fix it up. They're practically givin' 'em away."

"But . . . but a milk truck? What girl is gonna wanna ride in a milk truck?" I asked.

"We can paint it competition orange like Pete wants, with pinstriping. Cut holes in the sides and put in more windows so I can look out, get big fat tires with chrome rims, put glass packs on the thing, maybe even drop in a bigger engine. We'll be the only one in town. And we can stick a sofa in the back if ya want."

We left that day shaking our heads and giggling. But as promised, Pete and I talked with our parents. At first they laughed as much as we did. Then they talked with Rich's parents. Less than two years later and after countless hours working with our fathers, our Orange Uttermobile sat in Rich's driveway, ready to roll. We'd added a boss AM/FM radio, red dice around the rear-view mirror, and yes, blue lights in the wheel wells.

I got my license first. The look on the DMV guy's face was priceless when I showed up for my driving test in the orange bomb. Our fathers had already put plenty of miles on the thing. They acted as juvenile as we did.

The truck included extra seats and a special tie-down spot where Rich would watch the world go by, chat up the girls we took to ball games, dances, and on make-out sessions off Camino Cielo. Rich never ran out of ideas for having fun while being careful to steer around trouble. But he also learned to trust our judgment, to lay back and enjoy life without trying to control it.

In two years the three of us split up: Pete to Fresno State to study Physical Education, Rich to Cal Tech on an Engineering scholarship, and me to UCSB studying Psychology, then to South Vietnam to practice survival.

But we never lost touch, celebrated each of our weddings. Rich expanded his parents' house and moved in with them, with his wife and their two adopted Vietnamese children. The west end of Calle Poniente once again had another generation of little kids, the start of a new mini-fiefdom.

Rich died at fifty-four from renal failure and a bad ticker. We scattered his ashes under the oaks and the long-abandoned remains of the tree house. In my barn-like garage sits the Orange Uttermobile. It awaits its second life under the hopefully vivid imagination of the little boy asleep in my second wife's womb. I start it up now and again to keep the Three Amigos alive.

LOVE
RUN
HALF MARATHON
NuVu

IV.
FAMILY

JO MARIAN GOING

UNCLE JOHN

Memory is the equity we have in our lives, says the poet Jack Gilbert. Memories, whether pleasant or not, are a reminder of the pathways we have walked through the mystery of our life. Memory helps decode that mystery, giving glimpses of ourselves from another vantage point than the present. And out of such glimpses we make of our lives something of abiding shape and meaning.

I am writing from the wilderness of interior Alaska where I have lived now for eighteen years. Something deep in the soul of my youth called me to the far north, its forms, light, and spirit giving substance to the practice of painting that is my life. An unconventional life in many ways, it is for me a good one, keeping me in touch with my purpose and bliss.

And the long days of silence and solitude are suited to the wanderings of memory, which like migrating caribou return often to the calving ground of first beginnings and the people who gathered there, who in some very special way, stay with us on our journey. There will often spring up from some unbidden depth, like snatches of a half-remembered dream, familial remembrances of time past. Today as I was hiking in the mountains towards a favorite painting spot, from some hidden wellspring deep inside there came unbidden but clear a flowing stream of remembrance of my Uncle John.

There are some people in one's childhood who do not necessarily play a central role, but none the less an essential one, and Uncle John was definitely that person. He was a quiet presence in a family that tended to be volatile. There was a gentleness about him that did not force or impose, that created a calming in the midst of turmoil. It was that quality that allowed me to feel safe with him, and I can remember the peace I felt sitting in his lap, playing with the translucent " last drop" of his Maxwell House tie tack. I have a faded photograph of me at the age of five, holding his hand at his wedding to my father's sister, Angela. The expression on my face, pure joy, shows clearly I had found a friend. He was a humble man. In a family in which men become physicians and assume upward mobility, he worked as a dyer in a local mill. His work was always something of a mystery to me as child, and I used to imagine him standing over a big pot stirring cloth with a wooden spoon as my mother did when she dyed fabric on the stove. As I was extremely sensitive to color, foretelling my life as an artist, I knew my Uncle's job was important, saving me from a life of grays and beiges. And I was also very aware that his job did not keep him continually absent: he was present, and had time for me.

It was Uncle John who taught me to play baseball. He gave me a tiny wooden bat, showing me how to swing, hit, bunt. And he taught me to throw, practicing with me in the summer evenings in my grandparent's lot. He had somehow understood how very badly I wanted to learn, as in those days, athletics was not something young girls were thought to consider. I wanted to play sports with a passion, and Uncle John must have sensed that, for I don't ever remember vocalizing my desire. Sometimes when he was playing with the men's league in our summer community, he would, seeing me on the swings, call to me to come to bat, the entire team of young men pitching to and accommodating willingly my tiny bit of blond pigtailed self, ecstatically running the bases after a high fly into three feet before the plate.

Uncle John took me fishing in his small wooden dinghy that he kept on the brackish pond behind Nana's house. Carrying our fishing poles and bait we would walk to the pond through a tunnel of elephant grass and cat o'nine tails, an adventure of African safari magnitude. I can remember just sitting quietly in the boat for hours, as Uncle John was a person of silence. With a sensitivity to animals that would mature into my being vegetarian, I dont think I actually liked to fish, but I did like being with this man, with his quiet calm and tranquil spirit. Watching the swans and cignets glide across the still water, I was enfolded into the greater rhythm of the natural world, a pulse that was to determine so much of my lifes journey. And there were many times while climbing the cliffs by our summer house that I would come upon my uncle as he stood alone on the rocks fishing for ocean bass, tall and slender in a loose fitting work shirt, his red hair ruffed by the breeze. There was a zone of silence around him at these times that I never interrupted. Hiding behind a boulder, I would watch for a while, then silently leave him to his peace.

Children know intuitively when they are liked. I knew there was a place for me in Uncle John's heart, though our friendship was unspoken. Sitting in the rocking chair with him, together we would sing, "we're poor little lambs, who have lost our way . . . ," bringing a palpable longing beyond my years to my childs soul. To this day, with my thoroughly versed classical music education, I cannot hear that song without crying.

Uncle John died when I was in high school. When taps were played at the dedication in his memory of a neighborhood baseball field, I struggled with a growing lump in my throat that I still feel. I often wonder what would have become of our friendship had he been with me into my adulthood. I doubt he would have understood me, as the shape of my life is very different from the expected familial norm. Yet I do believe we would have remained friends, that he would listen to my dreams, and pitch a ball to me now and then across the distance.

STEPHANIE HART

MEDITATIONS ON GOODNESS

I never met my maternal grandmother, Sonia Tolchinksy, a Russian Jewish immigrant, who escaped the fiery pogroms of her village, to make her home in Newark, New Jersey, along with her husband and five children. She died before I was born. Nevertheless, she has had a profound effect on my life. When my mother spoke about her own mother, she would say, "My mother was an angel." Stories of her kindness and generosity were legendary in my family.

In the mornings, my grandmother worked along with my grandfather, who was the owner of a small successful grocery store. It was a job which allowed her to meet many members of her largely Russian Jewish Community. Carefully putting away a portion of her household allowance, she would deliver clothes, food, and money to needy families. These were private acts of kindness; she never spoke about them to anyone. At her funeral, recipients, talked about her visits: She would sit down at their tables, accept tea in a glass Russian style, and encourage the women to talk about their lives; not only did my grandmother help support these families, she also brought them solace. They thought of her as an angel too. I came to think of goodness as connected not only to kindness and generosity but also to humility.

I was named after my grandmother, Sonia. In the Jewish tradition, it is customary to name a child for a deceased relative. Thus the first letter of her name became the first letter of my name, Stephanie. I have always had a special affinity for her.

When I was a child of five or six, my parents, on the rocky road to divorce, were mean-spirited to each other and to me. I adopted my grandmother as my guardian angel. At night, I could feel her presence like a warm light around me. I would speak to her in my mind. She knew how angry I was at my mother and father and that I wanted to run away. Yet the light kept shining. Goodness and acceptance of another became synonymous in my mind.

As I got older, I was eager to learn more about my grandmother and my mother was a good source of information. Born in Moscow, she moved to Odessa where she married my grandfather, Joseph Tolchinksy, a blue-eyed debonair tanner with a fierce temper and a surfeit of charm; he loved and revered her for her beauty and gentility. Five years later, to escape attacks on Jewish villages, Joseph sailed to America to set up a business. Sonia, who then had three children, followed by ship a year after that. Terrified of the tall waves and the raucous sea that in a storm sounded like thunder, she kept her children close to her in steerage, comforting them and herself. On a clear day, she finally ventured out on deck with her youngest daughter, Ada, in her arms and her older children, Rose and Philip, beside her. She watched the ocean spread around them, like a continent she wanted to explore. (In the new world of summers on Bradley Beach, New Jersey, she would become a powerful swimmer). On this crossing, my grandmother took her children on deck many times. Overcoming her fear, she was able to treat them to the majesty of the sea and sky. Sometimes goodness takes courage.

My grandmother was a diabetic who lost a kidney giving birth to her fifth child, my mother; she died of a heart attack when my mother was fourteen. In her lifetime, not wanting to upset her family, she rarely complained of being sick. She got up early, got dressed neatly and carefully, and sang in a sweet voice as she went about her business. Her fortitude and consideration for others spoke to me of goodness.

My grandmother was not an angel. At times my grandfather ran roughshod over his wife and children, hurling commands and criticism. She was loath to stop him. Worn down by life, sometimes she was not able to give my mother, her youngest, the time and attention she wanted to. But on Friday nights, seated at the head of the Sabbath table in a white prayer shawl, Grandma Sonia was the glue that held the family together.

When my friends and I talk about goodness, some describe it as shared artistic expression in writing and in painting, others as political activism, designed to nudge the world into a better place, still others as attunement to the force of good in the universe. A few friends support the idea that goodness is coded into our DNA; we have it or we don't. I have reached the conclusion that while it is not perfection, goodness is a quality one can choose to develop and practice time and time again as my grandmother did, one which requires tolerance and patience with others and the self.

My mother like her mother was quick to help others; she visited friends when they were in the hospital and stayed the night if necessary. She would open doors for the elderly and walk them to where they wanted to go. I remember her spending an entire day with a stranger in the emergency room. She nursed me back to health with love and tenderness when I had hepatitis. My mother had a strong social conscience; she crossed race and class lines in her friendships and encouraged me to do the same. She could be rageful, even insulting, but the desire to help others was a definitive part of her character. From her, I have learned that lending a helping hand and respecting differences, are core elements of goodness.

My mother kept her mother's picture by her bedside while I keep the same picture of my grandmother on my desk. My mother assured me it was a good likeness. Now, I study my grandmother's broad face, her high cheekbones, her full lips with just a hint of a smile. Her hair, parted in the center, is tied back in a bun. She has on pearl earring and a white lace dress. Her eyes are brown and pear-shaped like mine. She has become my guiding light, my moral compass (and I suspect was my mother's too), and a damn hard act to follow.

Few people, I included, have her largesse of spirit. I have come to think of this as fine because part of goodness is self-acceptance. Yet, by example, my grandmother has influenced both my small and pivotal choices. When I give to charity, I give anonymously. I assist others, if I can, in deeds and words. Although as a writer I am often abstracted, I try to be considerate of my friends and life partner, David.

The most important career choice I have ever made has my grandmother's fingerprints on it and my mother's too. In my twenties, casting about for satisfying work, I tried editing magazines, writing YA fiction, and doing office work but often felt unfulfilled and empty. Teaching, a helping profession, became my ticket to happiness and satisfaction. In my mid-thirties, I acquired an MA degree, which allowed me the privilege of teaching international college students, who also happened to be artists and designers. A multicultural world opened up for me as I taught them to find their written and spoken voices in English. I have learned that giving can be gratifying and reciprocal.

The decision to take care of my stepmother, Annette, in the last months of her life, when her relatives were living in Nebraska, was based on what I perceived to be my grandmother's code of honor: it was the right thing to do. Annette and I had had a checkered relationship. While my father was alive, we had locked horns, once almost come to blows, and then learned to be cordial to one another. After his death, we gradually became friends, frequenting New York museums and restaurants. When she became ill, I accompanied her on late night visits to the emergency room, to doctor's appointments, and sat by her bedside during hospitalizations. We talked personally about ourselves and got to know each other well. She introduced me to the nurses as her daughter and that pleased me. As she got weaker, I would walk over to her bedside and stroke her cheek, her forehead, feeling a swelling of affection. I was bereft at the time of her death. The bond between us would never have formed if I hadn't chosen to come to her aid.

While my relationship with my own mother was often painful and contentious, once she became ill, I wanted to spend time with her. Every few weeks, I would fly from New York to Miami Beach to see her. In the mornings, we would sit by her window, overlooking Indian Creek and watch the Miami University rowing team power canoes across the water. The atmosphere inside her apartment was as quiet and peaceful as the scene outside. One day, as if on cue, we stood up at the same time. I noticed her cheeks were drawn; her eyes a faded blue. I walked over to her and put my arms around her; she slipped her thin arms around my waist. I stroked her back, the nape of her neck, which felt birdlike and tender. Compassion chased away resentment.

My mother sensed my good will. "God bless you," she said.

All at once, I felt renewed, joyful, and forgiving as if a weight had been taken off my shoulders; anger and blame fell away. I was aware only of the warmth of our hug and the love between us.

It was a moment I think my grandmother would have understood.

PATRICK CABELLO HANSEL

THE SWALLOWS RETURN TO EAST 28TH STREET

Not with trumpets, or portents or exactitude,
as at San Juan Capistrano, where the winged
heralds arrive right on time for St. Joseph's
Day, two days before spring. Nor in a whirl
of wings at dusk on the soccer pitch, phantoms
skimming inches above the grass, as my long-
legged daughter sprints goalward. The swallows
do not *arrive* at the old church tower on East
28th Street. They *appear*. One morning, they
are there, as I walk bottles and cans to the
recycling bin; one night, as spring stretches
its tongue over the long, dying winter, and
awakes joy, they are simply *there*. They are
there, skirting in and out of the cornices,
the nooks where their sisters, the sparrows,
have founded a nest to lay their young. They are
there, dwelling high enough above the thawing
earth to shield their eggs and hatchlings from
raccoon and rat, yet tucked into corners where
the tower meets the arched roof, tidy avian
hermitages too small for the red-tailed hawk—
that fierce remainder of souls—to enter and
plunder. The swallows return to East 28th Street,
not by clockwork nor command. They appear,
they tarry, they praise. Their wings whisper
each summer twilight. And then, of a season,
they are gone. Not having flown away, or departed,
but simply—and unnoticed for a time—they are
absent, as fall falls slowly towards another winter
and leaves us with just a slight rift in the sky,
where our longings for birth, for rest, seek shelter.

THE SECOND BREAKFAST, 1924

Bacon, pancakes, ham.
Fried eggs, sweet bread, milk.
The women brought coffee
in steaming pots, wild berries in thick
bowls, sugar, a tablecloth
to spread about the harvest field.
Men and boys up since five
commanding horses rightly swooned.
It was the late summer family wedding feast:
a marriage of toil and rest,
the hungry mind hailing the harvest.
Wheat, barley, oats—the ripe heads
snipped by the combine, chaff
driven to the wind, grain gathered
by hard work in silence, the winter
secured, shoes bought for half the family.

From beyond the second rise,
the cry of the harvesters:
Here comes the second breakfast!
Reins tugged back on the horses,
the combine geared down
with sputters, grace pealed from
lips for cream, butter, jam, the tongue's
delight. Your mother was still

alive at the last breakfast, bouncing
along on the hay wagon, her thick hair
streaming, the son who will burst
her kicking in the womb, his lost family
waiting beyond the horizon.
But not a whisper of the pain
on this September Saturday:
only beans, cheese, apple butter
and the cool breeze the earth
sends up to its victors.

LORRAINE JEFFERY

BEYOND NEED

Three of them floating the breeze
from the door we just opened,
like apple blossoms, gauzy pink, white,
and red blouses hang from the curtain rod,
where Mother and I see them on entry,
and gape—*Who brought them?* I ask.

She slowly shakes her head, reaching
a tentative hand to touch them,
seeking a pinned message.
She finds no hint
in the cluttered dining room
where we don't eat,
or on the open sewing machine.

She gazes at their slow undulations,
lowering herself into a wooden chair.
New, from Sears or Pennys, where
we buy school clothes with earnings
from picking cherries, beans and walnuts.
Her size—not her children's. She calls
her sisters on the black phone—*no* and *no*.

She doesn't consider the one
who brings the same paycheck
home each month,
each dollar counted.
A child of the Depression,
she has enough.
Her children are fed, they have
a house, a car, her sisters give her
an occasional skirt. She has a blouse
from last year. *Who needs three?*

Still, she wears them, her shoulders
alive to their feathery film,
till they are threadbare,
with only a hint of their youthful beauty,
always searching familiar faces for
the author of those
floating angels of wonder.

MY UNCLE'S LIGHT

Cutting beet tops
like I had seen grownups do, my
five-year-old world went black and

I screamed. Dad hitched
horses and Mother cried. Even
after the doctor, only shadowy

people, my world opaque.
I listened—*school away*,
sotto voce voices. I was afraid. Rails

on school walls guided me while
I learned with my hands
and fingers. Away from family

in the coldest winter in Utah
history, the new baby didn't know
me, my brother shot his trophy

buck alone. My ears read
the words of college professors,
but what about books? She

of the soft voice spoke
the words, her laughter an aria,
her speech, a lullaby. When

we told the others,
I heard the long pauses,
but my world blazed bright.

Osteopathy. Hands-on
manipulation in
medicine? I had hands—and hope.

She read textbooks, drove,
cleaned house, fed children,
watched news and smiled

with her voice. Much later
I put *doctor* on a plaque, my
world still bright.

FOR IAN

We siblings laugh louder as we age,
having scrabbled up summits,
and dug furrows to earn it,
our kids now plowing their own futures—

except Ian, my middle
brother's son. Thirty-four,
he rocks when he sits
cross-legged on the floor.

Our arthritic ears hear
ticking like a clock' pendulum,
as we revel in doing what we couldn't
when the yoke of parenthood rode our shoulders.

My writing gets me up in the morning, I say.
I get up to garden, says Art scratching his arm;
I still have to go to work, the youngest grumbles.
I wake up just to know that I don't have to,
quips John as our laughter rocks the room.

What about you?, I ask,
turning to Mark, my middle brother,
who barely whispers, *I*
get up for Ian.

JENNIFER L. FREED

IT ABIDES

in the enormity of sky
and in the slanted light
silvering the maple leaves,

in the girl on the grass, singing
into murmurings of green,
and in the woman, curved into the doorway

of the yellow house, silently gazing
at daughter
and tree and cloud,

holding back her call
to chores,
knowing

this

must be allowed
to last.

MARION DEUTSCHE COHEN

BRYN AT 5 AT GRAN'MA'S HOUSE

I hope Gran'ma's house is a magical place.
I hope the legos are enough, or the brightly colored
dominoes
piano, fruit you can play with, special Bryn-cookies.
And down the cellar Gran'ma keeps a doll crib, doll
stroller, doll highchair, and dolls.
Bryn always asks me to bring up the cellar things
and then, back upstairs, she selects two babies
one for the crib, over which she hovers, and slowly,
very slowly
she lays the little blue blanket over that first baby
then she takes the second baby
and wordlessly tiptoes over to Gran'ma sitting on the
piano stool singing lullabies.
With but a slight glance she hands me that second baby.
I hold and rock it
keep on singing lullabies.
And this isn't a soccer lesson
or ice-skating lessons
or piano lessons.
This is just holding babies and singing lullabies
and it's very quiet today
at Gran'ma's house.

LORI LEVY

WHEN FLOWERS CRY

She is their flower, beautiful, delicate,
but on this summer day, as she protests the *unfair*—
a perennial in her world—
she wilts in her car seat
as though crushed or torn or chewed.
Her mother soothes from the front
while her father signals, moves to the right,
as if it's crucial that he stop for a moment,
water her roots by the side of the road.
He swings her door open, scoops her up,
asks, "What can I do for you?
What will make you happy?"
Her sobs fade to whimpers to sighs to breath
as he rubs her back, kisses her head, her cheek.
He, too, revives as she blooms again.

I am the aunt in the back seat
watching them tend her,
wishing I, too, could be a child
someone stops by a roadside
to console like that.

HUGS

For Ruby Lou

I have a new teacher: my two-year-old granddaughter.
"Come on, Savta," she says, when we arrive at the playground.
Lesson One is as clear as the shine in her eyes:
no sitting on a bench as a quiet observer.
She grabs my hand, and the adventure begins,
my introvert self pulled straight into the action.
She rushes to greet other kids. Hands-on, close,
she touches a face, pats a print on a T-shirt,
a flower, a princess. Fingers a necklace. Hugs.
I note Lesson Two, toss out a few hellos, swap names, ages—
nothing like her hugs, but, still, there I am, exchanging
pleasantries with mommies, daddies, grandmas, nannies.
She doesn't wait to be invited, just joins in—Lesson Three—
chasing balls, pushing dolls in strollers, trying out
deserted tricycles. She sits down to check a truck
in the sand. Plays with pails and shovels.
Takes. Gives. Shares or doesn't share.
On the swings, beside another child, she sings along
with the child's mother, "The wheels of the bus
go round and round," while I smile and push,
smile and blush, still too shy at sixty-four to sing
in front of strangers. Lesson Four: sing!
She takes a toddler's hands in hers, spins, dances.
Some kids back away, not used to such affection.
One runs to escape, shouting, "I need space from you!"
I watch my little teacher, pretty sure I would have
cried, cringed, retreated. Lesson Five: her response,
how she follows, frolics, loves. Doesn't give up.
So many hugs, given freely, whole-heartedly,
all of us deserving. But no mistaking Lesson Six:
she beams extra warmth at her chosen ones.

GARY YOUNG

"HE WAS DRINKING"

He was drinking in the airport bar, and I asked, are you coming or going? I have been there, he said, and I almost didn't get back. He said, the engines failed, and we seemed to be falling forever; I've never been so afraid. Then he took a sip of his drink, and rolled back his sleeve. He'd printed his name down the length of his arm, and below that he'd written, Honey, I love you. It's strange, he said, what goes through your mind at a time like that. I hope to God this washes off, he said. My wife just loves to worry.

"I HAD NEVER SEEN HER SO ANGRY"

I had never seen her so angry, and her rage revealed a measure of love I had missed. There were many times she might have hurt me that way, and didn't.

"TREMBLING AND FURIOUS"

Trembling and furious, the baby screams. He's tired, and his own body frightens him. I hold him by his shoulders and sing. It's a sad song, but he finally sleeps. It's a sad song, but even silence can be a terror, and a violence, and I keep singing.

"I DISCOVERED A JOURNAL"

I discovered a journal in the children's ward, and read, I'm a mother, my little boy has cancer. Further on, a girl has written, this is my nineteenth operation. She says, sometimes it's easier to write than to talk, and I'm so afraid. She's left me a page in the book. My son is sleeping in the room next door. This afternoon, I held my whole weight to his body while a doctor drove needles deep into his leg. My son screamed, Daddy, they're hurting me, don't let them hurt me, make them stop. I want to write, how brave you are, but I need a little courage of my own, so I write, forgive me, I know I let them hurt you, please don't worry. If I have to, I can do it again.

"KITTY SMILED"

Kitty smiled, pressed my hand against the fleshy knot in her belly, and said, it's the child we always wanted, or as close as we'll ever get now. A malignancy, not a pregnancy, was swelling inside her. She'd caress it with her palms, and as the tumor grew, she mothered it; she brought it to term. One night she woke with a fever, and I carried her into the hospital. Her wasted arms and legs made her belly seem even larger than it was. A woman asked, are you in labor? And she said, no. Then the woman asked, but are you expecting? And she said, yes.

ANDY ORAM

KNOTS

Waves are swelling toward the coast back home,
So I have to return soon.
But I appreciate the chance to have our visit.
    I became wistful while sorting through what you left to me.
    Surprising, how fast I could travel so far to see you.

I couldn't have even read your handwriting,
Had you not taught me the old songs.
    They don't play them on the radio anymore.

Furthermore, it was a boon to learn how to tie knots.
And perhaps even more crucial, how to untie them.

Because I am hemmed in by so many knots.
My children, my employers, the politicians I argue with,
    Even an occasional poet.

Although most of the ones I disparage have already died.

Well, let's get back to the topic.

You also taught me to drop a plumb line,
And to dowse for items more precious than water.
Most of what we pulled up was pretty ugly,
But they were worth the long trips to barren horizons.
Don't worry.
    I have saved them all.

And finally, that last bit about retaining dignity.
Or correspondingly, relinquishing needless pride.
I'm sure I'll use that in the future.

So now I hear the torrents urging me back
To scan for survivors.

But thanks for the time spent, which I'll gather with me
    Till we are next together.

JOHN GREY

TO BE GOOD

Mama used to smack me hard
with her religion.
"Damn that kid," she'd say.
Across the rear with a paddle mostly
but it felt severe and unforgiving as a Bible.
Lying there in bed,
I'd be feeling the jabbing pains of Jesus,
the soreness in the saints.
And there was that old heat-riddled night sky
to deal with from atop of sticky sheets.
Felt like I was shrinking into it
though she insisted I was the one
who was wearing her out.

Back then, people had their nature
as much as snakes, as gators, did.
"Go wash hands," "clean behind your ears". . .
like fangs, like sharp teeth.
And so was the hair-cut
trimmed so close it threatened skin.
And school, the punishment
I slowly traipsed to
under a sun thick and red
as a bloody boil
that it took a thunderhead to burst.

The enemy was everywhere
and what did I have to fight back with . . .
a child's breath, a picture book of *Charlotte's Web.*
I trapped a bullfrog in a bottle

just to have someone on my side.
So luckless being born,
a face at the screen door
when the men were fixing engines.

And then people started dying
and that really found me out.
No tears for wax-dummy corpses,
just a hankering to be outside
away from the gloom.
My mother tried to stare
a serious look into my face
but it came out as a half-cooked grin.

More punishment to come.
Old people got nothing but choked up tears
for death but I paid a price for living.

A child had to be good
like no child could be.
The clean face, the perfect manners,
the grades better than a cousin's . . .
these were the invisible thieves
who stole from me.
And it was religion that told them
where I kept my most rebellious thoughts,
that listened in when, under my breath,
I hissed, "I ain't doing this no way.
OK, well maybe when I'm dead"

NICHOLAS SAMARAS

I AM CALLING FORTY YEARS AGO

into this telephone I hold now
like conscience and memory, an urgency of time,

calling our old house number from first memory,
praying into the tiny altar of the speaker,

to hear your voice once again alive
through the wires and years, to hear

your voice say hello, so I can tell you forty years
of everything—gratitude and grief, desperation and desire

of a son for his father, to say
I lived because of you.

I have a son named after you,
a daughter I pray you know and look after still.

I call our old house number of my childhood,
almost-seeing you stand in our tiny kitchen

in Quincy, Massachusetts
where my childhood survives,

where the impossible kindness of your voice says
hello, who is this?

YUROK CLASSMATES

The blessing of summer school—history, creative writing—to get me out the house of bruises and strap marks. A safe space in which to plan and execute. The Yurok girl who taught me her dancing. The Yurok girl in my class I confided in. A week of daily walking down to Hidden Beach, hiding a sack of my clothing in the underbrush, tip money—freedom money—folded in my pocket. The July 21st morning I went to the summer school bus stop and didn't get on. My fear like trembled breathing. My walking off the world. The swallowed days and nights. The scary hours in warm darkness. As the daily summer school bus slowed around the bend by Hidden Beach, myself hiding in the tree line, the brown arms of my Yurok classmates who threw their lunch bags out of the school bus windows for me. From this distance now, I forget their names. I don't forget their kindness. How I had food and lived a few more days.

THE KIDNAPPED CHILD LEAVES THE JUDGE'S CHAMBERS

Named. I am named.
You have no idea what it means

to finally be named
and belong to somebody, to have a family—

to be someone in relation to someone else.
To have a voice outside yourself who talks to you

kindly, without force or aggression.
To no longer live for flinching or apologising.

To be legal. To have a piece of paper
legitimatise you. To be adopted

by your real parent after all
the lost years, the desert wanderings.

The sun glints off the buildings' windows.
The road cruises down the road to home.

Named. I am named.
No longer the kidnapped child,

I am born old and young, reparented
with a life to begin for real.

THE KIDNAPPED CHILD IN THE HOME HE WILL NEVER LEAVE

My father brought me to Quincy, Massachusetts—
Executive Apartments, 1025 Hancock Street, Apartment 11-M—

an address that stayed and didn't move,
a home before memory began,

a home furnished with self-esteem.
The two-bedroom apartment, a cornerstone of Heaven.

Every day, my father taught me how to eat food,
how to hold a fork, how to brush and wash.

Every day, his soft voice reassured me
until I could begin to trust and recognize what was normal.

I had my own room that I knew
would still be there when I came home from school.

I had my own brass-gold key to our door,
my own address, my own parent.

Nobody to welt and bruise me for control.
Nobody to violate the air, the days.

There was no agenda but care.
No voice raised, but safety. No voice raised.

To know what it's like to be a life saved.
To know that stillness.

In houses, there are people.
In homes, there is God.

DON NOEL

THE REDHEAD

Guy found it vaguely unsettling that Terry was the child knocking herself out to help dear old dad transition to a new life. The two boys—the children he *knew* were his—were too busy or too distant to be of more than intermittent help. It was the daughter he'd never been sure about who rose to the occasion.

He'd never expected to need help. When he retired, he and Myrtle moved to a roomy cottage in a huge Florida retirement community. They made new friends, learned to play a sport called pickleball, bought a modest motorboat, and enjoyed life. For the first fifteen years, between taking his new pals fishing and inviting couples to evening drinks, they almost lived on the boat.

When they both began to have balance problems, giving up the boat wasn't as big a deal as he'd feared: Getting aboard and ashore had gotten to be problematic for their pals, too. In any case, there were plenty of shorebound pleasures, and life continued to be good.

Nor did they feel cut off from family. Howie did enough traveling for his Seattle company that they could count on him to stop in for a night or two every year, take his parents to an expensive dinner and spend the evening regaling them with the adventures of modern-day corporate brass. Charlie and his wife Beth were huge cruise vacationers, flying down annually from Minneapolis. They often spent a day or two afterward, sharing their latest port conquests—often, in later years, with endless photo shows from their busy smartphones.

And Terry—Teresa, both the name and nickname Myrtle's choice—brought her whole family to Florida for a whole week every year. She and Dick and their boys usually came during baseball spring training, renting a motel nearby, and took him and Myrtle to several games, which the kids never tired of. They also found nearby places where the boys could practice baseball themselves while their grandparents applauded.

Guy never expressed aloud his doubts about her paternity. Those grandsons were as vividly red-haired as Terry had been in her youth, though, and their visits never failed to remind him of a rough patch in his marriage.

He was born Guido, with dark Italian good looks; he made it Guy when he became the first in his immigrant neighborhood to be accepted at an Ivy League college. When Terry was born with blue eyes and flaming red hair, the marital tensions he'd thought resolved suddenly re-emerged, and came near the breaking point.

In the years before that birth, he admitted to himself and ultimately to Myrtle, he'd spent too much time climbing the rungs of the company ladder, devoting too little to her and the boys. She took to bitching about his absence; he reciprocated with a surliness that, looking back, he knew she didn't deserve. Their love life suffered.

Then one night he came home late for dinner—again—and she surprised him by not complaining. Instead she was again the loving, sympathetic and supportive wife of the early years. She brought him a glass of wine to relax with while she warmed up dinner, then sat with him at the table, seeming eager to hear about his hard day.

Then, while he read the boys their bedtime stories—at her urging—she took a shower and changed into a negligée he hadn't seen in years. They spent the night like newlyweds—including, he realized only later, not bothering with the clumsy birth control of those days.

It didn't seem long before she announced she was pregnant again. He had already resolved to be a better family man. A new child, he thought—maybe this time a daughter—would be a welcome incentive.

Myrtle's labor pains started earlier than expected, but she said the ob-gyn had said that might happen at her age. The new baby was born without any problems, and was indeed the daughter they'd hoped for. But she didn't look anything like the two boys. Myrtle claimed to remember an Irishman in her family, several generations back, famous for his Celtic red hair, whom she'd never mentioned until then.

He flogged his brain, trying to think of redheads he or she might have known. He went to the town library to do research, and learned that the gene for red hair is "recessive," which didn't tell him as much as he wanted to know except that red hair can skip several generations.

Still full of doubts, Guy finally went to see Father Antonio.

"You wanted a daughter?" the wise priest asked.

"Yes, padre. Partly for Myrtle's sake, but I thought it would be great to have a little girl."

"And if the opportunity had come along to adopt a baby girl, what would you have done?"

Guy remembered that conversation the rest of his life. "Padre, we probably would have adopted her. No, definitely would have."

"And you would have loved her?"

"Of course, Padre."

"Unreservedly?"

"Certainly."

"My son, God has given you a daughter to love unreservedly. You must never give her any reason to think she wasn't wanted, or to wonder if you are her father. She is your daughter."

So Guy put the doubts out of his mind, making himself a better husband and a loving father to all three of his children. He decided he had reached high enough on the corporate ladder, and could stop climbing. He began attending PTA meetings with Myrtle, and volunteered to coach Howie's baseball team. When Charlie took up soccer he boned up and coached that team, too.

And without slighting his sons, he made his daughter a special child. He attended her lacrosse and volleyball games, her glee club performances, even her spelling bees. If there was a Terry event he missed, he could not now remember when or why.

And it was this daughter who now came to his rescue.

Their Florida retirement village lost its charm in small steps. They had mostly done things in foursomes, with one or another of several couples in their circle of friends. When a few of those favorite companions died—a wife here, a husband there—it became awkward to arrange dinners or outings.

Then Myrtle died; he was desolate. All three of the kids came for the funeral, and Terry stayed a few extra days to help him ease into single existence. Even with her help, it proved a hard transition to a life that no longer felt good. He had not been a bachelor in six decades, and being one now felt as though his right arm had been torn away.

And on top of all that, it seemed as though every few months another of his pals died. Life in Florida was gradually, inexorably, becoming intolerably lonely.

His stroke was the final blow. He was alone when it happened, but the village's system of routine checks found him soon and got him to the hospital in good time. Both the boys harried the doctor and nurses by phone, insisting that he get every possible help to overcome the affliction, and Terry came to reinforce the message in person.

He got the attention his children demanded, and it by and large worked. With Terry helping and prodding him to maintain a demanding exercise regimen, he made great progress walking and talking, visible even during the week before she went back to her family.

The stroke had also affected his eyes, though, too. He could only focus at the periphery of his vision, like people with macular degeneration, which meant he could hardly read. He had to "watch" television mostly with his ears. He felt isolated, abandoned in an empty cottage that he could barely navigate, let alone manage. The Florida place was for people capable of independent living. He needed more help.

Terry found a place near her in Connecticut that had the right level of assisted living, and the kids rallied again. Charlie flew down from Minneapolis to join her in getting him downsized. His new lodgings, less an apartment than an efficiency bedroom, would be a third the size of the Florida cottage, so a lot had to be sold or given away. Charlie and Terry then got the rest of his stuff packed up to be trucked north.

Howie came from Seattle, just before the three of them flew to Connecticut, to take over selling the Florida place and managing financial details. Then both the boys flew their separate ways home, and Terry was again in charge.

She had chosen well: It proved to be a place with a competent and caring staff. Except for the vision, the effects of the stroke dwindled to almost nothing, and even the vision was improving. It turned out that his right eye, which had lifelong been the weak one, wasn't as affected by the stroke. His new aides devised exercises to help that eye strengthen and take over.

And in other ways this new place was better: He was far from alone in suffering the afflictions of age; he had plenty of company. And his new neighbors set him good examples of making the best of what God or fate or Charles Darwin (as one resident skeptic put it) had left them. There were daily group activities that he actually enjoyed, and to his surprise he soon found he had several real pals, both men and women.

And best of all, Terry kept coming: For dinner every Friday night, drop-ins for an hour or so during the week, usually Sunday mornings to drag him to the chapel service and stay for what they called brunch.

Yet the paternity thing kept popping, unbidden, into his mind. Did she know or suspect she wasn't his? Did she know who sired her? Was she in touch with another father?

It was an itch. He remembered when a six-year-old Charlie hadn't known about or recognized poison ivy, and suffered a head-to-toe rash that he and Myrtle took turns slathering with baking soda or oatmeal or some white commercial liquid whose name eluded him now. "Don't scratch it, Charlie," they'd urged him, "you'll only make it worse." The little boy couldn't resist scratching, of course, and made it worse.

Even remembering that history, Guy couldn't resist scratching. Father Antonio might have talked him out of it, but the priest was long gone. He kept rehearsing, in his mind, how he might broach the topic with Terry.

Finally, one Sunday after the service but before they left the chapel—spontaneously, unstoppably, with no finesse whatsoever—he blurted it out. "Terry, did you ever wonder where you got your red hair?"

"Oh Dad," she said, with a kind of mournful resonance that seemed appropriate for the chapel, "Mom wondered if that question chewed at you. She never knew if you'd guessed."

"You asked her?"

"We were learning about genetics in my senior year at Waverly High. I wasn't worked up about it; it just seemed a logical question."

"And she told you? Confessed?"

"You could call it that. She could have fobbed me off with that Irish ancestor story. Instead, she told me how lonely she'd felt because your work seemed more important than your wife or family."

"It's true. I was a jerk."

"So it just happened. You were away at some conference, and she met a guy from out of town at a church meeting, and . . . ."

"She fell in love with him?"

"Daddy, she never loved anyone but you. She never wanted to see him again, and didn't."

"Never?"

"Never."

"Did you?"

"I didn't want to, at first. Then, at college, I began to think I ought to. Mom resisted. Let sleeping dogs lie, she said."

"But you persisted?"

"Yes. Maybe there was some genetic disorder I should know about, I argued."

"So she told you his name?"

"Yes. That was almost all she knew."

"Did he know about you?"

"Absolutely not, Mom said. She'd never spoken another word with him."

"But you looked him up?"

"It wasn't as easy as it would be now, with the Internet, but I found him, out in the Midwest."

"And . . . ?"

"Daddy, I never contacted him."

"After all that?"

"I realized, finally, that he didn't mean anything to me. I had a real father who loved me, and who I loved. That's what matters, isn't it?"

There was a catch in her voice. He couldn't see her, which had nothing to do with the stroke. He wondered, as he reached out for a hug, if her vision was blurred, too.

"It is," he murmured. "It's the only thing that matters."

DC DIAMONDOPOLOUS

LIFE WITH ANGIE

My sister Angie gives me outrageous material for my standup comedy. She's a bona fide nut case, a paranoid schizophrenic, bipolar, manic depressive—you name it—Angie fits every disorder that isn't wired to reality.

The voices inside her head tell her to run from anyone trying to help her—except me. I take my sister's sorry existence, find the humor in it—in the loonies of my own mind—and make people laugh. Do I feel guilty? I'm half Jewish, half Catholic. Humor is my way of coping. Hell, I'm a female stand-up comic, and there's no higher hurdle in show business.

Growing up, bullies at school called me circus girl. I'm 5'10", big boned, with short blond hair. I was gay and Jew bashed. I rolled in the hurt, turned it inside out, and now make people laugh. I'm a babyface dykey-looking pansexual, gender fluid, LA Dodger and Laker fan.

There have been days and nights when I've had to search for Angie. I've become an expert on underpasses—the noisiest, the filthiest, with the latest graffiti art. I could be a docent, leading tours. I'd recommend disposable shoes, cheap socks, and a jar of Vicks VapoRub to hold under the nose because the bouquet is out-of-this world.

When the audience leans forward, I know I have them. They're waiting for the punch line. But I let the tragedy of Angie's existence sink in. Like the time the cops took her into custody after she stole a crossing-guard paddle, and used it to direct traffic on the 134 freeway. Angie caused gridlock for hours. At the mental health facility, she was a model of "rationality" with anger issues that she promised she'd address. She's instinctive that way—knowing when to sane-up.

Truth is, the worry and stress have turned my comedy into a commentary on homelessness and the mentally ill. I've become an observational comedian, like my idol, George Carlin.

My 5 p.m. visit to Angie's crib, an appliance box near the Golden State

Freeway, is timed before my 7 p.m. call for *Anything Goes,* and with her reading of the sun's angle, "the *real* watch," she calls it. When I asked her how could she tell time when it's dark, she answered, "When I sleep, there is no time." Angie's mind is a labyrinth, catching words that relate in a flow all her own; "Are you hungry?" "My stomach's vacant." "Are you safe?" "My deposits are empty." I weave that into my stand-up, too.

I visit Angie every afternoon. It's a short ride on Interstate 5 from my apartment in Glendale to the Zoo Drive off-ramp. I'm passing a homeless camp along the Los Angeles Aqueduct. People are visible through the chain-link fence. Outside their tents, they eat dinner from cans and talk to their neighbors. Angie won't live in a tent, and she won't be around people. She's a fugitive, always running from the voices in her head.

She was like the rest of us until a year ago, when she turned twenty-five. Her transformation happened gradually, soon after my father's death. I've wondered if that triggered her illness. She'd withdraw, hear voices, tear out clumps of her hair, be ecstatic, then sink into a black hole where no one could reach her, not even me. We're more than sisters. We're best friends. Angie has always been willowy but would stare down anyone who'd make fun of me. I'm three years older and have always taken care of her.

My air-conditioning is on full blast in the bumper-to-bumper traffic. I find humor everywhere. Right now in front of me is a garbage truck. Scrolled across the back in a flowing script are the words, *Nothing Like a Good Dump.* I'll use it tonight, when I warm up the audience before the filming of the sitcom, *Anything Goes.* I'm a laughter lube, bringing the audience to the edge of their seats, so they're ready to cheer for the stars. I love my job. The pay sucks but I recently scored a weekend gig at Flappers Comedy Club, and I have a roof over my head that isn't made of cardboard.

I snack on saltines and a smoothie, hoping my ulcer doesn't act up. In the passenger seat is Angie's care package: water, trail mix, granola bars, Lorna Doones (her favorite), toilet paper, five packs of wipes, a clean sweatshirt, and underpants.

I pass the same old billboards. No matter what they advertise, everyone smiles. For once I'd like to see families like mine. I'd like to see some genuine family friction, arguing politics and money, iPhones to the right of their knives, something candid, not canned. Nowadays, if we do eat together—with my father gone, and my sister out to lunch—it's just my mother and me. "*Ronnie, you're head of the family now. It's up to you to look after your sister.*"

Thanks Mom. If you took care of your heart problem and diabetes, you could help me roam the underpasses searching for her. Of course, I'd never say that. She has no idea how bad it really is.

I shift my Honda into the right lane for the off-ramp. Someone grabs my attention as they run across the overpass. It's a woman. She stops in the center of the bridge and holds up her middle finger to oncoming cars.

"Holy Shit!" It's Angie!

My hand sits on the horn. I drive up the ramp and hook a left hoping she doesn't climb onto the ledge of the bridge.

She's on the south side of the narrow walkway facing downtown. She's giving the finger with both hands. I'm on the opposite side of the street. I roll down the window and yell, *"Angie!"* She turns, and my heart breaks. Her swollen eyes are black and blue. Her lip is bleeding. I drive straight ahead into the zoo entrance and park.

I race across the street with the flow of traffic. Adrenaline sweeps away the pain from my ulcer.

"Ahrah!" she howls a wild animal yelp.

With her fists, she pounds the ledge.

"Angie!"

Vehicles speed seventy miles an hour or more under the bridge. Vibration from the cars shakes the overpass. Gas fumes, noise, the height, and the power from the traffic zooming under—my mind is swirling. I'm dizzy; my sister's battered face comes into focus.

I grab Angie. She wails as I force her skinny arms to her side and pick up all one hundred pounds of her.

Cars stop on the overpass.

"Down! Put me down!" she shrieks, kicking her legs.

"Stop it."

"Let me go, asshole."

"I called 911," a man shouts from inside his truck.

"No!" Angie screams, freeing her arms, and scratching my neck.

"Damn it."

She thrashes. I'm losing. She's wily, presses her hand into my abdomen right where my ulcer is. I let go. She darts across traffic and takes off running toward Griffith Park.

I'm racing after her, dodging cars, "It's going to be okay, Angie."

Not until she's treated will she have a chance for anything near okay.

But no one can force her. That's the law.

❦ ❦ ❦

Angie stops at the end of the bridge at a bumper-railing that curves down an incline to her nest. She's sobbing. Bruises circle her arms. I want to kill whoever hurt her.

"You need to go to the ER." Blood and dirt are caked in her long blond hair. Her cut lips tremble. "We've got to report this." She mumbles, flicks her fingers. "Who hurt you? Do you know him?"

"Stop," she screams.

"My car's across the street. I have a first aid-kit. We'll clean you up. I've got food and clothes." This is the worst. My poor mother, she'd die if she knew what happened.

For a year, Angie's survived on the streets and always by a freeway. She says the noise helps to muffle the voices. She's afraid of automobiles. For her, they're rooms with walls, moving in all directions where she'll never find her way home.

On rare occasions, she'll let me drive her to Denny's for a hamburger and fries. I've never betrayed her. I've always taken her back to her roost.

A siren blares then cuts off—the 911 call.

Angie runs.

I sprint after her, catching up, and gently take her arm. "C'mon, over there. To my car." We cross the street and into the parking lot.

She mutters to herself, twitches her fingers, laughs. She needs a doctor. I've thought of taking a couple of my mother's Xanax pills and dropping them into Angie's water bottle. Then what? She'd wake up in the hospital, play lucid, and run. I'd have to hunt for her all over again.

She's lived at the same off-ramp for months. It had my approval, until now, being the cleanest and safest—the Beverly Hilton of off-ramps and underpasses. It's her favorite because she loves the zoo. On a couple of occasions, we've gone inside, walked around, watched the gorillas, and eaten hot dogs, just like we did as kids. But she can't go back to her nest, not now.

I open the passenger door, toss the care package in the back, and ease Angie into the seat.

I'm a mixed bag of rage, sorrow, and relief that she wasn't murdered.

Inside the car, I reach for the packet of wipes and clean her face.

"What did he look like?" I open the glove compartment and take out the first-aid kit. "When did it happen?"

"Oh, blah, blah, blah."

"C'mon Angie. You want to see what you look like?"

She laughs, mutters to herself, and plays air-piano with her right fingers.

"It needs to be reported," I say, taking a close look at the wounds on her face. From the first-aid kit, I remove an antibiotic ointment and dab it around her eyes, cheeks, and mouth.

"It stings." She winces, turns away and says, "NSFL." Angie loves acronyms. *Not Safe For Life,* is a favorite.

Every smell in the city—car exhaust, cement, garbage bins, dirt—has oozed into her pores. I run a cloth over her arms, take another wipe, and clean her hands.

With her eyes closed, she lifts her face toward the late afternoon sun and says, "5:17 p.m."

I'll be damned, just like my watch.

"It's over, Angie." Her face was once beautiful—she looked like a young Cate Blanchett—but has now been toughened by the sun, the streets, her sickness. Seeing her beaten makes me want to rip out the heart of the fucker who did this. "You hear me? It's over."

"Don't cry Ronnie," she says.

I flip down her sun visor and slide open the mirror. "Take a good look at your face and tell me you don't need help."

Angie flips up the shade.

It's tempting to feel sorry for her, but that would be a further assault. "There are places that can give you medicine, a roof over your head. Make you feel better."

"You make me feel better."

"I'm just a Band-Aid. I don't make you *get* better. Let me look at your scalp. I need to know if it's still bleeding."

"IDC," she says.

"I *do* care," I answer.

One afternoon when I took Angie to Denny's, our entire lunch was spoken in acronyms: ICYMI, OMG, FYI, BTW, EOD. I remember being amazed by, ILYRSIPYB—that she tossed off in a second, and then hugged me. She flinches when touched so when she embraced me, I felt honored. It took me days to figure out the acronym; *I love you Ronnie someday I'll pay you back.*

"Let me look," I say.

Angie turns her head. I separate the clumped strands and find the wound. It's clotted. I pour water onto a fresh cloth and dab it.

"What was he wearing?" She looks out the window at Griffith Park and the Santa Monica Mountains. "I can report him. But I need information."

She covers her ears with her hands.

I know when to back off, but this is different.

"The schmuck who hurt you is out there."

"Blah, blah, blah, blah blah," she says, shaking her head.

We sit together in silence, although what's going on inside of me is a roaring chaos of *WTF.*

"Do you want aspirin?"

"No."

Silence. I'm tense, Angie's in shock, and neither one of us knows the way out.

"I've got a cool apartment. You can take a hot shower. Brush your teeth. I've told you about Carlin. He's the big fat tabby. You'd like him. Wanna meet him?"

"I wanna go home."

"You can't."

"My estate needs me. I want my stuff."

"Here," I say, reaching behind and taking the package. "Put on fresh clothes. Then we'll get your stuff and come back."

Angie changes.

"I'm hungry."

"Cookies?"

"Jogger mix. Currency. You have me some?"

"After we come back to the car."

"LOL," she says. A crow has swooped down and helped itself to a man's French fries. We laugh. The moment is an escape for both of us.

I open the trail mix and hand her the bag. She pours the dried fruit and nuts into her mouth. Pieces fall on the car seat. Hamburgers are the worst. She stuffs as much of the burger into her mouth and then eats with her jaws open. Angie's social graces fly over the cuckoo's nest. I can't help but compare her to who she was in the past—refined, even prim, as she'd dab the corners of her mouth. She went everywhere with several bottles of hand sanitizer. She had a boyfriend and worked at Macy's to help put herself through college. Her last year at USC she made the Dean's List. Peri Software hired her as a technical writer and then fired her when she sent out a mass email to her coworkers with pornographic images. If her sanity returned, she'd be shocked by her behavior.

"I should have let the cops take you to the mental health facility."

"That place wears a headache."

"You faked it."

"It's Hollywood."

"They wanted to help you."

Angie leads the way through brush and foliage. We swipe away branches and forage through dense vegetation. Nearby there's a trail that passes through a small narrow tunnel and runs parallel to the aqueduct. It's 6 p.m. I need to be at the studio by 7 p.m.

What's so important for her that she'd come back to the place where she'd been attacked? Or was she assaulted somewhere else?

Angie's nest is in a small clearing. The four-sided jumbo Sony TV box she calls home has been smashed. My old bed quilt is in a heap. A filthy tarp covers a partial area of the ground. Water bottles, food wrappers, and banana peels litter the area.

She's down on hands and knees squaring the edges of her house, reminding me of a bird; her thin limbs, darting eyes, the quick sudden movement of her hands, if only she had wings.

"Who crushed your house?"

She shrugs.

I crouch down and say, "Take what you need and let's go."

"You go," Angie says.

"You're not staying here."

She puts the piece of the tarp inside the box and flattens out the cardboard she uses as a roof.

"Angie?"

Her right eye is almost shut.

"Give me my finances. My parcel."

"That wasn't the deal. C'mon, take what you need." I'm not sure what

I'll do once she's back in the car. I just want her away from here. "We'll find a new home."

She wobbles to her feet, crosses her arms, and gets in my face.

"You'll jab me a knife."

"I just saved you from being arrested."

Angie sucks on a strand of hair like a sulking child and moves her hips side to side.

Sometimes I've wondered what's stronger, love or guilt?

"If I'm late for work, they could fire my ass. C'mon."

"No."

"I'm not going to end up homeless like you."

Angie giggles. "You're mad."

"I'm not sleeping in this shithole."

"Dirty word. Daddy's angry."

The mention of my father startles me. She knows he passed away. It's been a year and a half since he died. I wish he were here to help.

"You come. Or no money or package."

"Naughty naughty pants on fire."

"I'm not going to live like Tarzan and Jane." I bend forward trying to relieve the shooting pain in my abdomen.

Angie covers her ears with her hands. She's testing me, making sure she's the centerpiece of my life.

"I want the night here."

She moves in closer. We're nose-to-nose, so near I can smell the alcohol on her skin.

"You're older," Angie says. "You *have* to take care of me."

The truth explodes from my crazy sister's mouth, a belief I've lived with all of my life. It's so clear. How could I have missed it? I've become an enabler.

Letting go of rage, my own truth explodes, "Why don't you act normal like you did at the mental health place?"

Mumbling, she gets inside the box. She glances up at me and says, "Could you bring Carlin here?" And curls into a fetal position.

Defeated, I shake out my bed quilt and cover her.

"I need my roof."

On my knees, I lay the flat piece of cardboard on top.

"Sweet dreams, Angie."

I make my way down the bank of overgrown weeds to the road and head toward the park.

✾ ✾ ✾

I need to calm down. I'm walking fast, past the zoo's parking lot across from the Gene Autry Museum and enter the picnic grounds in Griffith Park. I've been holding my breath for a year. I inhale, take in the fragrance of the eucalyptus trees and the approaching chill of the night. It seems there's no exit out of this hell, or could there be one, and I don't know it? What would you do, Dad?

I pass a couple on a bench. The woman kisses her man. I'd like to fall in love. I'd like to go places without worrying, live as big and wide as I can, change my stand-up into broader experiences than just commentary on the mentally ill and homelessness.

The pain in my abdomen subsides. Then I think of my sister curled up in a box like a kitten and the ache returns.

There's a homeless man sitting under a tree, talking to himself. His fingers flick like Angie's. Does his family know where he is? Or have they given up on him?

I won't give up on Angie. Will she ever trust me or talk to me again? I turn around, take out my phone, and call 911. Where's the humor in this?

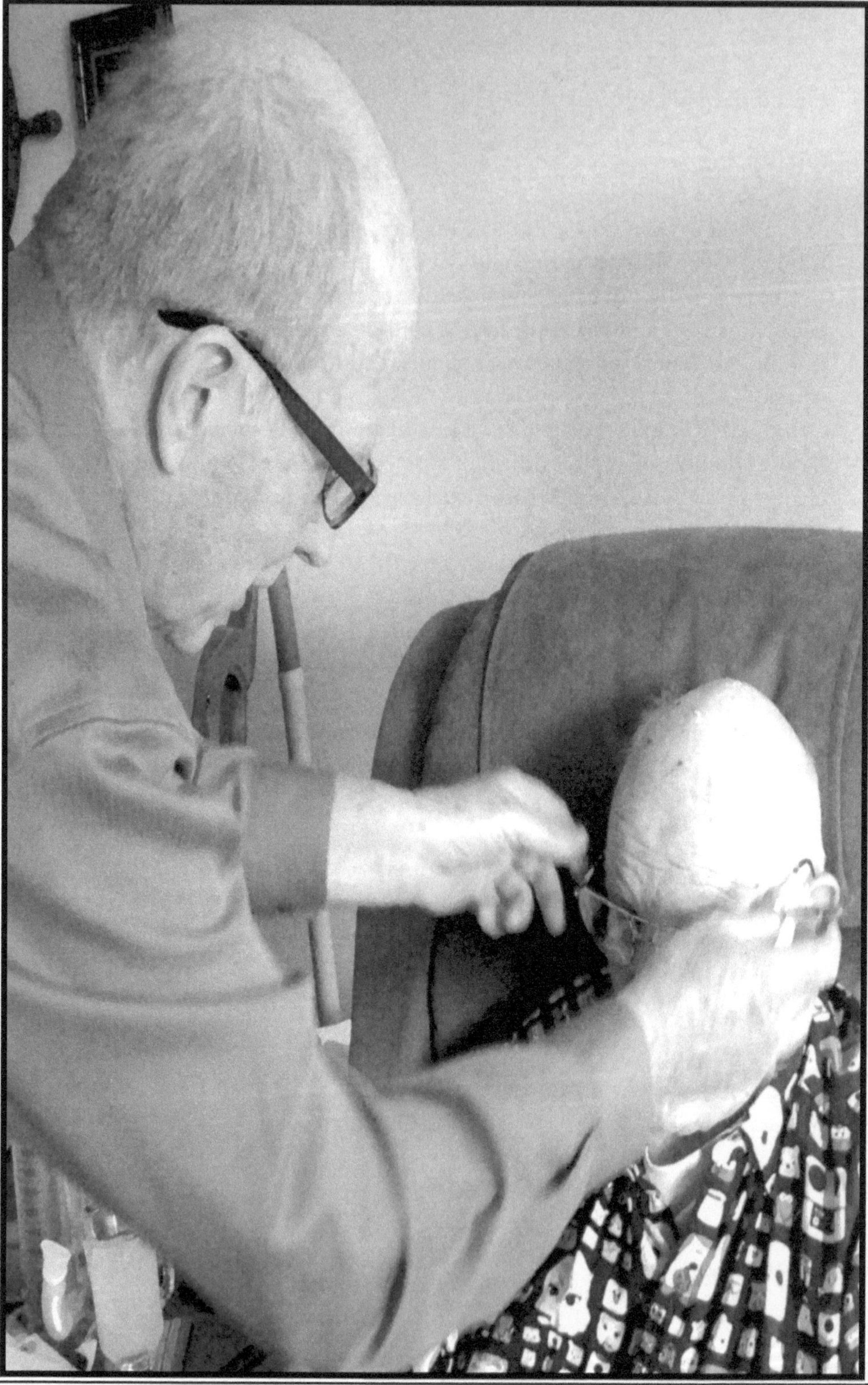

V.

ILLNESS/CARE

DOROTHY OLIVER PIROVANO

THERE WHEN WE NEED THEM

It happened again today.

The relatively smooth street we were crossing as we were heading three blocks away to an important doctor's appointment was suddenly pockmarked with shallow dips where the asphalt cracked and washed away, making it impossible for his new combination walker and transport chair to budge. A wheel settled firmly into a deep one. Stuck, we wiggled and tugged and fretted, and were magically unstuck as four strong arms materialized from nowhere and lifted 193-pound Larry, chair and all, onto the sidewalk. Rescued once again by strangers who can't even accept a grateful handshake in the midst of social distancing, and who receive heartfelt thank yous muffled by masks.

He's gotten used to being rescued by strangers who appear in the middle of a street or the sidewalk outside the barber shop, in the elevator that takes us to our 44th floor apartment or the gym where he's determined to do five more sit-to-stands to keep strength in his weakening legs.

It's hard for the guy I've always called "my big strong man" when I needed a jar opened or a screw turned. It's more than hard for this proud eighty-one-year-old who has had Parkinson's Disease for an exhaustive twenty-three years yet only in the last few needed more than a walking stick or a couple of canes to get around. The three-wheeled walker gave way to a four-wheeler that was put in storage when we replaced it with one with bigger wheels and greater stability. We added to the collection with the fancy red combo model that converts into something he can sit in when we go for a walk or an excursion and next steps aren't possible. He can rest and I can take over, pushing man and machine forward, always vigilant for the crack, pothole or uneven sidewalk that will stop us.

It started about six years ago with an occasional fall. Larry's left foot would turn in unexpectedly and down he would go. He kept a journal to show his doctor when, where and how often but stopped when it didn't matter since "a lot" became the simple answer when he was asked if he had any falls since the prior appointment. A physical therapist taught him how to go down gracefully so he wouldn't hit his head and, if something were nearby that he could grab onto, how to get back up. I learned how to become a bench on hands and knees in front of him when that something was not there, how to lift with my legs, how to grab his belt and pull up with all my strength so his legs could find a footing.

What a team.

But more often than not, we have our share of helpers.

He was heading into the barbershop when he tripped and fell as I scrambled out of the car to help. Two twenty-somethings quickly approached, hefting up his left side as I took his right. Assured that he was okay, the smaller of the two kept patting his shoulder as she showed him a small cut on the palm of her hand and told him she knew what it was like to fall and be so embarrassed you don't even want anyone to know you're hurt. "I'm okay," he said as she gave his arm a little hug. "And I'll try not to be embarrassed."

We got our wires crossed one day and he wasn't waiting for me at the spot I thought we agreed on. I was later than planned and he figured he could spare me by taking a bus home. Thank God for cell phones (a convenience he often forgets to use). When he wasn't at the appointed corner I called him, he explained his bus escapade and we agreed he would get off and wait for me to pick him up. As I was pulling up, he started across the street to meet me, falling half-way into the intersection. Within seconds, a gentleman in a business suit was at his side. Traffic stopped in all directions as they watched Larry being helped to his feet, making his way to the car with a stranger's firm arm under his. Before the car door closed, the man disappeared.

If there is a police officer anywhere around they always rush to help, calling him sir and offering to get an ambulance. Nothing they are doing takes precedence over their making sure he gets to wherever he was going and they tend to remain nearby until they feel confident he's safe.

We needed more than one rescuer when we broke the "walker rules" and he sat down on the walker seat, facing me, legs lifted off the ground so I could push him along the beautifully smooth sidewalk outside the zoo. There are two labels on the walker commanding you to not use it this way for it can tip over backwards and they don't want to be responsible. But he was tired and we weren't going to go far.

It was one of those magnificent summer days and we'd spent it at our favorite place, welcomed by the gibbons, who we were convinced had come to know us from our frequent visits; checking on the progress of the gorilla baby; and being transfixed by the flock of flamingoes who stand in a tight knot, stock still on one leg until one troublemaker puts his leg down, disturbing his neighbors who immediately put their legs down, flap their wings and cry out in indignation. Soon, everyone is squawking and flapping, until a bird on the perimeter draws up a leg and one by one, they follow suit and return to quiet repose. They are always the highlight of a zoo visit.

We knew I shouldn't have been pushing him but I was going to be extra careful and our destination was only two blocks away, a romantic rooftop bar atop a favorite neighborhood restaurant where we could watch the sunset and toast our good fortune. When we hit the crack, he went over backwards in what seemed like slow motion as I hung onto the handlebars trying to stop his descent only to wind up sprawled on top of him. His shoulders protected my arms and elbows from the cement, and he'd pulled his head up in time to avoid cracking it on the concrete. Not a scratch on either of us, we could only laugh as we tried to untangle our legs and figure out how we would get up.

A jogger was the first to appear. Within moments another was on the scene discussing with the first how best to extricate my shoulder from under the handlebar that was holding me in place. A third young man darted through traffic from the other side of the street and the three unwound our legs, pulling me up by the armpits. Our trio of do-gooders hauled up the walker with Larry in it, checked him out for signs of blood or broken bones and, after many thanks, resumed their jogs. We stood together quietly, knowing once again luck was with us, hailed a cab and headed home.

It was a bleak January day nearly twenty-four years ago when we met with the neurologist who provided the Parkinson's diagnosis after a series of questions, limb manipulations and dexterity tests. We went home, sat on the side of the bed and cried—a not uncommon reaction for me; the first time I'd ever seen him cry. We had just started a new chapter of our lives, having left our suburban home for a five-story townhouse on the near north side of Chicago, close to my downtown office and made to order for an easy transfer of his real estate practice. Like us, others of his clients were ready for a move to the city or their kids were, keeping Larry satisfyingly busy.

We decided not to tell anyone, even our kids, until we came to terms with this day and our future. We read pamphlets and books; found a terrific, positive doctor in a hospital-based practice that was aggressively involved in

Parkinson's clinical trials, enrolled Larry in a trial for a drug that turned out to be one that stalled the onset of symptoms and lived such a normal life it was easy to forget that he had anything going on.

We told the kids, our Brady Bunch of five (two of mine, three of his) who were young when we met–8, 7, 6, 5 and 2–and 13, 12, 11, 10 and 7 when we finally married. Now grown, with all but one living in other states and starting families of their own, they took the news well for they had seen no changes in who we were and how we were living, working, traveling and getting on with our lives.

His gait began slowing and our long walks around our neighborhood were taking longer. He would begin to lag behind if we were out with a group but not so far that it couldn't be explained away with window-shopping or a bird sighting. He wound up in the emergency room after trying to scale the wall that separated our patio from the sidewalk along the street and caught his foot on the ledge as he tried to get his leg over, sending him down, head-first onto the deck. He'd forgotten his housekey, he explained to the ER doctor, and knew he could get in through the unlocked patio door. He'd done it before with no trouble. Just clumsy, I guess.

It was the falls that signaled that "normal" was really changing. We were hiking one day when his foot turned as we were climbing up a rocky path and he flipped over, his fancy Nikon smacking into the side of a boulder as he skidded down backwards. It was the first of what would be many more dramatic falls that he miraculously emerged from with barely a scratch and many reassurances that he was fine, just a miscalculation. A bandage or two and all set. Soon after, he decided he'd better start keeping a journal of his falls. Then came the cane, then two, then the walkers and a lot more falls.

Other than our mishap today, we have had less of a need for outside rescuers in our new world of masks and distancing. We canceled our airline tickets and instead watched virtual graduations of our grandkids online. We eat at home instead of going out with neighbors and now have Zoom cocktail hours before some dinners and a family Zoom call every Thursday night. We're watching the progress of our new great-grandson virtually and are waiting for the day when he can see our smiles in person and feel our kisses. There are fewer falls as there are fewer outings and we have the stools and chairs and places to grab onto in our apartment to get him up again.

When we returned home after his rescue on the street we once again found ourselves sitting on the side of the bed. "What do you think we'll be doing the rest of our lives?" he said with a seriousness that rarely surfaces.

"What do you mean?" I asked. "We'll be doing this until the virus is under control and we go back to the old normal."

"No, I mean, how much longer can this go on—the falls, your pulling me up, the street, the people . . ." He trailed off.

"I'll always be there. It's that old for better or worse, in sickness and in health thing we agreed to forty-three years ago. And if I can't . . ." It was my turn to trail off.

And if and when I can't, they will be there. They, the caring. They, the rescuers. They, the kind of people who take a moment to be kind. They will be there. I'm sure.

NORITA DITTBERNER-JAX

RELIC

A sliver of wood
encased in a locket.
a fragment of the true cross, he said,

My father pinned it on the gown
near my mother's heart
whenever she seemed near death.

Hers a long dying, his a matter
of hours. After they both died,
I asked for the relic.

My brother said that if you gathered
all the relics of the true cross together,
it would rival Noah's ark.

The only truth I know is my mother's heart
and how we used everything
in our power to keep her with us.

S J ENGSTROM

TRAIN BOUND FOR GLORY

She was wailing. "Why didn't one of YOU die?" Her eyes were scrunched tight as if to shut out her world. Seven-year-old Bethany looked at my sister Janice and me."You two are older. Why didn't one of YOU get cancer, instead of Daddy?" She still cried, then sniffled, wiping her nose and eyes, beginning to compose herself. Her mother and grandmother flanked her in the cozy suite in Evergreen Hospice in Seattle, where yellow roses bloomed outside. Then Bethany faced the doctor, seated beside my brother Mark's still body, lying under a hand-made quilt. It was sunshine yellow, Mark's favorite color. "Are you sure he's dead?" she asked. "Maybe he's not."

"Would you like me to check again to be sure?" the gentle hospice doctor replied, his dark eyes locking onto hers. "Yes, please," she nodded. He knew just what to do, as if he had memorized this protocol along with the Hippocratic oath to do no harm. Although he had declared Mark dead just minutes before, he picked up his black bag and turned toward Mark's body. After putting on his stethoscope, he solemnly placed it on four places on the lifeless body. Silence. Then, as he took the instrument from his ears, he turned to the hopeful child. "I'm sorry, Bethany, so very sorry. Your Daddy really is gone." It was August 1, 2005. *How had we arrived at this unspeakable place in just four months and four days?*

On Good Friday, my parents and I had gone out for coffee and pastry after a church service. They had something to discuss with me. "What's it called, again?" I asked my eighty-three-year-old parents, after hearing the summary. I was across the table, gazing into my mother's gorgeous blue eyes, now glossy melancholy. Mom and Dad had just recapped their last five days during which time my sons and husband and I had escaped to a ski resort in Michigan's Upper Peninsula during spring break. The last I'd heard from Mark was that he had an unrelenting sinus infection and had reluctantly agreed to go to a second Ear, Nose and Throat doctor, who had sent him to an oncologist.

"Rhab-do-my-o-sarcoma," my thorough mother read from her notes. "Very rare, in adults; it's a child's cancer." Her lip began to quiver. She stopped and dabbed at her liquid baby-blues. Dad's turn. "It's bad, Sherry, Stage 4. The prognosis is less than two years, eighteen to twenty-four months, the doctor said," Dad reported, trying to maintain his stoic demeanor. Less than two years, twenty-four months max. That meant one or two more summers, Christmases and birthdays left to spend with his beloved little Bethany and son Sam, aged twelve. *What now? What to do? What does Mark do, when he knows he's going to die long before he ever imagined?*

Besides having a magnetic personality, Mark had been born restless in body and soul. As a baby, he rocked his playpen back and forth, jangling the colorful plastic bells around the edge. Before his first birthday, he was driving his wooden auto-playpen to the far end of the living room, then back again to the other side. His quest for movement and things that move was life-long. As a three-year-old, he named cars, like an avid collector, while we traveled the highway in the family's 1954 Chevy Biscayne. As an adult, he moved from job to job and career to career every few years, sometimes more often. While between jobs once, he bought and drove a new red pickup truck from Chicago to Central America to work on a mission project. He had a sharp, inquisitive mind that needed to dissect and master many subjects. A close friend called him a Renaissance man. As a two-year-old in his highchair, he tried to capture the grapes on his tray before they rolled off the edge onto the floor. "Mommy. Why don't grapes be square?" as he pronounced it toddler-style, without the "r." Somewhere in his teen-aged years he discovered bicycle racing. As a church youth leader, he commandeered high-school boys around Lake Michigan twice. Most everything he learned seemed to be self-taught, with the exception of his academic studies. He completed his BA degree and then earned a master's in theology at the University of Chicago. While there he took up sailing, owning several boats during his life, progressing to bigger and more intricate ones to match his need for adventure. He sailed often on small waters such as Geneva Lake, but his favorite was Lake Michigan. And the windier, the better. Why be a sailor if you weren't going to embrace the challenge of the unpredictable winds of Chicago's grand Great Lake? Mark was also a gifted musician, so naturally talented that he could play from a huge repertoire by heart on guitar or piano. When he had children, they both started instrument lessons at an early age. It was mighty hard for him to understand why just one of his kids couldn't intuitively pick up a guitar or violin and play like he did.

And now, here we were, his family of origin—healthy elder parents and two older sisters—trying our best to comprehend the enormity of this new monster in Mark's life. He had endured plenty—depression, anxiety, job loss and two divorces—but this would prove to be the mother of them all. The cancer was not only infecting his sinuses behind his handsome face, but way too close for comfort to his expressive sea-blue eyes and his fascinating mind that was always excavating some new idea or concept, rarely settling for the mundane or conventional.

After that dismal Good Friday, we all set out to make the new day a bright one. Saturday would be Sam's thirteenth birthday and Sunday was Easter, Mark's favorite. *Ahhh . . . The Resurrection. New Life. Spring. All things green and healthy. Really?* My response was to host a pre-Easter and birthday dinner on Saturday. Mark's ex-wife, Mona, came along, rallying to the cause, for the sake of her boundless mother-love and her tenderness for a charming man who had once stolen her heart when they met on a mission project. Our parents also came along, maintaining a celebratory mood, despite the foreboding news. One of our family strengths is knowing how to make the best of a bad situation. Mother had her every-gray-cloud-has-a-silver-lining philosophy, and Dad's stiff-upper-lip thinking from his WW II experience and passage through the School of Hard Knocks, had overcome obstacles in the past. So, Easter Sunday on Saturday with birthday cake, music, tears and laughter to boot got us through day two. Mark even played his guitar. Cancer be damned, at least for a while.

I was working half-time, so I quickly accepted when Mark asked me on Easter Monday to co-navigate his new journey. I felt honored somehow, like I had been commissioned for a sacred mission. Who wants to walk through the Valley of the Shadow of Death alone? We had had lots of conflicts through the years; contention seemed to be a necessary power base for him, particularly with his family, and people he viewed as having a leg-up on him.

He was maddeningly obstreperous in his self-righteous opinions. But he was my brother, my only and younger brother, and I loved him, pure and simple. We readily debated and discussed ideas, art, theology, politics, music and especially parenting, as our sons were a year apart. And his sense of humor rocked me. He was funny, sarcastic, ironic, absurd and downright silly. But what I most cherish, even today, is his laugh—his very own unique, hearty, raucous, nothing-else-matters-in-this-moment laugh. Our relationship was a far cry from smooth sailing and sometimes stormy, but it certainly wasn't mundane or boring. It remains a treasure in my memory, through all the ups and downs. We knew that we loved each other.

At the time of the diagnosis, Mark was an anxious single parent, underemployed and fighting a custody battle. I tried to pitch in, sometimes with parenting suggestions when he had the kids, but often my help was unwelcome. One time we met to talk in a park on a public square. We were standing near our cars, preparing to end the conversation, when he said something accusatory. When I called him on it, he exploded with anger. I retreated, knowing the discussion was useless; as I did so, his powerful and brawny body blocked me from getting in my car, with his toddler daughter watching from his car. And then there was his opposite side, often irrational with love and generosity. One Christmas Eve, while he was unemployed, he played Santa Claus by buying dozens of new sweaters and taking them to a homeless shelter. He came to our family celebration late, with a yellow sweater for each of us. That was Mark. Likable, spontaneous, unpredictable, always conforming to his own inner truths.

Mark chose the University of Chicago medical center for his treatment. It was his Alma Mater, his beloved Soul Mother. He loved the Hyde Park campus, old buildings, culture and Rockefeller chapel. He had lived there for two years, twenty-five year earlier, so this seemed like a homecoming. He latched onto the university medical compound as if it were his own healing angel in scrubs—the best of all things medical, spiritual and intellectual. His primary doctor, an ENT specialist, was young and petite with fiery, full red hair. "She looks like a teeny-bopper," Mark quipped. There were five experts on his team: the oncologist, ENT specialist, neurologist, and two surgeons. *Yikes, that many?* But Mark liked the thorough attention of an academic consulting team. He loved knowledge for its own sake as well as to solve any problem on his path. Only a week or two had elapsed since hearing his diagnosis, time Mark had spent researching alternatives such as herbal remedies, and an expensive treatment in Mexico. But here at this first appointment at his new home away from home, he got more bad news. The cancer was already noticeably spreading, so fast that action was required pronto—radiation, surgery, chemotherapy, and a clinical medication trial. Anything to stop this Abominable Cancer in its tracks, or at least to slow it down. When we left the clinic, we faced a new reality. *Prognosis: 12-18 months.* "God Almighty!" I said in anger. I threaded my arm in the arm of my big, strapping baby-boy brother and walked out to the car. Mark wept. So did I.

There was no relief in sight. Mark's cancer was brutal and aggressive, a tumor on steroids that lived only to take him down. After treatments of limited radiation—too dangerous—and chemotherapy, the tumor was reassessed. Surgery was the new prescription, the last resort for this otherwise healthy strong man who was weeks away from his fifty-first birthday. By this time, the sight in his left eye was impaired and the eyelid droopy, due to the tumor winding its sadistic path into his eye socket. The surgery had to come soon because the outlook had changed. *Prognosis: 9-12 months.*

June 1 was a beautiful sunny day with azure skies. "Heavenly," Mother noted. My parents and I accompanied Mark, my father taking his usual chauffeur seat. We left Woodstock at 5 a.m. for the 7 a.m. pre-surgical appointment at U of C hospital. The pain, grief and tension were palpable and unforgettable. No one knew what to say. Try to be cheerful? Listen to music? Let Mark talk first? Distract? Pray? *Just shut up for God's sake because what the Hell is there to say in these dire circumstances?*

In the pre-op room, a nurse asked me, "Are you Mark's Power of Attorney?" "Yes," I replied. "Do you understand what that means?" "Yes." I barely knew anything, but I DID know that I wanted to resign from this God-awful job I had accepted. Mark was dressed and prepped for a surgery that would cut into his face. "We need you to understand the risk factors of this procedure and indicate your willingness to accept these risks by signing here and here and on the next three pages. "Mark, you may lose your left eye.

Do you understand that?" the nurse continued. *Oh, for crying out loud.* We said yes, yes, we understood every devilish detail and we signed the damned disclaimers.

Mark was wheeled off into the room where four surgeons awaited him. Our only hope was that the Cancer Monster might be arrested before it was too late. The eight-to-ten-hour surgery actually took eighteen. Cutting and stitching. Mending and grafting. Skin was taken from his leg to patch over the empty eye socket that no longer held one of his beautiful blues. After struggling through the night and until the doctor could see us, while Mark lay in recovery, we finally heard the news. The cancer could not be contained any longer. It was snaking its toxic way into Mark's amazing brain. Mark would learn two days later that he had lost an eye, only when he was conscious enough to recognize the one-eyed man staring at him from his hospital room mirror. *Post-surgical Prognosis: 6-9 months.*

Four days later, I had successfully persuaded Mona to let me bring son Sam to visit his Dad. Sam had been begging for days; it was time. Mark would be released that day and Sam wanted in on the action. I booked a nice room in a plush Hyde Park hotel. After settling, we drove to Chinatown, his first outing there. We ate, walked, talked, bought souvenirs, then returned to our room to relax and sleep. We had successfully distracted ourselves to pass the evening before Sam would see his father the next morning with only one eye and cancer attacking his brain.

After breakfast and checking out, we drove to the hospital. At Mark's room, Sam grinned, "I'll help him get dressed, Sherry. You wait outside." "Sure. And here's the eye patch. Let's see how he likes it," I said. Vanity ran deeply in our family and Mark was strikingly good-looking, so I wondered how Mark could adjust to having lost an eye. I hoped he would agree to my effort at mitigating the shock; maybe the patch would arouse a little levity. Wouldn't he rather be a dashing pirate with a walking stick, than a man with a cane and one eye? On the way home, I suggested ice cream. Mark hesitated, but resolved to go in with us. Relying on his cane, he joined us saying, "I guess I should get used to people looking at me like I'm some kind of freak."

Back home, real life kept kicking us in the shins, making each step a living Hell for Mark. Staying temporarily with my parents, their small condo was laden with medications and supplies. Perpetually overwhelmed, we attempted normal daily living while simultaneously helping Mark adjust to his diagnosis and prognosis. We took shifts caring for him because we didn't want him to be alone yet. His mood was dark. His pain was intense, primarily in his chest. *Why there? Is the cancer metastasizing more?* The next clinic visit confirmed our fears. After an x-ray of his chest, I stole a glimpse at the x-rays while Mark talked with the radiologist. I saw two round tumors that were the size of tennis balls, each filling half a lung. That bastard Rhabdomyosarcoma had now invaded his lungs. No wonder he breathed like an old Marlboro-smoking man. New Prescription? Oxygen. *New Prognosis: 4-6 months.* My beloved brother, father of two young children, was losing his one and only life right before our eyes. My poor parents watched and wondered over and over why it couldn't be one of them who was the victim. "I'd give anything to take your place," my father said. "Mark, you know that, don't you?" "Yes, Dad, I know." Finally! These two men had experienced more conflict than connection for decades. But now at last, the unspoken love was breaking through before it would be too late. Hallelujah.

"What do you want to do with your one wild and precious life?" asks Mary Oliver, in her poem "Summer Day." I've loved that line for years and now it granted poignant new meaning. By this time, our sister Janice had joined us in Illinois. We agreed that it was time to ask if Mark wanted something special before his life would end. "Mark, what is something you'd really like to do before . . . before you get too sick to enjoy things . . .," I trailed off. I was tiptoeing around saying "death," despite the fact that I believed in speaking directly. But I'd read in hospice materials by then, that generally we can follow the lead of the dying person, that he or she will say *"I know I'm dying"* or something similar, giving permission for others to talk about it concretely, not remotely. Eventually, he did state his three wishes. One, he was determined to take his children along to our family reunion over 4th of July weekend; two, a cross-country train trip, to tour the lush area and visit Janice in her Seattle home; and three, he wanted a final sailing venture on Lake Michigan. Against cautions and intense reluctance from parents and others, we Scheming Sisters set about our task of getting this guy his final wishes. One of our greatest supporters was Mona, even after a contentious divorce and child-custody struggle. She was fully on board with supporting Mark to chase his dreams. Even as risks heightened due to his fast-declining condition, she remained steadfast in her agreement. Her love, faith and courage, and putting Mark's desire above all else, served as a lighthouse to us all as we trudged through these treacherous dark waters.

The first wish was the July 4th family reunion. Our parents and offspring now numbered a dozen, so we coordinated our three-car caravan to Cedar Lake in central Minnesota where maternal relatives had a lovely lake home in a bucolic island setting. We had enjoyed countless weekends and vacations there during childhood, having grown up in Minneapolis, so the setting was overflowing with memories, some including our maternal grandparents. This time was a little different. We still had the love and joy or family gatherings, but underlying the talk, meals, music and water fun, was the unmistakable bittersweet knowledge that Mark was likely near death. To deepen the grief, another cousin, barely forty, was battling breast cancer. She and Mark were sometimes spotted in quiet conversation under a pine tree, sharing what only they could know.

Another cousin, Dan, a calm and healing presence of a man, arranged a prayer circle. We had always been a family of faithful Christians of one sort or another, so why not put our praying hearts where our beliefs were? We met outside—three dozen—in a circle amid a flowering meadow, where both cancer patients spoke their requests—to be healed, God willing, to live. We listened, prayed and sang, concluding with smiles, hugs and consoling communion. The moment seemed healing indeed, especially in light of Mark's deep disappointment of the morning.

Although we three siblings had been avid water skiers all our lives, Mark had failed at pulling himself up on skis as the boat roared on. Our hosting cousin had said Mark would need someone in the water with him to get started. Mark chose me for support. *Me? Four years older, seventy pounds lighter, me? This was my brawny and brainy brother—long-distance cyclist, football player, swimmer, master sailor, theologian. Me?? Okay. Let's do this.* After all, we were raised with the spirit of competition and resilience, accepting challenge as a fact of life. So with supportive family fans cheering from the shore, we tried. And tried. Three times, but to no avail. He was just too weak. After that incident, there was one last time I did witness his physical strength in action. When Janice and I had returned from the reunion to his apartment, where he was then living, he realized his key was inside. When he mentioned that he had a hidden spare down in a deep basement window well, I offered to jump down and retrieve it, thinking by now I was stronger than he was. "NO," he insisted. "I've got it," as he jumped down. Indeed, he did, muscling himself up five feet. This picture is etched in my mind. After that victory, Mark's cancerous decline proved relentless, sucking the vigor out of him week by week, day by day.

Mark's second wish was the Amtrak project. Against all conventional wisdom and cautionary advice, the trip was still riding the rails in Mark's imagination. After all, he still had a few months to live, albeit having his lungs drained of fluid weekly and on oxygen around the clock. And Mark's hospice doctor had approved the plan and was coming the next morning for the final check-up and consultation. *Good. Janice and I could bear witness to the doctor's comments about our own crazymaking.* Mark's doctor had already okayed the trip, because one of hospice's chief tenets is that people be allowed all control possible in their last weeks of life. It wasn't her place to say no, but it was her job to advise the patient and family about possible consequences, while monitoring the evil demon consuming his body and spirit. After the vitals and meds were checked, another set-back. *Prognosis: 1-2 months. What?? That doesn't add up. Two weeks ago, it was four to six months. Now it's thirty to sixty days??*

"Doctor Redman, so that means no train trip, right?" I asked. "Not necessarily. It's still Mark's decision. Of course, the children must be strongly considered," she said with her usual steely patience. Silence. Only the ticking wall clock seemed alive. Mark sat speechless in his comfy chair in his modest apartment. My once-dashing, smart, engaging brother now had one eye, an ever-present oxygen tube in his nose, and lungs and head full of killer-cancer. My vivid memory is the numbness, the darkness, the silence. I felt hopeless, faithless and joyless. Fear, anger and hatred for this new truth filled my consciousness. The cancer was winning. My brother was dying.

"Mark?" she queried. Pause. Then, "I'm going. I'll talk to Mona, and the kids again, but we can still do this," he answered with a hint of his swagger back. "All right," the doctor said, as she pulled out a file labeled DNR. She slowly began her explanation of what Do Not Resuscitate means and the options Mark had. She detailed possible scenarios of what might happen if Mark were to become very ill on the train. "Do you understand, Mark? You will need to decide whether or not you will sign the DNR papers if you were to need emergency care on the train. And it's imperative that you explain all this to Mona and the children. The social worker can join you in that discussion. And you absolutely must have a caregiver and several oxygen tanks for the two-and-a-half-day trip. And I recommend that you change your reservations, move them up, so you'll be able to enjoy the trip more. Mark, you are a very ill man. Do you understand that?" I raged in my head. *No, he doesn't, he can't, I can't. How can anyone really comprehend one's own death when it's lurking around the corner?* But Doctor Redman was so kind, present and hospice-trained that I kept my bitter words inside my furious self. "Okay, Mark, lets' get going. It's time to eat and take your meds. While you rest, Janice and I will start making some calls. We don't have time to spare," I finally managed. "Let's get cracking," as Mother says.

Another of our better family traits is perseverance. I'm convinced that it comes from our four Swedish immigrant grandparents composing new lives across the Atlantic as young adults. It seems as surefire as our DNA. Or as Mark's son Sam quips about many of our quirks, "It's hereditary. Why fight it?" So, with various rounds of assistance, plus abundant grace and grit, the Amtrak trip stayed on track. All things needed were supplied, and ten days later Mark was packed and prepared. Against multiple odds, it was a solid plan. "Well, I guess it's Providential, after all," Mother declared.

The eve of his departure, I was with him to help, support, check the list, and look after last-minute details. I was ready to bed myself on his sofa when Mark called from his bedroom, "Sherry, want to sleep here with me? There's plenty of room." He was right. He had a huge king-sized bed. I was a bit surprised, but then, this was one of those, you-have-to-say-yes moments. We had a few laughs and tears, and then I read aloud his requested Psalms until he drifted off to sleep, for what would be the last night he would sleep in his own home.

The next morning, bags and four large oxygen tanks were lined up at the door for departure. My parents had said their good-byes, not without fear but still holding faith that somehow this decision would be right. "Well, maybe it is Providential," Mother had declared. They were prayer warriors, so they had Mark's back, and had chosen to trust that their grandchildren would be okay and leave the trip in God's hands. By this time, Janice had returned to Seattle, preparing for Mark's visit. Her husband, Jonathan, also a sailor, was creating an unforgettable sailing voyage on Puget Sound so that Mark's third wish, a last sailing trip, could be fulfilled.

Except that it wasn't. The reunion, check. Train trip, incredible as it seemed, check. Getting to Union Station in Chicago on time seemed miraculous. Tension. Lateness. Rushing. Forgotten items. Angry words. Traffic. Lugging the oxygen machines while literally running for the train. Victory. Mark sank into his seat, raspy, deep breaths audible. We said our goodbyes and I-love-you's. "God bless you," Mona called before the door closed. *My amazing, strong sister-in-law who really wasn't my sister-in-law after the divorce five years earlier, seemed more like an angel.* "Come on, hermana," she said, glowing, as we locked arms. "Let's go get coffee. My treat."

Two and a half days later, word came that the mighty Empire Builder had arrived. *Yea! The kids were safe and sound. The oxygen supply lasted through forest, desert and mountain. And my brother was still ALIVE! How do I say thank you for this miracle?* I'd heard from my sister that Mark had gotten off the train very depleted and asked to go to bed. When I called him the next morning, he was as joyous as his exhausted body allowed. "How was your train trip?" I asked. "Wunnerful!" he slurred. The curse of The Monster had now affected his vocal cords. "And the scenery?" "Beautiful!" He slid through the word without the "t" sound but who cared? He had gotten his trip, his ultimate longed-for wish. And the kids had loved their spectacular train ride.

Mark saw a doctor right away. The new prognosis: days to one week. He would never go back to his home. His life was indeed ending. He would be hospitalized immediately and added to the hospice wait list for a place that could house his family and him until he died. My mother flew immediately to Seattle alone. Dad, who had recently returned grieving and fatigued from burying his brother in Boston, chose to stay home. Mona and I arrived the following day.

Mark had declined rapidly since the trip, in and out of awareness and conversation, due to the cancer, morphine and anxiety. Mostly he slept, but when awake, he succumbed to making a few funeral plans with Janice, finally coming to terms with the inevitable. He talked to his children and to Mother, then slept again. On Friday he had a "good day" as it is known—an energy surge that often comes to dying people two or three days before they die. It was a gorgeous summer day and Mark asked to go outside. His caregiver wheeled him to the lush floral gardens under sunny skies. Returning, he requested a special dinner—salmon, green beans and something peachy for dessert. His favorites.

After dinner, he asked to be wheeled to the grand piano he had spotted in the spacious hospital lobby. He wanted music, *live* music, to *play* music with his own two hands. He didn't need strength or perfect vision; he just needed to let the music in his mind flow out to others. Straightening his ridiculous gown behind him, he sat. He played, and played. Show tune after show tune. Hymn after hymn. Spirituals. Love songs. Beatles. Sinatra. Scott Joplin. Even classical. It seemed unreal. We watched, mouths agape, as people gathered around, stopped talking, listened, smiled, even applauded. Janice ran to buy an Instamatic camera at the gift shop, so fortunately we have a photo of that perfect indelible Kodak moment, that no one could have predicted. Mark playing the piano, one of his greatest treasures, using his God-given gifts—his hands, his mind, his courage. Mark would exit his life only after he had given his final performance, playing and playing as if his life depended on it. Or maybe his death did.

In two more days, a hospice patient died, so the family had a suite for that final night of life. Early in the morning the labored breathing set in, the kind that says *it's almost finished.* Mona, Sam and Bethany held his hand and serenaded him with Spanish folk songs. Mark took his last breath at 9:04 on Monday morning, August 1. Peace at last. Mark was aboard the train to his final destination.

[Names in this memoir have been changed for privacy.]

RONA FRYE

TERRY

Yesterday he could shift his old Ford truck! Just yesterday, he seemed fine. Now, sitting down to play a card game was confusing for him, a game he played hundreds of times before. Hand and Foot is like Canasta and Terry played it almost daily with our mom. Now dealing, laying out the cards and following along became complicated. Sue and mom were eyeing him, what were they were seeing?

Terry didn't act peculiar, otherwise. He still walked normally, ate normally, seemed to know everyone, so what was going on? Sue asked mom to follow her to the kitchen where they put their heads together and tried to come up with an answer. There was no answer, only questions. The only option was to take him in to the ER for analysis.

They hopped in Sue's Tahoe telling Ter that they wanted the docs to have a look at him. He was a kind, gentle, trusting soul so there was no balking at this sudden, new plan. And frankly, his thinking was off just enough that he wasn't able to discern what this meant. The drive, about half an hour long, went smoothly; no one was saying a word. There was reason to worry, but without answers what could they think.

The docs and NAs, RNs and technicians moved quickly taking a scan of his head, asking questions, checking his oxygen levels, doing eye/hand coordination, and the usual vitals. Then the waiting game to see the results. Sue and mom waited in the lounge, worrying and growing weary. Mom was no spring chicken, she was closing in on eighty-seven years of age. That made Sue close to sixty-nine. Both advanced enough in age to find this frightening occurrence exhausting.

They called me and clued me in. I was a nomadic sort, never staying put for long, but was in town at the moment. They likely forgot they could count on me. I dropped everything and drove straight to Sierra Vista. The regional hospital on Wilcox Boulevard was the location. I walked in and spotted them sitting quietly, sagging in their chairs, exhausted and troubled. I said "Hi" and sat with them to hear their concerns, then walked into the cubicle Terry was in and found him sitting up on a bed with the oxygen clip on his nose. Hmm, that was not what I expected, but it informed me that something was wrong. The techs came by just then and said that they read the report and found seven tumors in his head. That was a situation out of their range of care, and they advised that the next step had to be a move to Tucson and a hospital equipped to handle this.

A transport vehicle showed up, Terry was strapped in and loaded into the back and I stood watching. Suddenly the sight made me cry. What was happening to my brother!!!?? The poor guy had no idea what was going on and yet he completely trusted those men. That broke my heart. I told Sue and mom to go home to rest, that I was going to follow the transport vehicle to Tucson and stay with Terry.

Ninety minutes later, we were there. Terry was being unloaded and rolled inside. I parked and went in, staying close. Whatever was going to happen I would be a part of. I knew, without really knowing, that he was not capable of understanding where he was, who he was, or what was going on. I didn't want him scared or lost. He was set up in a private room on the third floor and quickly the room was filled with machines hooked up to him one way or another. I let the nurse know that I would be staying there, in the room with my brother, and would need a cot, blanket, pillow, and water. She promptly busied herself getting me set up and showing me that she was happy to make me comfortable there. Plopping down on my new bed, I began to watch Terry. I tried to wrap my head around what I was seeing.

He began to pull on the IV tube, toying with the machines and playing with them. I asked him to stop. "Leave that stuff alone," I said. He just grinned and continued to pull on tubes.

I asked him who I was."You're Jennifer!" he said, grinning. Jennifer is my daughter. He doesn't know me right now! The nurse popped in and asked her own set of questions. "Where are you?" she said.

"Madison, Wisconsin," he said

He had lived in Arizona for the last twenty years.

"What day is it?" she said.

"May?" he said. It was September.

The nurses and doctors who came in and out hoped that I could keep my brother under control, it seemed, but I couldn't. They didn't seem worried so

I calmed down and breathed.

There was a flurry of activity as the staff came in and began to package him up for a test. I asked about their plan. "I will be going with him on all tests," I said. They looked at each other and concluded that I was not allowing my brother to go anywhere without me. Accepting this outcome, they simply informed me of how things would be done, where we were going, and what gear I had to wear in order to be present, that the machines would be very loud, and then said, "Let's go." The first test was the CAT scan and yes, it was loud. I wore a lead apron and watched him be rolled inside a large tube. The intent was to locate and count the tumors in his brain.

That test revealed eleven tumors. The Diagnosis, given to me over the phone later, said to me : We cannot save him. "He has eleven tumors in his brain, he smoked, there are too many to operate." I had to beg to get that answer.

Subsequent tests were set up, and finally he began what was considered the best protocol, radiation. Terry was fitted with a helmet to wear for each treatment. That way the tumors could be targeted with the rays. Two treatments down and release date was upon us. I drove my brother home to what would become our family compound for caring for him.

Sue provided a home for us, one of her vacant mobiles, and I furnished it with items from my previous place. My mother, my brother Pat and I moved in with Terry and began to live a life that unfolded in a brand new way.

Our family had reeled off in many directions at that time and none of us was close. We were a family loosely connected by blood. Loving, nurturing, open and honest, deep and connected, we never were.

There was a lot of dysfunction in our childhood home and we all got our own version. None of us ever worked through our baggage alone much less together. Now we were going to dive into something that would require us to live close and deal with the unknown. Where it would lead and what was required of us was a mystery.

Our days unfolded in a manner made for reality TV. My mother became the cheerleader, rising every morning, chirping to Terry, asking what he wanted for breakfast. In this way I saw her nurturing and loving him in a way I had not seen before. Taking on this project at her age was commendable. I was awed by how she took on this role bravely, with no possible way to understand how it would unfold.

Pat, as it turned out, was more psychic than I knew and during his sleep at night he dreamt of how it felt to be Terry. He felt the crowded brain. That helped him see and it helped me see what Ter was going through. I had the good fortune to witness how Pat's depth was being exposed to me. In the midst of problems, gifts were revealed.

I took a week on and a week off, taking turns with Sue. She moved an RV onto the property for herself so she had her own space. I chose to be right in the middle of it all to keep a close watch on what went down.

To begin with, we drove the ninety miles to Tucson twice a week for radiation treatments. The longer they could shrink the tumors the better chance Terry had to continue living and "being Terry." The in-between days we lived life by the seat of the pants. We took turns cooking dinner. My mother loved making casseroles and roasts so that was what she did to feed us. Pat and I liked to cook on the grill so our meals centered on that.

Every night we built a bonfire and gathered around it in lawn chairs, drinking cocktails and, for some of us, smoking. I smoked cigars at that time and Pat liked unfiltered Camels. Misha, a shy, middle-aged neighbor woman, joined us most nights and found comfort in our nightly communing. Vincent, another single neighbor, joined us most nights sharing dinner and drinks. Terry was always in the middle of our circle tipping over lawn chairs trying to make sense of things. We let him smoke when we were close. He often tried to light his cigarette with his phone. Those moments were both sad and humorous, and very telling. He seemed to be able to talk to us just fine but was dragging his left leg more and more and his hair was almost gone. What touched my heart so much was that no matter how he looked, he didn't seem to have an ego and thus didn't seem to care about his hair or his new limp.

He was the kindest, sweetest, gentlest, most agreeable guy I ever knew. He had a great sense of humor and was always ready to help who ever asked for it. He was a dad with two adult sons, divorced for years and estranged from those sons. Because he didn't have good role modeling as a young man he had no idea how to be married or be a father. His sons grew up without his guidance.

There was a wisdom about him that I never saw until we moved in together. On rides to Tucson we asked him how he wanted his death handled. Those questions had to be asked. That was hard but he seemed to have made the decision. He wanted to donate his body to science and he wanted to be remembered as "himself." Because we, as a family, never talked intimately about anything, doing it now was very hard. And we really didn't know each other. Superficially we did, but what I learned through this process was that I missed really knowing Terry for who he was on the inside, what his dreams were, whether he was happy. Watching him live in a drunken stupor most of his life made me think his life was wasted. I couldn't see meaning in it from a distance.

As days wore on, and the treatments were done, Terry started tripping, falling, and getting more confused. I called the doctor on Terry's case and asked if we could get another round of radiation. He said we could not. "Now you have to contact hospice and make him comfortable," he said. "Terry has lived longer than we expected," he said. We had never asked that question. It was better not knowing. I hung up and swallowed hard. The next call went to our local hospice office. I had introduced myself weeks earlier, to inform them that we might one day need their service. The day they showed up to begin helping us, I cried fearing that now Terry would know he was dying. We were given a vast array of meds for everything from constipation to sleep meds, morphine, and anti-seizure pills. The nurse took us on as a family and shared everything she knew to gently guide us down this road.

Every night was pretty sleepless for me. Terry spent hours foraging in and out of the kitchen cabinets and fridge looking for something. He took out whatever caught his eye and added it to a bowl, mixed it up and added other ingredients. After a long period of mixing and adding he sat down to taste the concoction. It was disgusting, of course. He soon stood up and walked into his bedroom to sleep.

Sleeping wasn't a happy time for him and I never knew why. Since I was too afraid of overdosing him on sleep meds, I always gave him too little. His tumors were probably causing pressure on his brain causing the sleeplessness.

The day came when he no longer knew when he had to urinate so it fell on me to introduce Depends. I gingerly walked into his room and said that we had to start using these. He was appalled by that so I told him we were all using them now. He said, "Well, that's the shits." Poor guy. I helped him put a pair on and helped him get into his pjs for the night.

Soon his Depends got too wet during the night, and he took them off and either put another one on, put two on or threw them all, soaked, around the room. I walked in one morning to see him naked, sitting on the bed, Depends strewn about the room, and cringed. I knew I had to get him up on the bed to put a fresh pair on. I asked my brother Pat to help me. Somehow, I knew that Terry couldn't follow directions. I asked Pat to take Terry by the upper body and I would take his legs and we would move him up onto the bed. Pat grabbed Terry's wrists, not wanting to touch him and tried to drag his whole body that way. I was irate feeling like he was going to break Terry's wrists. Somehow, we managed to move him up enough so I could put new Depends on him. I laid him down, pulled the blankets up to his chin, ran my fingers through his hair and touched his face. I realized that it was time to touch him and 'love' him. I brought him his nightly pills and asked him to lift his head to take them and a sip of water. He couldn't lift his head and shook so hard I knew I had to hold his head and help him like I would a little child.

I turned off his light and walked outside to sit by the fire. I began to cry and that infuriated Pat. He was repelled by my sobbing. The more I cried the more he yelled at me. I said, "It's time to start touching Terry." We fought viciously and then Pat went to his room. I sobbed so hard snot hung from my face to my knees. Our mother was there in the circle around the fire, but what happened right there had to come out. I was seeing something and though I didn't know exactly what it was, it made me know that things had to change.

I wondered how Pat would be the next morning. He woke up the next day like our fight never happened. We rose and made our coffee like we always did, sat on the little deck that Terry made, facing the rising sun and savoring the coffee. The deck was small so we sat close.

I noticed that Terry's eyes were darting back in his head and didn't know what that meant. In no time, like magic, hospice showed up and as the nurse witnessed Terry's eyes she told us that if he ever did drugs in the past, he thought he had put himself into this place and didn't know how to get out of it. He had, indeed, been a user of drugs and alcohol. She said that we did not want to see him suffer like this so we needed to begin giving him morphine.

It was time to give him his morning meds, and as I tried to feed them into Terry's mouth I saw that he couldn't swallow. Not sure what I was seeing but knowing it was not good, I sat down to think about what to do. We decided that we should take him inside and asked him to stand up. He couldn't!! He could not stand up anymore! Suddenly everything was going away. We called for a hospital bed and when it was delivered, Pat and I took Terry in our arms and carried him inside, putting him in the bed we placed in the living room where we could keep a close eye on him. Pat held Terry in a new way without the previous fear of touching him. I covered him up and dripped morphine into his mouth. He slipped into what must have been a coma. I sat by his side like a sentinel never wanting him to suffer any seizures or suffer again. That whole day I sat by him and watched him for any twitches or signs of seizure. I dripped morphine into the corner of his mouth at the slightest movement. He twisted his blanket one time trying to drink it but otherwise slept or went deeper into a coma. I changed his diaper and Pat said he couldn't believe I could do that. I said, "There's no option." It had to be done.

Our sister came over the next morning to take her shift and I left to stay at her house and get ready to process my Top Secret Clearance with the United States Government and send my application on to Washington, DC. I went to Fort Huachuca and met with the security officer to process the clearance. I turned off my cell throughout the meeting and turned it on again once outside. There were several messages—all from Sue, all saying "We lost Terry." That confused me at first and then I knew.

The drive back to the house took twenty minutes and once inside I looked around at the circle of friends and family surrounding Terry, now dead, in his hospital bed. They all had time to process the death. The hospice nurse stayed with us to help where she could. I sat on the side of Terry's bed and began to touch his face, his eyes, his head, his legs, his arms, and really look at him. He was gone and I was crushed. Why didn't I see it coming? How could I have missed that he was near death while I was dripping morphine into his mouth? Now I reasoned that the tumors grew and squeezed off his brain stem. His last breath was taken in my sister's presence.

In working together for Terry's care, my mother, brother, sister and I found a balance that was foreign to us. I learned so much about Pat and kept a photo journal of our life so I could look back at the moods and precious moments we walked through like the blind leading the blind.

Terry's body was taken by the local morgue in preparation for his transport to Science Care in Tucson where his body would be used for medical research and the cremains would be shipped to his sons.

Our next step was to plan and carry off a memorial. I had never experienced one but my sister seemed to know exactly what to do. She invited everyone she knew of that knew Terry. She planned a big meal and then suggested that Terry's son Keith and I make up speeches to deliver to those who attended. We did so and found a flow to it.

As people showed up and filled the room, I was stunned by how many people came for Terry. Keith and I sat on the hearth by the fireplace facing the room. I began first with my speech feeling small and yet surrounded by so many of his people. Head down, I delivered my heartfelt words. Keith took over when I was done and his speech was so tender that no one could help but cry. I sobbed. Keith was Terry's oldest son and he had never really had a dad. Terry was so occupied with drinking that he was absent for most of Keith's childhood. And yet, Keith delivered his speech with great emotion and found a way to add humor to it. Next, one by one, people spoke up about how they knew and loved Terry and how he touched their lives. The outpouring of love for him made me aware of how meaningful and important Terry's life really was. It wasn't a waste like I always thought. Now I was disappointed in myself for never really knowing him and for not having a memorial while he was alive so he could see all the love people had for him. I vowed that in the future, for those I loved and participated in their last days, I would request a pre-memorial of sorts, like a "going away party."

HEATHER TOSTESON

THE AIR YOU BREATHE

I know many people disapproved of my parents' choices. The psychiatrists and psychologists I was sent to regularly in my teens to treat my severe agoraphobia and social anxiety all made it clear—explicitly or implicitly—that they did and that they found in those choices of my parents sufficient cause for all my symptoms. My last three lovers might concur. I myself am not so sure.

Consequently, I've found it is generally wiser not to share the particulars of my upbringing anymore. This isn't denial. It just doesn't help me clarify my own responses. Certainly, I know I was shaped, permanently, by the events of my late childhood and prepubescence. I believe I would have been whatever choices my parents made. I'm not sure I see that formation as negatively as did Drs. Robinson, Freed, Smith, Dalton, and Ellis.

But it came up this afternoon in the conference about Sophia Greene. I found myself taking her side—to the surprise of everyone at the table. Sophia is fifteen. Her sister Chloe is seventeen and in severe heart failure. She is on a transplant list, but is very low on it because of uncontrollable pulmonary hypertension. Chloe is eligible for hospice, to her mother's great distress, but that only involves a weekly nurse's visit and monthly social worker's visit. She doesn't like staying home alone, and it also worries her mother if she does. Chloe isn't eligible for home health because she is mobile and able to care for herself. She is in virtual school. Her mother wants Sophia to go to virtual school with her sister Chloe this year so they can have as much time together as possible.

The girls are close and Sophia is fine with this plan. Sophia is a smart girl, extroverted and generous, and her homeroom and English teacher Annie Hughes's pet. Annie Hughes is the one who has insisted on calling in DFACS—and me.

"It isn't forever," I said. "Chloe's already in hospice. That gives you a time range. Six months, a year at most."

"Her mother's going to continue working because she's used up all her leave. There's no adult oversight," Annie protested.

"Virtual school is all computerized. You've said Sophia is disciplined. If you're worried, you can call her periodically or stop by once a week to review her work."

"They're locking her up in a sick room just so her *sister* doesn't feel isolated. They're sacrificing *her* life."

"It isn't forever," I said.

"It was Sophia's suggestion," Julia Greene, Sophia's mother, said when Annie called her to object. She repeated it in the conference. "Sophia says she thinks it will help everyone. I won't have to worry about getting her to and from school. We'll save on fees. Chloe and she will have fun. She will be able to go at her own pace, maybe skip a grade."

"What do you think Sophia will gain from the experience?" I asked Julia before Annie could say anything.

"What she would say herself: that she hasn't missed a minute of her sister's precious life. And that however tough things are, she can always care for others, make their lives a little better. That's not a small thing, you know." Julia Greene, a thin woman in her late forties with blond hair going dark at the roots, spoke to her crossed hands, then looked up at Annie with a look beyond grief or contempt.

Annie opened her mouth to protest. I shook my head. We had talked to Sophia earlier—and she had said pretty much the same thing. Although the person she saw herself helping was her mother.

"They need me and I want to do it," Sophia had said to us. She shook her bangs from her eyes briskly as if to wake us all up. This was common sense to her. "Chloe wants to stay home. She doesn't like the hospital. She can't stay home alone—and mom has to work."

"Legally, you have to go to school," the social worker said.

"If you're worried about my slacking off, two-thirds of my work needs to be done on computer for virtual school. It can be checked on every day. But look, I spend a lot of my time at school just hanging out. I'd rather spend that time with Chloe. *I* will feel better." Sophia sounded calm, sure of herself. She made eye contact with each of us as she spoke, a gentle smile lighting her face.

"Who came up with this idea?" the social worker, Andrea Moran, asked

Sophia.

"Honestly, I can't remember," Sophia answered. Again, she flashed that wonderful smile, and her interesting dark blue eyes weren't hesitant to peer into our own. There's something straightforward and good about her—which makes me understand Annie's protectiveness. But she also projects a self-assurance that she may well feel. "Does it really matter whose idea it was? It *feels* right to all of us. Whatever happens, we'll know we've done the best for Chloe. Mom and I can be at rest about that."

"And *you*," Annie Hughes said. "Will *we* have done the best for you, Sophia?"

"If *we* haven't, we have longer to get it right," Sophia said. "The decisions for Chloe, those are probably lasting."

"Are you making Sophia pay for her good health?" Annie bluntly asked Julia Greene in the conference we held alone with her. "Is Chloe?"

"Chloe loves Sophia. The girls have always been good friends. They're even closer now. Sophia can make Chloe laugh like no one else."

"I can see how this might be the best choice for Chloe, Mrs. Greene. But are you sure it is the best choice for Sophia?" Andrea Moran asked, backing Annie up. She was a robust red head with a permanently flushed face but a deep, comforting voice.

Julia Greene stared at her hands for a second, then turned her own stormy blue eyes on me. "Best is a ludicrous word in these circumstances. Almost obscene—"

"Death happens," I said to the far window, the tree branches tossing in the wind.

The three women looked at me.

"Dr. Bellamy?" Andrea Moran asked.

"Josh?" Annie added.

"Death happens," I repeated. "It's a fact. In itself it's neither a tragedy or a blessing, obscene or pure. It's a fact that leaves an astonishing void at the center of most of our meaning systems. Most likely Chloe is going to die by the end of this year. All the love in the world isn't going to stop that. Neither is medical science. Neither is Sophia's personal sacrifice, if it is that. Chloe has to live with the knowledge that the world as she knows it and she as she knows herself are going to stop existing."

I took a deep breath and looked directly at Julia Greene, who looked away. I looked at Annie and Andrea and continued. "Mrs. Greene has to live with the loss of her child, with the knowledge that she brought Chloe into this world to experience an inescapable early death and that another child, no more or less worthy than Chloe, is going to live a longer life whatever her relative affection for the two might be."

I could see Julia Greene open her mouth to protest but went on. "She has to live with the reality that, because Chloe needs health care now and she and Sophia need a future, she must keep working, can't spend every minute with her beloved first born. And Sophia," I began to conclude staring at my hands, "has to live with the gift of her own good health, the weight of her sister's irremediable illness, the injustice of this difference, her love for her sister and her mother, and the reality of a future with her mother that extends beyond Chloe's."

"Care to apply this, Josh?" Annie asked. "It's like you're reading from a script here."

"To the extent that *anyone's* choices are based on denying rather than accepting that—independent of our will or wisdom or actions—*death happens,* those choices are probably distorted. Why *should* Sophia's life go on 'as normal,' meaning as if death, especially the death of a beloved sister very close to her in age, isn't happening? Why *should* Chloe feel that she can ask Sophia to give up her social world if death happens, it just happens? Why should she ask Sophia's life to stop too?"

I have a nice voice, people often remark on it, ask me if I've ever considered radio. I could see all the women relax as I spoke. But my own right leg was doing its bouncing thing, and then my fingers began their tapping.

Annie was looking at my hand with a little smile, both sad and satisfied. "It makes you as uncomfortable as it does us, Josh."

But I know, I wanted to tell her, exactly what I'm talking about. It's just that there are no words there, never have been.

"Death happens," I said again. "When it does, it makes mockery of our law of averages."

My father died at seventy, leaving two families, six children, four adult, two not, and the impact was exactly like Chloe's death here. Astounding to everyone concerned. Should it have been? That's the question I have been asking myself for years now.

The women all looked at each other. Was Annie rolling her eyes at the social worker to say, *Just like a man. Making it all abstract. Law of averages. Death happens. What crap.*

I don't know what happened. My hands got still, my leg stopped jiggling. I stood up to my full height of six feet. I'm thin and hold myself straight, so I can appear taller or smaller depending on people's focus.

"Let me tell you where I'm coming from. When I was nine my father was diagnosed with ALS and given a year at most to live. He was sixty-eight. He had retired two years earlier and was looking forward to spending more time with me and my older sister. My mother, twenty-four years his junior, a social worker, had recently retooled for a career in public administration and had just started a new job. My father had been a college professor. They were all analytic types—my father, mother, sister. Their responses were pragmatic. They learned about voice storing and Hoyer lifts. I was the one who freaked. I was afraid to leave my dad alone, afraid that something might happen to him. I couldn't concentrate at school. I began to fail. The solution they came up with was for me to stay home with my father and be schooled by him. As he became more incapacitated but didn't die, questions were asked about my parents' choices, especially toward the end, by well-intentioned people like you. My parents persuaded everyone they were doing it for my good. At the time, I agreed. I felt both responsible and very privileged."

"And now?" Annie asked softly.

"Look at me," I said, smiling broadly. "I have a doctorate in child psychology. I've made a career of wondering, exploring all sides. There isn't a choice we make when young, or that is made for us when young, that doesn't shape us, perhaps permanently. But many of these choices are inescapable. Death happens. Illness happens. Poverty and wealth and disability and general weirdness *happen.* Who is to say they shouldn't?"

The trees and I nodded to each other.

"Point, Josh?" This is one reason Annie and I stopped seeing each other. There was too much explaining involved.

"If they stop enjoying each other's company, separate them. Until then, find the choices that enrich Chloe's present and safeguard Sophia's future as much as possible. It seems as if the family may have come up with a good working solution."

Annie looked at me like a disappointed lover, which she is. "You're satisficing, Josh. And in this case, it really is the same as sacrificing."

❦ ❦ ❦

"Egotistical bastard," is what Annie said about my own father. "Thinking he was the only one who could help you. Using you as an excuse to keep hanging on at any cost."

Annie's the blackest of Irish with a redhead's skin—the thick white kind that doesn't flush and bright yellow-green eyes whose perceptiveness I actually find restful although other people can experience it as scornful. The oldest of six, with two alcoholic parents, she is enraged by parental lapses, or what she perceives as them. She is five years older than me, thirty-seven, and without, as far as I can tell, a functioning fertility clock. Perhaps it was replaced by her ten nephews and nieces, her affection for her students, her passion for teaching, the care she generously but caustically distributes equally to her divorced, ailing parents.

We weren't involved for very long: three months soon after I came to work at Greenwood Academy. She was uncomfortable with my open bisexuality, but more so by what she said was my lack of resistance.

"I *need* strong personalities," she told me. "With you, Josh, I keep looking for the wall, and all I get is foam pillow. I *need* the push back."

This might have bothered someone else, but I know the calls I've been able to make in my life. I don't feel I need to share that knowledge with the world. The question that engages me is could I, if necessary, make those choices again. I doubt I'll ever be able to be really intimate with anyone until I'm sure.

Annie and I decided it was best just to be friends—and for the last three years we've considered ourselves good ones. I've seen her through a serious relationship with a married man. She's seen me through my mother's death, my sister's wedding, and four short trysts, three with men, one with a woman. She called me into this conference because it is my job as school counselor—and also because she was counting on me to be the cushioning between her rock and Andrea's hard place.

Annie called me into the conference knowing my own story and assuming that it would naturally mean I would support her. Instead I provided a door out of the either/or cage she keeps building as compulsively as bees build hives. She didn't expect me to find my grounding in the *and*—or to stand there so openly. Truly, Annie who is so busy defending the helpless and the hopeless has far less knowledge about how to protect herself than me.

After my father died when I was eleven, I was forced to go back to school because I was too young to stay home by myself. Not too young to stay home, mind you, with a man who couldn't speak or breathe or eat or piss without mechanical assistance. And they were right, however much I protested, however unbearable the alternative felt to me then. For how can a boy of eleven possibly describe the rarified existence I experienced for a year and a half as my father's primary caregiver?

I understand that my sister and my mother never saw it that way. Honestly, I don't know what planet they were living on. Of course, I do. They were seeing it as my father did. My mother lifted my father into his chair, attached his catheter and diapered him for the day. She poured a can of nutritional supplement into a plastic glass and fed it to him through a straw. I did the same at noon. She returned religiously at five-thirty, the first year with my sister Sabrina, who was a junior in high school. My mother and I made dinner while Sabrina filled my father in about her day. My mother interrogated my father and me about ours at dinner. She talked to us in the same voice she used for her welfare clients. It's hard to describe but easy to recognize, and it's one I'm careful never to use myself. It grates on me like you wouldn't believe. All that faux respect, that pretence of "can do-ness," that bonhomie. At least my father had genuine hopes for me—and for himself. I was the son who was going to know him in sum. I was the one whose gifts, as yet invisible to the larger world, he would identify, protect and nourish.

I keep trying to see what the world saw in me back then—both positive and negative. I know afterwards my therapists saw me as vulnerable, isolated, exploited. But I think *I* saw myself as in the thick of it, as remarkably indulged, treasured, crucial. That's a wonderful thing to feel at any age: *crucial.*

It was happenstance that learning about my father's illness, experiencing the existential vertigo of his imminent (or so they said then) death, and the fourth grade agony of having Miss Mary Lovejoy as my language arts teacher coincided. Miss Mary Lovejoy, you had to use both her names, was more than contrary, she was cruel. She read aloud the names of anyone who failed a test, "These are today's big losers, class." Then she passed our tests back with a smile that made me cringe. Our school straddled an economic divide, so it didn't help that she was also drawing a color line. In solidarity, my own scores in spelling and grammar began to fall by Christmas, but it wasn't until I returned in January that things fell apart.

My father's diagnosis had been delivered over our Christmas break, and my mother spent her nights in the garage heroically muffling her sobs. My sister obsessively ran laps around the block when she wasn't practicing her violin or researching at the library or talking compulsively with my dad about her college plans as if nothing had shifted.

"Don't look so sad, Josh," my mom would say coming in from the garage, red-eyed. "We'll all help your daddy. It's going to be all right."

It was so obviously not going to be all right, all I could do was pat her arm, at which she grabbed me and pulled me to her and wept into my hair until my scalp began to crawl, a poignant form of water torture. Since escape wasn't possible, I hugged her closer.

Within those two weeks, I discovered my own indispensability and what it consisted of. Whenever anyone else looked like they would break, it was my job to break first—not into tears, but into activity of one kind or another. For example, I used my savings to buy my mom food for Christmas—sausages and cheese and crackers and cake so she wouldn't have to cook. I had Sabrina practice with the Hoyer lift my parents had immediately ordered, lifting me from the bed and dumping me on the floor with a rapidity and force that soon blotched my buttocks and back with bruises. When my mother put a stop to that, I had Sabrina try to teach me the violin until the parakeet's horrified shrieks put a stop to that as well. With my dad, I read through all the information the doctor had given us about ALS, asking really simple questions, hundreds of them, so he could use his quiet teacher's voice. I held his hand after he said, "I'm so sorry, Josh. I was counting on our having another decade together. I've been so looking forward to this time with you and Sabrina."

My father was a small man and at that age I looked as if I was going to take after him. My sister, at sixteen, had obviously inherited my mother's more statuesque genes and at five ten with a well-rounded figure looked as if she were already in college. She almost was, for she had inherited more than her fair share of the smart genes in the family and was already getting A's in all her advanced placement classes. She had scored a perfect score on her math SATs and was now feverishly trying to get a matching score on the verbal.

By the end of that vacation, Sabrina too understood the role she was to play. Family star. Nothing was to disrupt her practice or study schedules or her prep for the retake of her SATs. Colleges were already writing her. She and my mom and dad would laugh about it, but leave the letters lying around like get well cards. Which they were. They said there was light at the end of the tunnel. Sabrina ended up graduating early after taking an extra English course over the summer and then heading off to Swarthmore a month shy of seventeen. "Don't you worry about us," our parents said to her. "You go on out there and do what only you can do."

I, on the other hand, was to be the light *in* the tunnel, hesitant, wavering, and real as the line between life and death.

But to return to language arts and Miss Mary Lovejoy. It wasn't what she did to me that drove me to act (it rarely is). It is what she did to my best friend Jesse. Jesse was a thin, funny boy with a hyperactive bladder. When he asked to go to the bathroom, Miss Mary Lovejoy would make him wait so long he'd have his whole desk bouncing up and down, then he wouldn't make it in time and when he returned to class with his pants wet, she would order him down to the office to call his mother to bring a change of clothes because of his lack of self-control. I can still hear her say that. She made it sound more serious than being a serial killer. Jessie's mom worked two jobs, his grandma, who watched him, had arthritis so bad she didn't leave the house, and his dad wasn't expected out of jail until Jessie was twenty-one. No one had time to bring him dry pants. Miss Mary Lovejoy knew that, knew that Jesse was going to have to parade down the hall to the office in his wet pants—and parade back in borrowed clothes from the lost and found. Girls' clothes sometimes. I had thought about this over the Christmas break and with my mom I'd come up with a solution, which was to bring some extra pants and underwear in my knapsack and let Jesse use them, but I hadn't had time to give them to him yet.

So when Jesse asked if he could go to the bathroom and Miss Mary Lovejoy gave him that sneer of hers and said, "All in due time, Jesse. Try and control yourself," something took possession of me and I stood up.

"Yes, Josh?"

"I need to go too."

"Fine," she said. Even though my grades were falling, at that time my mom was on the PTA board.

"Not unt-t-t-il Jesse," I said. "He asked first."

"Are you t-t-telling me how to run my classroom, young man?" she asked.

"You just look like a person," I said. I was looking around the class as I spoke. I can still remember the looks on the other children's faces. Little

Kayla's eyes opening wide, Dynetta bending her head to hide her smile, her beads clattering together. Emboldened, I looked back at Miss Mary Lovejoy. "But you're really a witch," I continued. "A wicked one. And I wish you were dead. Dead. Dead. Dead. Dead. Dead."

"Ohhh boy," Jesse whispered. "Ohhh boy. She goin to get you, boy. Shit hitting the fan now."

"Are you threatening me, Josh?"

"No," I said with a smile, channeling my sister Sabrina's precocious know-it-all voice. "I am expressing a heartfelt, well-considered opinion. I am exercising my right to free speech in a democracy."

And then I picked up my knapsack and opened it and just had time to pull out the bag of extra clothes and hand them to Jesse as Miss Mary, all contrary, grabbed me by the shoulder with her pincer fingers.

"Dead, dead, dead, dead," I sang as we walked down the hall. "I wish, I wish, I wish you were dead."

"He should be institutionalized," Miss Mary Lovejoy, her face as red and moist as a raw steak, told the principal, then the guidance counselor, and then my mother.

"And you should be fired," said my mother, her face as white as Miss Mary's was red.

"Just try it," Miss Mary Lovejoy said with a smirk.

"If I could, I would," the principal confided in my mother after abruptly escorting Miss Mary Lovejoy from the room. "She retires in June. Let's just find a solution for Josh until then."

Which is how I began attending home school, with my father taking the role of beneficent mentor. I can't tell you what bliss it was not to have to sit in a desk for hours at a time, not having someone always criticize my handwriting, not having to watch all the petty cruelties Miss Mary Lovejoy exulted in dealing out, being able to read about Prince Caspian and the Dawn Treader at any time in the day as long as I finished whatever my father assigned me by the end of the day. My stutter disappeared. My mom, who saw my dad's spirits rise with my presence, the demands of my education, stopped crying. My sister looked at me with respect because I was doing something she didn't dare—spend hours with our increasingly feeble father.

Neither my dad nor I were really big talkers, so what I remember of those hours are mainly the singing of our parakeets, the hum of the refrigerator and the air conditioner or heater, the occasional sounds of cars on the back streets, the sounds of my basketball hitting the wall of the garage when I took a recess, coached by my dad from his wheelchair stationed on the deck.

While I completed my reading or my math exercises or practiced my typing (we all agreed my handwriting was a lost cause), my father was busy recording short all-purpose phrases in his own voice so when the time came when he couldn't talk anymore, we could still continue our work together. I heard him saying, "How was your day?" "Tell me more." "Could you repeat that?" "Great job." "Try again." "I love you." "Thank you." "I'm sad." "I'm happy." "Water, if you could." "I'm hungry." "The joke is on me." "It's time to end this." "Tomorrow is another day."

I enjoyed my reading and writing lessons without the anxiety of Miss Lovejoy. The farther I got from her, the easier it was to contract her name, although I couldn't go as far as my father who called her Mean Old Mary All Contrary. I loved having the freedom to reward myself with a chapter of a favorite book whenever I tired of the formal assignments. My dad wasn't a task master. I just wanted to earn his smiles, which came most readily when we were on task and on time.

The first year, Mrs. Deal, my math and science teacher, came to the house once a week. She kept saying she looked forward to seeing me back in school next year. I liked Mrs. Deal and she liked me, but she looked at my dad in a way that made me nervous and protective. "My dad already checked that," I'd tell her as she looked over my math assignments. "He checks everything I do." Already, even though my father was still able to get up out of his wheelchair unaided and his voice was clear, I felt somehow we were doing something a little shady, a little under the table. It was too good to be true. The two of us on perennial hooky. Appearances were important, so I was always nodding at Mrs. Deal, looking as shy and withdrawn as I thought suited someone whose mother claimed he was too vulnerable to be in school.

My dad seemed oblivious to the threats I intuited, chatting with Mrs. Deal just like he would have before he was sick, always a little punctilious, with practiced charm.

"Josh and I are having a fine old time here," he said. "We've worked out our daily routines like two old bachelors. No surprises." He briskly wheeled his big new motorized chair around the living room, escorting Mrs. Deal in and through the house to the sunny back room we used as a shared study. "We have everything we need at our fingertips. Curiosity, peanut butter and jelly, pencils, erasers, spit balls."

But he knew what he was doing, he knew what to say to reel Mrs. Deal into our conspiracy. He looked up at her as she was leaving and said with a wave of his better hand, "You do know that my son's well-being comes first with me. Let there be no mistake about that. To the extent that I am the cause of his anxiety, it is my responsibility to relieve it."

Mrs. Deal was in her late twenties and pregnant with her first child. My father was older than her grandfather. You could see how she was torn in her responses. He was talking like a man in the middle of his life, and part of her wanted to respond to the parental authority of that voice, but her natural response when she looked at him was to humor him like she would her grandfather with his harmless delusions of control and influence. And when she looked at me, her response was too much like my mom's for me to feel comfortable. I felt she wanted to pull me right up against that bulging belly and start the water torture.

"I like being able to read at my own pace," I told her. "Every morning I get up and read some on my library book, then have breakfast and start in on my schoolwork. I can do my classes in whatever order I want. Dad lets me choose. But I have to do all that subject before I go on to the next. Dad makes our lunch." (Already this was white lie.) I took a deep breath and hurried on. "Then we have discussion hour after lunch. We talk about world events. After that I play basketball or run around the block five times and then practice my recorder. Then my mom comes back with my sister and she takes over."

I would smile my biggest smile and close with, "Dad says he wishes he had been home schooled. He says it is made to order for a shy kid like me."

Mrs. Deal would smile at me gently. She had this thick blond hair filled with curls and skin that looked very soft. "It always seemed to me that the other kids liked you, Josh, and you liked them. I wouldn't have described you as shy—just someone who needed to have his private thoughts from time to time. You always seemed to be having a good time when you were playing with Jesse and Louis and Dynetta. Don't you remember?"

"Do you want to meet my parakeet?" I asked her. "I'm trying to teach him to talk. His name is Jeremiah and when he learns to talk he can utter a jeremiad. And here's my dog, Jove, who you can see is very jovial. Look, he's smiling at you. He shakes hands too."

The truth was I couldn't remember the faces of any of those children. I couldn't remember what it had felt like to play with any of them. When I thought of school all I could remember was Miss Mary Lovejoy's wrinkled, spiteful face, her red mouth opening: "Are you t-t-telling me how to run my classroom, young man?" And then that merciful wave, equally hot and cold, of nausea, rage, oblivion. Honestly, I didn't remember what followed those words until I began writing here. I always assumed I'd just blacked out.

With Mrs. Deal, the situation was more delicate. I needed her to trust us. I needed to protect my father. I needed to project the same kind of have-it-all-under-control, can-do energy my father, sister and mother did and, with the crafty ingeniousness of a child, I did my best. The only problem was that the real resilience I did have, my essential optimism, began to feel fraudulent, as severed from real feeling as the responses of my highly cerebral parents and older sister.

Mrs. Deal, the last day she visited, slipped a piece of paper with her home phone number into my hand as she was leaving. "I'm not going to be teaching next fall," she said, patting her ballooning stomach. "I'll be on maternity leave. That means you can call me whenever you want to, Josh." She had just learned that my parents had decided it was best for me to spend another year being home schooled by my father, until middle school.

"Josh asked for that?" Mrs. Deal asked my father with more force than I thought polite.

"He didn't need to," my father said. "Many things here don't need to be put into words."

Truly, my parents saw themselves as making near super-human efforts to meet the special needs of their bright, distractible, adored, anxious, maladaptively shy, youngest child—all in the face of the deepest tragedy the family would ever know. My mother had been my father's student and she remained willingly in that position with him. "If it were only me," I heard her tell an old friend, "I would choose to go at the same time Bill does—but I have the children to think about."

That feeling of hers, I'm sure, changed over time, but it guided many of my responses. If it weren't for me, I often thought, *both* my parents would die.

"Bill is determined to do everything he can for Josh so that Josh knows, he'll always know, how much he is loved." I heard my mother saying over and over again, to everyone who asked how my father was doing, how we were all holding up, most especially to anyone who looked the least bit quizzical when informed that I was being home schooled.

That everything that my father did for me required certain things of me in return—one of which was that I should never imagine being anything but the family linchpin—we all knew but never mentioned.

❦ ❦ ❦

Originally, I think my parents just imagined keeping me out of Miss Mary Lovejoy's malicious clutches for the rest of the school year. I think they thought that was all the time my Dad had left. It was our relationship, the strength of it, that might have contributed to Dad's extended survival. Certainly that was the unspoken understanding between us.

I was the one, keying in on it, who insisted I stay home for fifth grade too. My grades on the standardized tests were improving dramatically and, although I had no dreams of matching Sabrina's achievements, I began to imagine that I might come in a presentable second.

As I said, Sabrina, after my dad's diagnosis, had gone into overdrive and, combining AP course credit, summer school, and a little administrative legerdemain, had graduated a year early. She was busily packing when I made my request. Mom, who had been acting on the assumption that I was going back to school, was trying to talk Dad, who now could not drive, not even with our new van with a lift, into accepting a home health aide.

"I'm a private man, Melanie," I heard him tell her. (Closed doors were as rare as psychological boundaries in our house.) "Dying is as intimate as love. I don't want a threesome."

Unless, of course, that threesome included me. At that point, my dad couldn't walk at all, but he still had some function in his arms and his voice was getting husky but was still clear. He was a high-spirited man, curious. He didn't make light of the limitations, but he never sentimentalized them either. He really was only asking for privacy.

"Look," he said. "Why don't we put in a feeding tube now. That way you can just hook it up when you leave in the morning, pour in a can or two of Ensure, unhook it when you get home. I have you on easy dial on my phone."

My mother began to cry. "That's no kind of life, Bill."

"It's a hell of a lot better than a hospice, for which I still don't qualify.

We said we weren't going to let this go on long enough for me to become a burden, Melanie. I have nearly seventy years of a very rich life to review. I have the riches of my library. And my memory. The other kids call me while you're out."

My mother wouldn't have it. "Let me see how much sick leave I qualify for."

My father barked at her, "I never want to see you sitting here just waiting for me to die—that's moral suicide for you, honey. You can't stop your life. Remember, we said quality of life would determine our choices. No trach. It can also include no feeding tube."

That's when I broke down and broke in, sobbing, acting as if I had heard none of the preceding, was totally engulfed in my own ten-year old misery. I couldn't stand going back to school, I told them. I wanted to stay here with my dad and Jeremiah and Jove. I wanted to keep on making 98th percentile on the standardized tests. I couldn't remember the names of the kids in my class anymore. It would be like starting all over again. Why couldn't I wait until middle school when it really would be a different group?

It only occurs to me now that none of us thought of suggesting that Sabrina might delay college for a year—or just go somewhere closer to home. I think the two of us had been given separate responsibilities for living out the two kinds of normal—life as it should be ideally and life as it is. I don't know what to make of the fact that Sabrina dropped out of college a few months after Dad died, moved to Colorado and worked at a ski resort as a ski instructor and member of a jazz band. She returned to live near my mother in her late twenties, earning a degree in physical therapy from the local branch of the state university. She works with young spinal cord victims, takes them deep sea diving and on wheel chair marathons. A year before my mother died, Sabrina married a physician, neither particularly wealthy nor handsome, a widower twenty years her senior with two sullen teenage children. My mother wept through the whole wedding although Sabrina looked radiant. But that was far in the unforeseeable future that day.

I was both plaintive and practical as I tried to persuade my parents. Dad could still review my work, answer my questions. I could heat his soup (he could still swallow though it was slow) and make myself a sandwich, staving off the need for a feeding tube for some more months.

It's a strange disease, ALS. Deeply debilitating, rapidly so in some ways, very slowly in others. Your mind stays clear, just all volitional movement deserts you—and then the involuntary ones, like swallowing, breathing. My dad had the slower kind that starts in your limbs. At first, when his legs went so fast, they thought he was going to be one of the ones who went quickly. But then, when the weakness went so slowly in his arms, they began to talk as if he were one of the outliers, maybe as much so as Stephen Hawking. Oh, we could only hope. Or dread.

Alone together the next year, my dad and I just took the changes on one by one. We stopped predicting or comparing. We just moved on. My father liked to write—and as long as his voice held out, he continued dictating letters to his friends (and to my mother, a love letter a day), which I would transcribe on email and send. He regularly wrote Sabrina. I never felt jealous, of course, because nothing was withheld from me. Indeed, my father made our days sound adventurous and happy. It was the background music of my days, my dad describing vivid moments in his courtship with my mother, or, when writing to his older children, with theirs. I knew the sweet victories of their childhoods as well as I did my own, felt his pride in their accomplishments, his gratitude for their being. My dad, you have to understand, was a very sweet and loving man. He was an amazing—inimitable—model, rather like my sister.

I got better and better at deciphering the sounds he made, translating so smoothly for my mother as we sat at dinner every evening that she was shocked when old friends visited and acted as if my father, no longer able to lift a finger to feed himself, were uttering gibberish.

I still can't identify when it was that I quietly, unnoticed, began to refuse to leave the house at all. Because we had a large backyard and I ran Jove there, a basketball hoop on the back of the garage, and, later, a trampoline, there wasn't a decrease in my level of physical activity. I had been going out with my mom to do errands on the weekend, or to church on Sundays—but I always avoided other kids, said I thought Sunday School was a waste of time and that I would rather maximize my mother's and my time together. It was true. My mom was working longer and longer hours. It seemed like it was always audit time or grant time or program review time at her agency. So our weekends were compressed, intense, sweet. But too nerve wracking.

Years later, she told me, "I began to imagine telling your dad I'd change places with him if only because it meant I could finally get a full night's sleep. Paralysis would be a small price to pay for adequate REM."

We never settled in, you see. For the first year, after the lifts were put in the bedroom to help get my dad in and out of bed, my mom slept on the couch. After Sabrina left for college, I made her sleep in Sabrina's room, but she always pretended it was on a night by night basis. She never moved a single thing around in Sabrina's room—the trophies, the stuffed animals, the movie posters.

I took the same approach to my self-imposed house arrest. "Maybe next time," I would say when my mom would suggest a walk in the park, a quick trip to the grocery store. "I have this chapter I really want to finish." And she never pushed me because the fact was she was as anxious as I was about leaving my father alone. And she was never *refusing* me anything, you see. She was offering, and I was thanking her and passing up the opportunity *just this time.*

✵ ✵ ✵

By the end of that school year, my dad was on a feeding tube, even soup was too hard for him to swallow. His voice had gone and the taped voice was laborious to use, haunting and limited if he did. The voice was his with all the life taken out of it. So, most of our time together, my dad and I just communicated with our eyes, my gestures. I wrote to him rather than speaking. I'm not sure why I decided to match his silence. I think it made me too sad to hear my own voice echoing alone there in the air between us.

Sabrina came for a few weeks that summer but it freaked her. I heard her talking to my mother. "He's like a zombie, can't you see? They both are."

I think it wasn't like that you know, whatever it looked like from the outside. We were like each other's seeing eye or PTSD dogs. It was all visceral, what we were exchanging. Shared gazes, smiles, silent laughter. I'd bring my book over and point to a page I especially liked and my dad would read it and then smile or just blink his eyes twice. When my mom was around, I did the voice over. But with Sabrina when she visited, I didn't. I don't know whether I just forgot or I just wanted to leave her out.

"It won't be long now," my mom told Sabrina whenever she complained.

Oh, I can't tell you how much I hated them both at that moment. There they were, sitting out on the lawn in the long summer twilight, their own bright worldly unit. My dad couldn't leave his wheelchair, but that also meant he couldn't leave me, who couldn't, at that point, cross the threshold of our house even to get the paper.

"They're able to give each other something no one else in the world can give either of them," my mother said softly.

"But what about you?" Sabrina asked. "I thought he said he wasn't going to prolong things, that he wasn't going to deplete the family."

"He doesn't think he is. He's doing this for Josh, all for Josh."

"You really believe that?" Sabrina asked. She was pacing the lawn, her voice low. My dad was asleep with his external ventilator, so he couldn't hear them.

"He does," my mother answered. "Josh does too. That's what counts."

"What's this talk about a trach tube? I thought that was ruled out from the beginning," Sabrina said.

"He says it is Josh's idea. That Josh isn't ready for him to leave yet," my mother answered. "Who am I to make that decision?"

"Who is he?" Their voices were so alike it was hard to distinguish them. It wasn't clear whether that *he* referred to my father or me.

That was the moment when I assumed full responsibility for my father's next breath. If it was a trach tube he wanted, it was a trach tube he would get. Only I knew that I had never asked for it.

The next day, as I blew out the eleven candles on my birthday cake, my mom asked if I had made a wish and I said yes. When she looked at me quizzically, I tapped my throat. "For Dad."

Strapped in his chair, my father blinked and nodded his head. Sabrina let out a huge, harsh breath and stood up.

"You *promised*," she said to my small, motionless father, to my overwhelmed mother. "You *promised*."

"What does it matter to you?" I said quietly as I began to pull the candles off the cake. "It won't make any difference in your life."

"But it will in yours," she said. She put her hand on my mom's shoulder. "And what about her? Just because you don't dare leave the house doesn't mean Dad has to go on like this, that Mom has to live for years in this kind of purgatory. What kind of life is this for *any* of you?"

I could see my dad was getting really upset, his eyes blinking and tearing, the oxygen mask fogging up. My mother was in tears. But inside me it was really quiet, you know that kind of stillness you can experience in the middle of a car accident just before the impact.

"He is *eleven* years old," Sabrina said. "You *cannot* put this on his shoulders."

When I think back on that scene now, I'm both amazed and amused. There was my sister tall as a Valkyrie, filled with righteous fury, and there was me, still small for my age, not even up to her shoulder yet—but we were a perfect match for each other and I knew it. We both did. Sabrina was the only one there young enough to respond to me as an equal, to put the consequences of my actions squarely on my shoulders, whatever she had said to my mother. Even as she spoke, I could see she was right. Who *was* I to make this choice? Who was my father to foist it on me? My mother to accede to that? And who was Sabrina, soon off to Interlochen, to object?

What Sabrina didn't understand was that, more than prolonging life, the trach gave us, we thought, control of the inevitable. Once in, life stopped rapidly when we removed it. There would be none of the soul-hollowing unpredictability we experienced now. Soul *hallowing* unpredictability. The two months that followed, in my memory, have no language.

My dad indicated that night, after Sabrina's outburst, that he wanted to go to bed. Sabrina and my mom used the lift to get him in and my mom diapered him. I went in to see him and stood there holding his hand. He held my eyes for a long time, and there was such kindness there and such defeat. I expect he read the same in me. *That* was the minute, you know, when the choice was made. I could have sobbed, begged him to reconsider. I could have badgered my mother. But I didn't. I stood there staring into my dad's eyes feeling the weight of the last year and a half lifting from my shoulders, all our determination, all our can-do. I also began to feel how *real* our lives were, that this was *our* air, my father and I, *our* trach, and we were both, at this moment, taking it out.

That was the moment my childhood died. But as I write about it now I wonder if it meant, as I always thought it did, the death of my manhood as well. I felt, at that moment that I was committing a terrible betrayal, one that deeply invalidated everything I might have hoped to become—but perhaps, it occurred to me today, I was keeping faith with something larger than either of us. *Death happens. Life does too.*

The last two months of my father's life were completely silent except for the oxygen mask, the involuntary sounds he made when we turned him to wash him. He made no more efforts to get up after that night, to use his voice, or even his eyes. My mom called hospice in. The social worker wanted to send me to friends but I went wild at the suggestion.

"He will never recover if you do that," my mother said. "His fear of death is devouring his life. And mine. His father's too. He needs to touch it, know it intimately, so it has no mystery for him anymore."

Or more—the kind of wonder that lifts us up like a tornado and sets us down unscathed in a completely new state.

❋ ❋ ❋

"You do not know," I told Annie this evening when she called to scold me about my scandalous performance in the conference. "Seriously, you do not know what is best for them."

"Neither do you," she snapped.

"I don't dispute that. But I believe, Annie, I really do believe, they are taking their next best step to find it—and they will know when they get there. Sophia, Chloe, and their mom too. Each of them. *All* of them."

"Like you?" she asked and then began to cry. "I really hate what they did to you, Josh. And what I hate most, truly, is that you don't see it. It's such a loss, to all of us."

"But I do," I said. "I do see what *we* gave, what *we* received. It's you who can't. I was in on this too. I had choices. I don't want to be saved from the enormity of it all, Annie. I just want to claim its beauty. It's the very air I breathe, it is what defines me. And it's sweet, Annie, it's really so sweet with possibility."

I took a deep breath. She did too. And we slowly let them go, in unison.

"Dinner?" I asked.

Annie laughed. "My place. Eight."

As I walked to the car, my step was heavier and quicker than usual. Turning the key in the lock as I was leaving my apartment to meet Annie, I realized that for the first time since I was nine leaving home didn't set off an ache that seemed to reverberate into infinity, an absence that was its own form of presence. For I knew now, I really knew, that what mattered was inside me, always had been, and would be until death.

And there was no way, never would be, to hang on to it. I had to let it go. Hope. Let it back in again. Ad finitum.

VI.
WHOLE OF LIFE

LENORE BALLIRO

UNTITLED

Mourning doves are first to appear in the spring, always a couple. If an egg
falls out of the nest, I am told to leave it, disregard my dream of hatching

it into a full life. Sometimes the egg is whole, sometimes cracked eggs open,
then the dog licks the slick tab of yellow protein off the bricks.

Soon enough a new brood of two putters around my yard, unafraid. I feed
them millet and place a small bowl of water under the lilacs.

We do our work side by side: I pull weeds, the babies poke around and
test their fragile wings. Parent doves sit on the telephone wire, noting every

movement. I am sure the mother would dive and peck my eyes out if
I hurt them. And she should. But no, she trusts me by now, never mind

that some say I should not place human motivation on a wild thing.
Maybe it's a new word we need. Or better, no term, just the
goodness between, among us.

Once my old dog discovered a bunny nest under the spent pea patch.
He grabbed a baby in his teeth and whipped it in a fit of primal memory.

Things we have to do. Leave fallen eggs behind. Knock the life out of a half dead bunny and put it to rest. Acts of kindness that mask themselves as cruelty, neglect.

I buried the rabbit where broken things get placed to find their way back to the elements. Like my friend told me once: We are all carbon.

TERRI ELDERS

GRANDMA FANG'S CLOWDER OF KITTENS

Fang appeared shortly after Thanksgiving in 1965. My eight-year-old son, Steve, found her curled up in the patio, blanketed with purple jacaranda blossoms. He'd gone out with his telescope to look for Pisces, his favorite autumn constellation.

"Look, Mom. I nearly stepped on this cat on my way to the gate," Steve said, cradling the calico tabby. "I saw its little white paw sticking out of the flowers. Then I heard it meow. It looks so tired."

Our last feline guest disappeared several months earlier, so I agreed we could keep this latest stray. That's how it was back then. Except for one neighbor with a purebred Siamese, people didn't actually *own* cats the way they did dogs.

Instead, these free-ranging creatures would surface, sometimes reproduce, and then simply vanish. My mother called them "nocturnal nomads" since they usually showed up on the porch at dusk. She'd feed them leftovers, called all the girls "Susie," and all the boys "Tommy."

"Don't get attached to alley cats," Mama cautioned. "If you fall in love with them, they'll break your heart when they move on."

I heeded her advice. I'd set out a snack for cats if they showed up, but I didn't pet them. I didn't mind playing hostess. That was basic kindness. But I wouldn't lose sleep once they wandered away.

While the newfound cat yawned, Steve's eyes gleamed. "I'm going to call it Fang! Just look at those sharp teeth." He rubbed its tummy. "What are these bumps?"

I leaned over for a closer look.

"Steve, Fang's going to have kittens," I said. "So, we need to make a nice soft bed for her. We could put a box outside the back door."

"Oh, no, it's too cold now."

"This cat's used to sleeping under shrubs or in crawl spaces," I reassured him.

Steve shook his head. "I'll take care of her."

He padded a box with soft old towels, carted it upstairs, and set it next to his bed. And that's where Fang stayed for the next few weeks, except when she made brief exits through a sliding kitchen window that we'd propped partially open to allow her to come and go.

By Christmas vacation, Steve hovered over Fang's box like a midwife. He even shredded newspaper to line it. I worried a little about her age. I guessed she'd had several previous litters. I wondered how Steve would feel if she had any complications or if the kittens were stillborn. He'd fallen in love with this cat.

One morning right before Christmas he rushed downstairs.

"There's three babies in the box with Fang, Mom," he cried. "Three! And they all look fine, except their eyes are closed."

For weeks Steve watched as Fang raised her young. When it came time to place the kittens, we decided we'd keep Twilight, a longhaired tortoiseshell who'd been napping in the patio when a wind gust blew Steve's bike over on her. Though she picked herself right up, we figured she'd had the sense knocked out of her.

She'd started to cower under beds or in the closet. Once I found her in the dryer in the laundry room. Fang tried to watch out for her not-so-sharp daughter. If Twilight didn't come back in the evening, Fang would leap out the window and go on the hunt. Soon they'd come home, Fang yowling like a scolding granny.

We realize we didn't need more kittens. Groups like the SPCA now urged people to spay and neuter. Besides, these cats seemed ready to stay put. Steve agreed to accompany me to the vet.

"We'll take them in tomorrow," I promised, picking up the phone to make an appointment.

Though we searched everywhere the next day, we couldn't find the pair. Steve seemed so downcast that my heart went out to him.

"There'll be other cats showing up," I said. "They always do."

"But these were different. I took care of Fang when she first came, and the babies, too. These were *my* cats, not just alley cats."

A few weeks later, as I peeled potatoes for supper, I glimpsed a movement at the side of the kitchen window. Fang plopped to the floor. Within seconds Twilight hurtled through the slot. She stared at me with her dazed copper eyes and made a strange chirruping sound.

Guess they're hungry, I thought. I'd long since put away their bowls, but dragged them out, and filled them with water and kibble. As the pair ate, I reached down and ran my hands across their tummies. Oh, no. More kittens.

Weeks later Fang gave birth first, producing two kittens. She'd been nesting for days, shredding papers in Steve's room. Twilight hadn't nested at all. She just loped around the house, looking for crannies to hide in.

One night she jumped into a wicker wastebasket and proceeded to deliver her litter. Fang wandered downstairs for her nightly constitutional and paused when she saw Twilight's head and shoulders poking out of the basket. I swear she shook her head in disgust before she jumped through the window.

Twilight wouldn't let us near her. I'd brought in a box and kept trying to lift Twilight out of the basket, but she'd claw at me. I decided we'd best let her be. It was a long, hard delivery, but Twilight finally clambered out of the wastebasket and lurched to a corner where she fell asleep.

We peered down into the basket at two apparently normal kittens. I lifted them into the box I'd prepared, and then placed Twilight next to them. She swatted them away and climbed back out of the box. After the third try to get her to nurse her kittens, I gave up.

Steve and I didn't know what to do. I'd heard of cats that refused to nurse their kittens and decided to drive to the drugstore to get an eye dropper and some goat's milk. I went upstairs to get my purse.

"Look, Mom," Steve called. I ran downstairs and gazed into the box. Grandma Fang was there, patiently nursing the newborns. Steve and I quietly went upstairs and got Fang's own slightly larger babies, and after Twilight's kitties were finished nursing, we gently moved them aside so Fang's could have their turn.

For the next few weeks, Fang raised the entire clowder of kittens. Occasionally she'd wander around the house, hunting for Twilight. When she'd find her, curled atop a bookcase or huddled behind a bookcase, she'd hiss and screech, like an old scold.

Apparently, she finally forgave her witless daughter, because one day when the kittens were a couple of months old, the pair wandered off together. This time neither returned.

Steve's classmates adopted Fang's kittens; we kept Twilight's daughters. We'd run out of names, so dubbed them Spot and Rover. Though it might have seemed a newfangled notion, we took them to the vet to be spayed.

Spot eventually strayed, but Rover stayed . . . loyal to Steve through a dozen years.

Fang? Surely, she protected Twilight until they crossed the rainbow bridge. Mothers do what mothers do. It's not just *human* kindness.

KATHIE GIORGIO

HOW YOU ARE REMEMBERED

When Pearl's brother died, there was nothing for it but to invite his two ex-wives to dinner. The ex-wives were from so long ago; Tad passed away at eighty-four years old and his last divorce was final when he was forty-six. There'd been a long, unbroken string of women since then, but none that he knotted in marriage. The two ex-wives, Margo and Mary, were present from Tad's age twenty-eight to forty, and forty-one to forty-six, respectively. Pearl used to comment on the similarity of their names. After the second divorce, she wondered aloud if the next wife would be Margaret, Marian or Marti. This caused Tad to become twelve again and punch Pearl on her upper arm. She laughed, although the punch raised a bruise.

Pearl hadn't given a thought to the ex-wives through Tad's sudden illness (brain cancer, gone in five weeks), nor when he died, nor through the wake or the funeral. It was only two weeks after, when all was quiet again and Pearl was trying to settle into brotherlessness after seventy-eight years of being big-brothered that she thought of Margo and Mary. It was disorienting, really. Pearl's husband was gone, five years now. Her parents, long ago. And now her brother. There were no other siblings; there were no children, no sons nor daughters, no nieces nor nephews. Now there was only Pearl who had never been an Only before. Maybe, Pearl thought, previous pseudo-family could take the Only away. During that on/off period of seventeen years, Pearl had had Margo and Mary. Sisters-in-law. Those hyphenated and implied relationships lasted until they were severed by the bang of a judge's gavel.

They all, Pearl thought, loved Tad. Margo during the first marriage, Mary during the second. Pearl for her whole life.

"I must have them to dinner," Pearl said. "They should know he's gone." And they should know I'm still here, she didn't say aloud. There was no one to hear, but still, she was selective in what she aired.

It didn't take too long to find the ex-wives. Neither woman had remarried. And both women were still in the area. Pearl carefully worded her email to each of them:

Hello, Margo (Mary),

This is Pearl, Tad's sister. I know we haven't spoken in a long time. But I wanted to let you know that Tad passed on of brain cancer a few weeks ago. It was very sudden. He was eighty-four.

I should have thought to contact you before his funeral. I'm the only one left and all the arrangements fell to me, and I'm afraid in the chaos, it just didn't occur to me to include you. I know Tad would have wanted you there. So I would like to make amends to you and to him by asking you to dinner. Would you come next week Thursday around six? I am living now in Mother and Daddy's old house on the east side. I'm sure you remember it.

Most sincerely,
Pearl

Pearl didn't know in the least that Tad would have wanted the ex-wives there; in fact, she was sure he would have been against it. Neither divorce was an amicable affair. And in fact, both were the result of an affair that was more than amicable, but outside of each marriage. Mary was what split Margo from the family. And Pearl could no longer remember the name of the woman who sent Mary running. At that point, Tad's women became nameless and faceless and they were never invited to family events. Family events returned to the structure of Pearl's youth: just Mother, Daddy, Tad and herself. And her husband, of course, but Pearl's husband was quiet and he mostly sat in the striped wingback chair in the corner of the living room and observed. Pearl had to admit, she liked it that way. Returning home for Thanksgiving or Christmas or the celebration of an anniversary or a birthday was like returning to childhood, at least for a few hours. To a big brother who laughed and teased and slugged her on the upper arm. To parents who spoiled her. These last years, with just Tad and herself, family events were spent looking through photo albums. And now . . . well, now, Pearl supposed, every day was a family event. She was the family. It was an event to wake up when the others were no longer around to do so.

But there were these two women. The wives. The ex- wives. Sisters-in-law.

In the email, Pearl neglected to tell Margo or Mary that the other ex-wife was invited too. When they both accepted by the next morning, Pearl decided it was best to keep it a surprise.

When that Thursday arrived, Pearl was abuzz with nerves. She didn't really like to cook anymore, so she went to a grocery store and bought everything pre-made. A ham she'd only have to warm. Coleslaw in a plastic container that she could transfer to a serving bowl. Mashed potatoes and gravy that would appear on the table in the family silver tureen and gravy boat. Rolls, of course. A pie she could heat in the oven with the ham and fill Mother and Daddy's old house with the scent of fresh apples and ground cinnamon. Apple pie was Tad's favorite.

They would eat in the dining room. Pearl got out the china. She placed herself at the head and Margo and Mary to her left and right.

Pearl wondered what the ex-wives would expect her to look like now and she tried to dress to achieve their expectations. She was neat, in style, and conservative. She was neat and in style back in their days too, but the conservatism, she felt, was expected to come with maturity.

Margo, the first wife, was the first to arrive, which Pearl thought was appropriate. "Oh, Pearl," Margo said when Pearl let her in. "I'm so sorry. I can't believe he's gone!"

Pearl was taken aback. Even though she knew she'd grown older, Pearl hadn't applied the advancing years to Margo and Mary. She thought of the ex-wives as forty and forty-six, the ages they were when she last saw them. But here Margo was, eighty-four, and obviously so. "It was very sudden," Pearl said. "I guess we all expect to live forever."

She'd just hung up Margo's coat and ushered her into the living room when the doorbell rang again. She let in Mary and received the same shock.

"Oh," Margo said, when Mary was let into the room. "I didn't know she was going to be here."

Mary said nothing, but folded her hands at her waist.

"I wanted to see you both," Pearl said. "You were the only women Tad ever married." As the ham warmed in the oven and the pie added its familiar ambience, she served the women wine and cheese and crackers and black and green olives fresh from the can in tiny crystal bowls and plates. She sat between the two women on the couch and showed them the photo albums. They laughed over themselves. But as the years paged by and the wives disappeared and Tad grew older, and so did Pearl, and the parents disappeared and so did Pearl's husband and then the photographs disappeared altogether because there was no one to hold the camera anymore, they grew quiet. Pearl closed the final album and she felt like Tad's casket was closed all over again. At the funeral, the priest did just that in the narthex of the church, right before the casket was rolled in on what looked to Pearl like a stretcher. The only friends left to be pallbearers were at least Tad's age and they couldn't bear the weight. They positioned themselves around the stretcher to roll Tad in. But before they did so, Pearl rested her cheek, just for a minute, against the smoothest of wood. Wood that was more final than any door. She stayed there until the priest gently handed her off to an usher who led her to her seat at the front of the church. All by herself. No one on her left or right. No one to pat her knee or hold her hand. No one. She was an Only in a sea of friendly mourners. Her big brother was gone.

Now, she set the last photo album gently atop the others on the coffee table. "I think it's time for dinner," she said, and led the way into the dining room.

When they were all settled, meals ladled onto the pretty china plates, the ex-wives looked expectantly at Pearl. Mother and Daddy used to insist on grace, but in the latest years, Pearl and Tad hadn't. When they were young, Pearl and Tad had actually kicked each other under the table during prayers, and made faces at each other while their parents' eyes were reverently closed. Once their parents were gone, Pearl and Tad didn't kick or make faces, but they dispensed with the prayer. Despite hearing it for years, neither one could remember the words. Tad compensated by always lifting his wine glass and saying, "Here's to ya!" Pearl shrugged and lifted her glass. "Here's to ya," she said and then clinked the ex-wives' glasses as they joined in.

"You're sitting in your father's seat, Pearl," Mary said. "And I'm in yours."

"I'm where Tad used to sit," Margo said and she seemed to take some pleasure at this. Mary frowned.

"I thought this would be more comfortable," Pearl said. "Less gaps. Plus, I couldn't put you in your former places. You both used to sit in the same seat. Next to Tad."

Both women busied themselves with their utensils.

Their tongues, blessed with the first bottle of wine that accompanied them to the dining table, loosened further with the second bottle and they began to remember Tad. Stories were told. Pearl noticed that Mary matched Margo tale for tale, but was careful to not include any memories that were from before the first marriage ended.

Pearl wiped away a tear. "It's just so hard to believe he's gone."

"Well," Margo said, "of course he's been gone for me for a long time now. He's just gone in a different way." She took a reflective sip of her wine. "Not all of the memories are good ones. When he told me about . . . well, about you, Mary, it was the last straw. I knew he'd had affairs, of course, but you were the only one he wanted to make permanent."

Mary almost preened for a second, but then she seemed to deflate. She rested her elbows on the table. "He might have married me, but the affairs never stopped. I didn't wait for him to replace me. I left when I found out about the fourth affair since our wedding."

Pearl blinked. She didn't know there were women during the wives. That didn't sound like her brother. Yes, he loved women. But he never meant to hurt anyone. She was sure of that.

Margo laughed. "You left early," she said. "For me, you were number eight." She lifted her glass again, and Pearl wondered if she was going to say, "Here's to ya!" Instead, she studied the small amount of wine she had left. Pearl wondered what she saw there. "When he told me about you, that he wanted to marry you, I said I was leaving right then. And . . . I called him a few names. Not very nice ones, but fitting." She shook her head and the wine swelled. "He hit me."

Pearl's head about swiveled off her neck. "He hit you?" But Mary, she noticed, didn't startle at all. She only ate another piece of ham. "That doesn't sound like Tad."

Margo shrugged. "It didn't happen often, but it happened." She rubbed her upper arm. "That one left a good bruise, too."

Pearl touched her own arm.

Mary said, "It was the nights he came home drunk that were the worst." She finished her wine, then held out the glass for a refill. "I'd hear the car squeal in. One time, he forgot to open the garage door and just drove right through it. He called the insurance company and blamed it on the ice." She laughed. "It was winter, but the only ice was the rocks in his glass. He got out of the car and into the house, and then he passed out partway up the stairs. I usually undressed him and tucked him in after he passed out, but that night,

I let him go. Let him sleep on the stairs." She nodded, but then she rubbed her upper arm too.

Tad did like his drink. But so did Pearl. When their parents were gone, she and Tad often spent evenings together with a couple bottles of wine and a fire. Tad had the old wood-burning fireplace replaced with a gas one so that she could have the comfort and company of the flames at the flick of a switch. Even when he wasn't there with her, she had the fire. And a good bottle of wine.

"That doesn't sound like Tad either." Pearl set down her glass with a solid thump. "Let me get the pie and coffee," she said.

As she sliced and served the pie, she reflected, "I chose apple because it was Tad's favorite."

"No, it wasn't," Margo said. "His favorite was pecan."

"You're both wrong," Mary said. "He hated pie. He liked chocolate cake best. He loved my frosting. I always laced it with strong coffee."

Pearl hesitated, but then continued with the serving.

"When I was six," she said, after savoring her first bite of pie, washed down by the strong coffee Tad loved, "I had to have surgery on my eyes. I had strabismus, crossed eyes, you know." Both women looked at her; Pearl assumed they didn't know. They were sisters-in-law, pseudo-family; they weren't around when Pearl was a child. "Tad was twelve. I had to stay in the hospital for two nights. They probably zip you in and out in fifteen minutes now."

The ex-wives murmured agreement.

"Tad came to visit me in the hospital after the surgery. I couldn't see him; both my eyes were bandaged. He brought me a gift. I had to reach into a bag like a little blind girl and pull out this stuffed animal. 'Guess what it is,' he said." Pearl reached out now with her hands, ran her fingers through the air. Her fingers caught at nothing, but her memory held on tight. "I felt a nose and legs, a tail. And these puffballs. They were light and they squished, but I could tell they were circles. 'It's a poodle!' I said. And Tad cheered. I held that poodle all night long. I didn't actually see it until the next morning, when the bandages were taken off. I called the poodle Bon Bon. Its puffballs were lavender." Pearl patted the air. "Mother told me later that Tad touched almost every stuffed animal in the gift shop. He wanted to find something that I'd be able to see, even though I couldn't."

The women finished their pie and coffee. They talked about the weather.

They touched on politics. And then Margo and Mary went home. The door closed behind them with a bang like a judge's gavel. Pearl held a hand to her upper arm. She remembered the bruises left by a teasing big brother.

Since she used the good china and serving bowls, Pearl washed them all by hand and then returned them to their proper spots, the places her parents always kept them. Then she sat in the living room with only the fireplace casting light and shadows and flurries of heat, and she finished what was left of the third bottle of wine. Her toes, slipped out of her shoes, rested on the coffee table on either side of the photo albums. When the bottle was empty, there was nothing for it but to turn off the fireplace and head to bed. She decided to take with her the photo album with pictures from when she was six. And Tad was twelve.

Pearl slept now in Mother and Daddy's room. When she and her husband took ownership of the house after her mother died, three years after her father, Pearl decided they would want her in the big room they loved, with the private bath, the bay window overlooking the park across the street. Her childhood room, on the other side of the hallway, was just the same as it was when she moved out to get married. Tad's room, next to hers, was also the same. Pearl didn't feel the need to change them into anything else, a study, a library, a media room. When Pearl's husband passed, quietly as was his way, there was only her in that big house. Tad used to stay over sometimes, especially on those nights when the fire burned long and the bottles of wine multiplied to more. His room was always ready. It would remain ready.

On this night, before going on to bed, Pearl turned right and went into her childhood room. She saw it all again even before flipping on the light. The pink ruffled bedspread, knotted with hundreds of lavender bows. The white furniture, a bed, a dresser, a desk with a bookshelf holding *Little Women*, *The Five Little Peppers,* so many others. And on the bed, a stuffed poodle.

Pearl scooped Bon Bon up and carried him with her to her parents' bedroom. She settled him on the pillow that used to belong to her husband and then she propped herself beside him and paged through the photo album. From time to time, she reached out and patted the toy on his topknot. Without looking. Without seeing. But she knew he was there and what he was.

And then she rested her hand on her upper arm.

JENNIFER L. FREED

THANKS-GIVING

From a distance, as you walk your morning miles, you begin
to watch the woman standing near the waves.
Hours before the crowds arrive, she is
aiming her camera at an unimpressive
sand castle. She is soft, pale, thick
through her middle,
and something more

than middle-aged, and you think without hesitation
that she is happy,
and you wonder why
so many photos—first from one angle, then another—
and you decide she's from some land-locked place
where she would not stand out for having moon-white shoulders
glowing down on densely freckled forearms,
or high-waisted floral shorts,
or that gray halo of tightly permed hair,

and you think, maybe
she's here for some family
holiday, maybe all of this is new
to her—this salty, gull-strewn air,
this fine, warm sand, these unceasing waves—
maybe that's why she is happy, is savoring
her sand castle,
and you believe she is at ease
with herself, and you believe
she is loved—you know
she is loved—

and lately you've been noticing
your dried out body, your face with its deepening lines,
how your youngest child, your only son
and his new wife will smile and shrug away
your conversation,
and lately you've been wondering
whether you have done enough, are good
enough, and it isn't that
you think your husband doesn't love you,
but for so long you've been wanting
him to touch you, touch you
into faith that you are,
still, good enough
for him,

and now you see this aging woman, so pleased
with her castle, so at home within
herself, and she is
beautiful,
and you fall in love with her,
and you give thanks
for her,
though you do not share a single word as you walk by.

LOWELL JAEGER

A PRAYER TO INVISIBLE STARS

On our rented motor scooter
weaving through the breeze along the shore,
we inhale forgotten simple joys
of youth once more—our skin toasted brown,
our hair bleached with brine, the horizon
so blue, so generous, so deceptively endless.

We are in love and long married, no
small miraculous adventure on its own, having lasted
past crashing along the long road. And now
we carry with us what survives. We wear it
like a flag, a truce of goodwill, the two of us
scooting inland toward our hotel, past military

guards posted at gates to the base,
their black rifles in hand, stern-faced
and dutiful. We see the danger; don't misunderstand us,
please. *They're just boys,* my wife says, and says it
with a heart full of hard-earned forgiveness, says it
like a prayer to invisible stars, the ones we know,

eternally burning through darkness. She waves,
and the soldiers lower their guns, just boys again,
smiling and waving. Don't misunderstand; we comprehend
the world is hemorrhaging sadness. Our small cause
is to risk our brittle skulls on an open highway
in a foreign land. We hold fast to love. We hold to the other

and won't let go.

DIFFICULT WILD TERRAIN

Cold wind blasting the truck broadside.
Threatening horizons of blue/black
encroaching storms. That image
sticks with me most, the pair of us

bumping along washboard back roads
in search of . . . well, in pursuit of . . .
well, hungry for difficult wild terrain,
sweeping landscapes so unforgivably gorgeous
we'd fallen hushed in reverence and awe.

She recalls we'd stalled mesmerized,
speechless in highland ranch country,
thrilled by an eagle diving through a dervish
of whirling grit, then winging heavenward,
fistful of prairie dog. Finally,

folding himself on a fence rail,
ripping crimson strips of flesh.
The blood, bone and gristle—terrible and revealing—backlit
with roiling torrents of violent sky.
She and I . . .
a snapshot of a lightning flash
long marriage. I, bedazzled behind the wheel,
and she beside me, reaching to take my hand.

Both of us goose-bumped
in the beauty of hell's wrath, thunder crack,
and cloud bursting downpour. Each of us sheltered
in loving the other. Alive in the world

we were born to explore.

RUTH SILIN

SMALL DISTRESSES

He is embodiment of goodness in all things
that matter, like trust and honor, loyalty
and generosity.
He never passes an outstretched hand
without responding.
He opens doors, pulls out chairs, remembers
my mother's birthday, and never forgets
to put out the trash.

Yet he manages to spill coffee
on the paper before I get to read it,
leave no milk for my morning cereal,
forgets to pick up towels after he showers.
Most annoying, leaves his shoes in
the middle of the room, a constant hazard
that I fear will some day trip me.
He has told the joke about the Priest, the Rabbi
and the Minister so many times that I fear
we will lose dear friends who pretend
they are hearing it for the first time.
I could go on about the things he does that
make me much annoyed, but take away
these small distresses and he would be
someone he is not.
And, not so incidentally, he thinks that I am
just about perfect.

THE SCORE CARD

The Pastor described his virtuous deeds,
tears falling softly on the faces of his friends.
stained glass windows filterering the sun.
I wiped my eyes and sank lower in my seat,
remembering the forsythia and flowering
shrubs he planted.
Did I take the time to hold his hand
as he did mine?

One day will someone see a flowering bush
and say with some affection, *I knew one*
who planted this, a generous and thoughtful
soul who left the world a better place.
Is there still time to plant a bush?
Who will remember me
as I remember him?

ANDRENA ZAWINSKI

IT IS ENOUGH FOR NOW, VILLANELLE FOR MORNINGS

It is enough in this first breath of morning
to lie here with you, light slipping between us,
our fingers laced, lids still swollen with sleep.

Enough to listen to the distant sound of the early train,
song of buoys in the bay, wind bells in the breeze.
It is enough in this first breath of morning

to talk about the night's dreams, and to dream
across seas, up rivers, into the wild hills,
our fingers laced, lids still swollen with sleep.

It is enough to hold onto each other,
to keep each other still and quiet in place.
It is enough in this first breath of morning,

enough to breathe in the sky, the bright of sun
crossing and washing the continents of our bodies.
It is enough in this first breath of morning,
our fingers laced, lids still swollen with sleep.

JOHN L. SILVER

PROSPERO

(from versions of the nursery rhyme "Ring Around The Roses" and also E. A. Poe's "Mask of the Red Death")

the eagle's on the steeple
lying to the people

we all fall down

prospero would blind us
with such lies of his to bind us

ashes ashes
we all fall down

rotting bodies stink
put on ice at Wollman Rink

we all fall down

knocking at the windows
knocking at the doors

we all fall down

give us distance, some distance
or we all fall down

with ashes many ashes
on your forehead cross the spot

then with rulers take a measure
to trace your family plot

please, again please
keep six feet back and round
a cloth to hide your visage
while the virus hunts us down

walking on the harbor
our great green lady cries

a tissue a tissue
he would knock her down

the cows are in the meadow
eating buttercups

for those who made great sacrifice
we all stand up

MARY KAY RUMMEL

A PANDEMIC STORY: SISTER THERESA LOUISE

It was 1917.
Just fifteen, you kissed your mother and sister,
climbed the street car to Randolph Street,
walked a path through the woods
carrying your small travel bag

Near the river at the stone convent
framed by trees,
you entered through the heavy door.

On the feast of St. Joseph,
you rose in the dark, a poem
composing itself in your heart—

In the early morning light
I will dress myself in white
To give myself to you
Who gave yourself for me.

You knelt at the altar,
with just-shorn hair, in wool habit
and veil, repeating your new name,
Theresa Louise, Theresa Louise,
getting to know the sound and feel.

You slept, hungry,
with other young novices,
in white night gowns,
lithe as birches in wind,

hidden from each other
by white curtains
in a forty bed dorm.

Days in silence. After prayers, you
scrubbed stairs, watched your sisters
climb, some growing weaker.

On calloused knees you scoured
bathroom floors, then prayed some more,
studied Mary and Joseph
in stained glass above the altar

Theresa Louise, young heart
storing-up light, your voice chanting . . .

When your sisters fell sick in 1918
and your superior refused them medications,
saying *God wants us to suffer,*
did you still believe?

The dorm became an infirmary,
healthy sisters caring for the sick,
until a storm of flu killed all of you.

You were my father's favorite cousin—
your death, he said, was the greatest grief
in his twelve-year-old life.

Is being dead the end of your story
the book closed?
Is this poem the end of your tale?
I hold on to your prayers
even as they slip away.

LORI LEVY

MEMORIAL SERVICE ON ZOOM

In memory of Blanche Rosloff

I witness your impact, Blanche. You are here in the sobbing warmth
of the gratitude expressed—the blessing you were to your daughters and
grandchildren, who you nourished with stories and songs, poems, art.
Who felt loved, heard, supported by you in their ups and downs.

If I could paint you, Blanche, you'd be the dancing waters
of the Bellagio, your water colored red, yellow, blue, green,
spraying high and wide, splashing on us all,
brightening lives the way your paintings brightened walls.
Because of you, the poor, hungry kids in your Head Start class
in Kansas City, Missouri, received their lunches on time.
Because of you, Blacks and Latinos in Los Angeles
were given their fair housing rights.
Many thank you today: mentor, role model. Many cry—
including the rabbi, who calls you a rare blend: strong
as steel, yet soft and compassionate, like your poetry.
She trembles when she holds up the love between you and Reuben,
how you cherished each other for seventy-six years—from the moment
you first touched in a meadow by the Hudson.
The cantor, too, wipes away tears.

You made white hair elegant, says a friend.
In your honor, says your oldest, your family wore aqua, turquoise,
lavender to your funeral. Favorites in your wardrobe.

I am left with memories of your laughter over lunches. Our sharing.
I am left with your poems: "meringue crested waves," hummingbirds,
tangerines from your garden—mixed with the darkness you met head-on.
Cancer in the family. Deaths. A mother too delusional to be there for you,
who threw to the floor the gloves you bought her for Mother's Day.
I am left with wonder at the trail you blazed. The love that bloomed
in a girl from the Bronx whose dad made her eggs with kippers and
onions every Sunday morning, the only dish he could cook.

GERARD SARNAT

APPRECIATING THE FIRST MORNING OF DAYLIGHT SAVINGS TIME

Mudita is my favorite inspiration in Buddhism.

In Pāli it roughly means Empathetic Joy.

I'm not sure if there's an equivalent single word in English.

That's one part of why I love it.

The other reason is that cultivating *Mudita* has been challenging.

The Buddha made lists:
Mudita is the third *Brahma-Vihara,* or Noble Abode.

It is surrounded by equally worthy goals:
Lovingkindness, Compassion and Equanimity.

Into my eighth decade, except when in physician mode,
I have had some difficulty not considering cripples They.

Now a grimacing pretzel, walking stick
in my left hand and lurching to the right, I am They.

Since housebound moving as little as possible,
it is improbable I will be your individual *Mudita* challenge.

But we are all around should you wish to try engaging
with simple acknowledgment, perhaps just a smile to start.

Although I appreciate your Compassion,
my purpose is not personal.

I'm able to maintain Equanimity on the whole,
and today if warm may try to sit outside in the garden.

Family and friends offer good will and take excellent care;
medical interventions very possibly will make me well.

And in the meantime using a walker is less dangerous
than a cane and allows me to maintain upright posture.

I am lucky compared to those of us who will never
be made whole, or have painful terminal illnesses.

Why do I write this now? Because once better,
like blind people who regain vision, humans might forget.

With *Metta* (Lovingkindness) for all sentient beings.

JOHN LAUE

MY LIFE AND THE CORONA VIRUS

It's not that I want to die, not at all. I'm still providing useful services in the arts and otherwise, but I'm at an okay stopping point. If the universe wants to take me, I'm ready to go.

Even if I lived to be a hundred, I couldn't equal the things I've already done, the friends I've made, goals I've achieved. I've been an outlier, taking opportunities others missed, attempting things few people have, getting some unusual jobs done.

My life to this point wasn't all good; it's been the polar opposite at times, but I'm grateful for it. I'm not perfect; there's always more I could have done, and probably should have, but I've come to the conclusion I haven't wasted my time.

It would be terrible if you were close to death and you'd played it so safe and accomplished so little that you felt you'd never lived. This might be stretching the metaphor too much, but I've known people I believe are examples of that.

My wife has a male relative who's able-bodied but lives off the state and does very little besides watching TV. He justifies his existence by saying, "What are we here for except to reproduce ourselves?" He's fathered two boys, both of whom are in serious trouble with the law and otherwise.

I also thought of an old acquaintance, Bill P., who was kicked out of a monastery and failed to become a Catholic priest. He constantly strove for some great achievement, his own "masterpiece" that would bring him acclaim and allow him to believe his life worthwhile. He was working on a new type of musical notation the last time I saw him. I doubt he was saved by that.

❦ ❦ ❦

The Covid crisis is here, lies like a dark fog over our future, makes us stay home, turns some of us philosophical, causes people like me to assess our existence.

I know people who are wiser than I, more intelligent, more grounded, more spiritually advanced. Some are at levels where they can actually cause changes in the warp and weave of what we assume to be reality, perform feats we think of as magical, alter local and general history in ways beyond my comprehension.

I believe once people reach for perfection and become fully enlightened, they have to do nothing else: they've achieved their purpose. As sitting buddhas or saints they make wonderful models for the whole world to emulate. People like me, on the other hand, like to be known not for what we are, which is flawed and may be seen as pedestrian, but for what we do and have done.

I value the role of the bodhisattva, one who aids people in their quests for perfection. With the limited avenues available to me, I do what I can to make the world a better place. I know that like everyone, I probably could have reached a type of perfection myself, but I didn't see that as a course I wanted to pursue.

Some like me see the lamentable state of the world and vow to do whatever we can to advance the cause of human evolution, We get our self-worth by doing good and helping to move people along. We suspect we could do better if we were more perfect, but instead of mourning our loss of potential, we turn to compensatory activities.

My spiritual father, Dr. David Shupp, whose therapy groups I attended for many years, once told me, "Give, give until you have no more to give; then give some more!" That may be overstating the case, but it sums up one way to live a meaningful life.

The Corona crisis is changing our lives now. I'm told my wife and I are quite at risk because of our ages (eighty and eighty-three). If we contract it, our chances of dying (fifteen percent or more?), are higher than for other age groups. My maternal grandfather died of the flu in 1918. I wonder if that makes me more likely to die from this new scourge.

So far Sandy and I are fine. I've survived every illness my close relatives suffered from: two major cancers (lung—my uncle, prostate—my father) plus heart rending periods of mental distress (my mother died in Greystone Park, the New Jersey State Hospital for the Insane after twenty-three years there).

Operations helped with the cancers. I lost the upper lobe of my right lung in the first; my prostate was excised for the second. I apparently still have some prostate cancer active although so far my PSA (an indicator of that) hasn't increased enough to be treated. So I'm a grateful survivor.

As for the mental illnesses, after my breakdown when I thought I was in hell even though I'm a humanist and not religious, and prepared to take my own life, I was lucky enough to be in a therapy group with the good doctor who I call my "second father." He put me on antipsychotic medications that I've continued for over fifty years. They allow me to work and play somewhat like "normal" people.

For the last few years Sandy and I assumed nothing was going to kill us very soon, so we could enjoy our older years without worrying. All we have is the "now" we said, and we must make the best of it. Our main concern, especially my wife's, was that we might run out of money if we lived as long as we might, say ten or fifteen more years.

By bringing death close to us, the pandemic forces us to assess our lives. Have they been meaningful? Taken as a whole, were we good citizens of cities, states, countries, the world? At eighty years old, I wrote a series of small poems about that. Just one of these will suffice:

Who's to object if
I say my life was well lived?
At 80 who cares?

Grappling with thoughts of death came early for me: while I attended graduate school at San Francisco State University, I worked in the funeral industry delivering flowers to cemeteries and services, earning enough to support my graduate studies. I was so moved by experiences doing this in Colma, the eighteen-cemetery city adjacent to San Francisco, that I produced a book of poems titled with that town's name, nominally about death, but really a series of meditations on the natural beauty I found in the cemeteries that I enjoyed as sculpture gardens.

A few times in my life I did things I believe were heroic; at other times, things others thought of as heroic didn't feel heroic to me at all—like when

I let second language Mexican students in my English classes speak Spanish, something my fellow teachers strongly condemned.

Years later I found out that the comfort this gave certain kids immortalized me in their eyes. A few of these children of uneducated field workers went on to have excellent careers in education and health services. One said I'd inspired her.

Sometimes I reached worthwhile, even almost magical goals, but got little approval or approbation except what I gave myself. As chair of the county's mental health board, I successfully lobbied in Sacramento to change the state's public schools' health curriculum framework to include more attention to student's mental health and welfare. This caused positive changes in the entire country's health textbooks. I consider this my own "masterpiece."

Of course my life hasn't been all that successful: I've failed miserably sometimes such as in my first marriage where I was without a clue how to be a decent partner, then much later, when I knew I should be a better teacher, but was too burnt out, angry, and depressed to achieve this. It struck me as ironic that some of my fellows still thought I did an adequate job.

I was fortunate enough to retire from teaching at fifty-five before I fell apart completely, an act which released me somewhat from my acute conscience pangs. This early retirement might have actually saved my life. At the very least it convinced me to use the rest of my time wisely.

As the little poem mentioned above testifies, I've given myself a passing grade for a life that swung like a pendulum from inspiring successes to miserable failures and back again. I'm still achieving positive results for society, coordinating poetry readings, sending writings and photos that are accepted for publication, supporting the arts in the Monterey Bay Area and the world. I believe I have nothing more to prove.

The most powerful event that brought me satisfaction was my eightieth birthday party, a dinner with about forty-five people attending. I invited folks from three different locations: Watsonville for the teachers' group, Monterey and Carmel for the poetry people, and Santa Cruz for poetry, prose and TV groups.

The eight-person Watsonville contingent knew me as a teacher, and not a very good one at that. Although I was sure I'd done quite well teaching Peer

Counseling classes, none of my colleagues and bosses knew what went on there because, like in a therapy group (I had many years of experience with those), the main rule was confidentiality. Watsonville people also had little knowledge of my successes in California and nationally.

Most of the people from Carmel and Monterey across the bay knew me as a magazine editor, poet, and coordinator of readings, but not as a teacher/ counselor.

The Santa Cruz group knew me mainly as a TV program director and interviewer, a prose writer, a poetry contest conductor, and mental health board member.

Almost no one from any of the three places knew about unusual events earlier in my life, such as winning Cal's 1959 Ina Coolbrith Poetry Prize, and before that being probably the only white musician in the entire 1950's black music scene while playing saxophone with singer Lord Luther and his Kingsmen, a prominent rhythm and blues band that gigged all over California.

I was fortunate enough to have my brother in spirit, Rick Jevons, as the master of ceremony for my party. He'd been an assistant principal at the school where I worked, and, at my bidding, had joined me in county mental health activities on boards and as mental health speakers in schools after we both retired. I hadn't given Rick a list of things I wanted mentioned and had little idea what he was going to say, but he managed to hit on most of my major accomplishments.

He even mentioned things I hadn't thought that important for the groups to know, such as my having out-of-the-closet gay speakers in my Peer Counseling classes, something I thought vital, but of which few of my colleagues were aware. There was no specific rule against it, but we all knew that no teacher was supposed to do this at that high school whose administrators feared parent and school board complaints.

I kept producing peer counselors for fourteen years with the class featuring many controversial speakers unknown to administrators until a new principal found out and eliminated it, fearing the possible repercussions if some of its activities became widely known. Losing this favorite class that I could see greatly aided students' mental health and happiness caused me to retire.

Rick, a blues enthusiast with thousands of records and tapes, also told the groups that while in San Francisco with Lord Luther's band, I'd been taken to meet Little Richard who had the whole penthouse at the Booker T. Washington Hotel set up for sex when I arrived.

Although the dinner attendees mostly sat at tables with people they knew, some mingled rather freely. It was as if these disparate groups of members representing separate portions of my life coalesced into one great body. With my psychology background (a degree from Berkeley), and interest in the brain, I pictured the scene as similar to completing a fabulous series of new neuronal connections.

I see myself as a "connector" introducing people to information, products of the arts (including my own), and other people. It fits the Buddhist bodhisattva role I try to embody, a person who helps others become more enlightened. At my party an analyst friend also said I fit the Jungian archetype of the "Wounded Healer." I took that as a great compliment.

In a certain sense, the party made me feel like my life had reached a benchmark of completion with my accomplishments now visible to everyone. This also made me feel vindicated because some people present had criticized me as a teacher (without knowing what was really going on) and still sold me short. Because of the party they became aware of my achievements outside their domains, feats I considered compensated for my years of borderline poor English teaching, One especially critical colleague even said to me later, "I wish I'd have done some of those things."

Today we're told to cocoon in our houses. During some years of my life, I wouldn't have obeyed those orders, taking the risks rather lightly because I couldn't imagine dying.

At other times I became so depressed and down on myself, I almost didn't care if I lived or died. But now at eighty-three, strong and relatively healthy and with Sandy healthy also, I'm taking precautions, convinced my life has passed muster and is worth saving.

As for "masterpieces": I don't believe everyone needs to achieve them to consider their lives worthwhile. Many have successful, stable existences full of small, positive acts without particular feats standing out. For some people like me who are diagnosed as mentally ill, just hanging in there can be a worthy accomplishment.

I've produced writing that won small prizes, had stories, poems, and photos I'm proud of accepted by local and international galleries and magazines, written and gotten published five books of poems and one full book of advice for people with psychiatric diagnoses, interviewed people for TV, put on local and national poetry contests.

As a non-theist, I've never thought myself entitled to anything, even breath, so I remain grateful for the qualities that enabled me to pull off these achievements. And as "wounded healer," I caused changes in national health education that I believe still improve millions of people's lives.

Usually successes of this magnitude are attained only by legislators or other "important" people, not semi-anonymous high school teachers or critically neglected poets. But Percy Bysshe Shelley called poets the "unacknowledged legislators of the world" and didn't limit it to "major" poets. As for high school teachers, we never know what effects our ideas might have, even on the world's future leaders.

Without experiences as both teacher and poet I probably couldn't have achieved what I did. My knowledge of the education system and my poetic ability to write convincingly combined to make me an effective instrument of change. The difficulties and setbacks that plagued me at times didn't prevent me from attaining this largest goal; in fact, they probably helped in my quest, generating the powerful urge to achieve beyond my everyday self and compensate for the times I thought I didn't measure up.

MILTON TEICHMAN

HAIRCUTS

She gives free haircuts to the homeless,
and then to people coming out of prison,
and then to battered women.

I am awed by such love.

And when I'm about to do a modest kindness,
I think a dozen times:
Is it wise, is it safe,
what's the cost,
what's the benefit?

So many internal battles
where none should be at all.

What's wrong with me?
Why don't I start giving myself away?

HEART CURRENTS

Strange the shifting currents in the heart.
I've seen bad flow from good, and good from bad—

I've seen love darken to jealousy,
piety turn to fanaticism,
faith harden to arrogance.

And I've seen lust become love,
contempt become caring,
indifference turn to passionate concern.

So strange to know that the shifting currents of the heart
are in motion everywhere—in my friends, my intimates,
in strangers I pass on the street.

More sobering to know these waters shift
within me.

I cannot have the faith of Abraham, the humility of Moses,
or the integrity of Job,
but I pray that in my own days the good in me remains good
and the bad becomes good.

HEARTS BREAK DIFFERENTLY

They can shatter like a vase
that falls from the shelf.
They can harden
like clay in the sun,
earth without rain.

Or they can break open,
become vessels
for pains and pangs of others—
for the mother who has lost her child,
the neighbor trapped in addiction,
the immigrant living in fear.

There must be other ways
hearts can break
I haven't even thought of.
If mine should break one day,
let it break open all the way.

HEATHER TOSTESON

TRUST THE EMPTINESS WITHIN

Trust the emptiness within
and the rain sifting gently
through palm, jacaranda and mimosa,
church bells tolling for joy,
east and west, north and south,
on *el Día de la independencia.*
For we never begin again. We beget.
And forget.

And beget again
watching hummingbirds hover,
then rest, wings closed
on the smallest twig
on the one dead branch
of the largest, most vibrant tree
in our borrowed garden.

The doves above take without stint
what the world freely gives,
leaf cover, air to breathe and spread
their wings in, yet one more
moment of perfect tranquility
fully absorbed into our being
like manna received for what it really is.

We are not here to be saved, redeemed,
transformed. We are just here to live.
Even the dove turns its back on us.
The hummingbird moves to its own
inner *ritmo,* and out on the street,
a world away, a minute, cars
and trucks slur through the residue
of a hurricane to the east of us,
a typhoon to the west.

We're drenched in goodness.
Fíjese. Just *fíjese.*
At our age. Let's stay this way
as long as the hummingbird,
and the dove and the light above.

CONTRIBUTORS

Lenore Balliro, a garden mentor and art maker, lives in Gloucester, Massachusetts. She has worked with adult literacy programs in the Boston area for most of her professional life, where she has encouraged the integration of poetry into the curriculum. Her work has appeared in a number of national literary journals and anthologies.

Kevin Stuart Brodie is a playwright, screenwriter, storyteller, and poet. Three of his plays have been produced and two screenplays have been optioned by production companies. He also recently won his very first story slam. Kevin has won fourteen scriptwriting contests and festivals and been twice nominated for the Pushcart Prize in poetry.

Bonni Chalkin is a Reiki master, intuitive healer, possibility coach, artist, and writer. Her work has been published in the anthology *Re-Creating Our Common Chord* (Wising Up Press) as well as *And Then* magazine, and her paintings have sold in various countries. She is passionate about helping people embrace their power and follow their intuition. She is currently working on a memoir.

Marion Deutsche Cohen is the author of thirty-two collections of poetry or memoir; her newest prose collection is *Not Erma Bombeck: Diary of a Feminist 70s Mother* (Alien Buddha Press). She is also the author of two memoirs about spousal chronic illness, a trilogy diary of late-pregnancy loss, and *Crossing the Equal Sign*, about the experience of mathematics.

DC Diamondopolous is an award-winning novelette, short story, and flash fiction writer with over 250 stories published internationally in print and online magazines, literary journals, and anthologies, inclduing: *34th Parallel, So It Goes: The Literary Journal of the Kurt Vonnegut Museum and Library, Ball State University, Lunch Ticket, Progenitor,* and *Blue Lake Review.*

Norita Dittberner-Jax has just published her sixth collection of poetry, *Now I Live Among Old Trees* (Nodin Press). *Crossing the Waters* (Nodin, 2017) won the Midwest Book Award in Poetry. Norita has won awards for her work, including several nominations for the Pushcart Prize. A poetry editor for Red Bird Chapbooks, she lives in Saint Paul, Minnesota. In regard to the poem, "Relic," in the division of her parents' household, she asked for the relic.

Terri Elders, LCSW, a lifelong writer and editor, has contributed to nearly 150 anthologies, including multiple editions of *Chicken Soup for the Soul.* She writes feature articles and travel pieces for regional, national and international publications. She lives in her native Southern California, not far from her beloved Pacific.

S J Engstrom's writing can be found in *Re-Creating Our Common Chord*, the Peace Collection at Swarthmore College, and *The Willow Review*. Her current non-fiction project about her father's WW II service in England is based on the daily correspondence between her parents. She teaches Humanities at College of Lake County, IL and lives in Lake Geveva, WI.

Kevin Fidgeon is a retired court administrator, community organizer, youth and family activist in Kenya and Washington, DC, and an active member of the Rehoboth Beach Writers' Guild of Delaware.

Jennifer L. Freed lives in Massachusetts. Recent work appears in *Atticus Review, Naugatuck River Review, Rust + Moth, The Worcester Review*. Her chapbook, *These Hands Still Holding*, was a finalist in the 2013 New Women's Voices competition. She is recipient of the 2020 Samuel Washington Allen Prize and has recently completed a full-length manuscript based on the repercussions of her mother's stroke.

Lee Gaitan is an award-winning author of three books, including her latest release, *Lite Whines and Laughter: Mild Rants and Musings on the Mundane*. She has contributed chapters to best-selling anthologies and her work has been featured on *The Huffington Post, Erma Bombeck Humor Writers' Workshop, Mothers Always Write, Enchanted Conversation,* and *Bella Grace* among others.

Kathie Giorgio is the author of five novels, two story collections, an essay collection, two poetry chapbooks, and a full-length poetry collection. She's been nominated for Pushcart Prizes in fiction and poetry, awarded the Outstanding Achievement Award from the Wisconsin Library Association, the Silver Pen Award and the Pencraft Award for Literary Excellence, and the

Eric Hoffer Award In Fiction.

Jo Going resides in a coastal Alaskan village after many years living in a remote wilderness homestead cabin. Her writing is published in many journals and anthologies. Her book of poems and paintings, *Wild Cranes* (National Museum of Women in the Arts), won the Library Fellows Award and is held in the permanent collection of the Museum of Modern Art. Her books combining poetry and paintings can be experienced at her website.

John Grey, an Australian poet and US resident, recently published in *Soundings East*, *Dalhousie Review* and *Connecticut River Review* with work upcoming in *West Trade Review*, *Willard and Maple* and the *MacGuffin*.

Patrick Cabello Hansel is the author of the poetry collections *The Devouring Land* (Main Street Rag) and *Quitting Time* (Atmosphere Press). He has published poems and prose in over sixty-five journals, including *Crannog*, *Ilanot Review*, *Hawai'i Pacific Review*, *Ash & Bones*, *RiverSedge* and *Lunch Ticket*, and won awards from the Loft Literary Center and the Minnesota State Arts Board.

Stephanie Hart is the author of *Mirror Mirror: A Collection of Memoirs and Stories*. Her essays and short stories have appeared in numerous anthologies, including *Re-Creating Our Common Chord* (Wising Up Press) as well as literary magazines, *The Sun*, *Jewish Currents*, *And Then*, *Home Planet News*, and *Ducts.org*. She is working on a novel about the McCarthy era.

J.O. Haselhoef is an American writer, the author of *Give & Take: Doing Our Damnedest NOT to be Another Charity in Haiti*. She has also written for literary journals such as *Storm Cellar*, *San Fedele Press*, and *Fiction Southeast*.

Lowell Jaeger (Montana Poet Laureate 2017-2019) has taught creative writing at Flathead Valley Community College for the past thirty-seven years. He is author of nine collections of poems and founding editor of Many Voices Press, a non-profit press promoting Native American poets of the West. His verse-play, *Someday I'd Write This Down*, was published recently by Shabda Press.

Lorraine Jeffery has a bachelor's degree in English and her MLIS in library science. She has won poetry prizes in state and national contests and published widely in various journals and anthologies, including *Clockhouse*, *Kindred*,

Calliope, Canary, Ibbetson Street, Rockhurst Review, Naugatuck River Review, Orchard Press, Two Hawks, Halcyon, Healing Muse and *Bacopa Press.*

Mary E. Kendig authored and illustrated the children's book *Wonderful Words: Fun Poems About Words* and recently completed its sequel. She has also served as a guest editor for Southern New Hampshire University's online literary journal, *The Penman Review*. Mary is a contributing writer in an upcoming anthology, *Letters to Loved Ones: A Journey Through Grief.*

Michael Konik is the author of many books of fiction, poetry, essays, and non-fiction, most recently *The Unexpected Guest: How a Homeless Man from the Streets of Los Angeles Redefined Our Home*, and a contributor to Wising Up's anthology *The Kindness of Strangers.*

John Laue has edited *San Francisco Review* and *Monterey Poetry Review*, and won awards for his writing beginning with the Ina Coolbrith Poetry Prize at The University of California. With five published poetry books, the most recent *A Confluence of Voices Revisited*, ((Futurecycle Press) and a book of prose advice for people psychiatrically diagnosed, he coordinates Monterey Bay Poetry Consortium readings.

Lori Levy's poems have appeared in *Rattle, Nimrod, Confrontation, Paterson Literary Review, Mom Egg Review,* and numerous other literary journals and anthologies, as well as in medical humanities journals. One poem was read on a program for BBC Radio 4. She and her husband live in Los Angeles, where they enjoy having their children and grandchildren nearby.

Janet McCann taught at Texas A&M for forty-six years before retirement. Her latest poetry book is *The Crone at the Casino* (Lamar University Press).

Wendy Jones Nakanishi has published book reviews, literary articles and critical monographs on the topic of English literature; creative fiction detailing her thirty-six years in Japan as an academic, the wife of a Japanese farmer and the mother of three sons; and, under the pen name of Lea O'Harra, three crime fiction novels set in Japan.

Don Noel is retired after four decades' prizewinning print and broadcast journalism in Hartford CT. He received his MFA in Creative Writing from Fairfield University in 2013. He has since published more than five dozen short stories and non-fiction pieces, but has two novellas and a novel still looking for publishers.

Andy Oram is a writer and editor in the computer field. Print publications where his writings have appeared include *The Economist* and *Vanguardia Dossier*. His poems have been published in *Ají*, *Arlington Literary Journal*, *Genre: Urban Arts*, *Heron Clan*, *Offcourse*, *Panoply*, *Soul-Lit*, and *Speckled Trout Review*. He has lived in the Boston area for more than thirty years.

John Pierce is a high school teacher from Central Texas who writes when he should be grading papers. Some of his recent work has appeared in *Workers Write*, *Time of Singing*, and *Right Hand Pointing*.

Dorothy Oliver Pirovano accumulated hundreds of bylines as a reporter and editor for a daily newspaper, taught journalism and free-lanced before joining a national public relations firm and rising through the ranks to become its CEO. Now retired, her writing has turned to memoirs, recording the past and present in short pieces that capture her family's history for future generations.

Mary Kay Rummel is a former poet laureate of Ventura County, CA. Her ninth book of poetry, *Nocturnes: Between Flesh and Stone* has just been published (Blue Light Press). She recently co-edited *Psalms of Cinder & Silt*, community poems by survivors of recent California fires published by Solo Press. She divides her time between Minneapolis and Ventura.

Nicholas Samaras is from Patmos, Greece (the "Island of the Apocalypse") and, at the time of the Greek Junta military dictatorship ("Coup of the Generals") was brought in exile to be raised further in America. He's lived in Greece, England, Wales, Belgium, Switzerland, Italy, Austria, Germany, Yugoslavia, Jerusalem, thirteen states in America. He writes from a place of permanent exile.

Terry Sanville lives in San Luis Obispo, California with his artist-poet wife and two plump cats. His stories and essays have been accepted more than four hundred times for publication in commercial and literary journals, magazines, and anthologies. Two of his stories were nominated for Pushcart Prizes and one for inclusion in the Best of the Net Anthology.

Gerard Sarnat MD won prizes/been nominated for handfuls of Pushcarts/ Best of Net Awards, authored four collections, is widely published including recently by Dartmouth, Penn, Oberlin, Brown, Harvard, Stanford, Columbia,

Chicago, Wesleyan, Johns Hopkins, *Review Berlin, New Ulster, Gargoyle, Margie, Main Street Rag, New Delta Review, Free State Review, Brooklyn Review, Los Angeles Review, San Francisco Magazine, New York Times.*

Ruth Margolin Silin, retired director of development at a pediatric hospital, has had her work appear in many journals and anthologies. She focuses on love, family, death, and loss while trying to maintain a light touch along the way. Her poem commemorating the tenth anniversary of September 11th won an award from Mount Wachusetts College. She resides in Newton, MA.

Mark Tarallo is a writer based in Washington, DC. His fiction and poetry have appeared in *Abbey, Asphodel, Angel Face, Beltway, District Lines, Innisfree Poetry Journal, Manorborn, Red Mountain Review, The Best of Vine Leaves Literary Journal*, and the Wising Up anthologies *Connected: What Remains As We All Change* and *Surprised by Joy.*

Milton Teichman, a retired professor of English and Jewish Studies (Marist College) has written on English literature, the literature of the Holocaust, and other literary topics. He is also a writer of fiction (*A Teacher of the Holocaust and Other Stories*, 2015) as well as of poetry. He has had a parallel career as a painter and sculptor and has shown his work in galleries in the U.S. and in Mexico, including a 2019 retrospective at the Cape Cod Museum of Art.

Johnny Townsend is a climate crisis refugee who relocated from New Orleans to Seattle in the wake of Hurricane Katrina. An ex-Mormon who volunteered two years as a full-time missionary, he advocates now for LGBTQ rights, women's equality, and racial justice both in his former church and throughout society. His latest essay collection is *Am I My Planet's Keeper?*

Gary Young's most recent books are *That's What I Thought* (Persea Books), and *Precious Mirror*, translations from the Japanese from White Pine Press. His many honors include the Shelley Memorial Award, and the William Carlos Williams Award from the Poetry Society of America. He teaches creative writing and directs the Cowell Press at UC Santa Cruz.

Andrena Zawinski has received awards for her poetry's lyricism, form, spirituality, and social concern. Her latest book is *Landings* (Kelsay Books); others are *Something About* (a PEN Oakland Award) and *Traveling in Reflected Light (*a Kenneth Patchen Prize) as well as several smaller collections.

ACKNOWLEDGMENTS

Charles Brockett and Heather Tosteson's "Together for the Long Haul" is excerpted from their book *Sharing the Burden of Repair: Reentry after Mass Incarceration* (Wising Up Press, 2020).

Jennifer L. Freed previously published "Golden Door" in *Amsterdam Quarterly* (2017), "Angel" in *Off the Coast* (2015), and "Thanks-giving" in *Eunoia Review* (2016).

Michael Konik's "The Porch Watcher" is excerpted from *The Unexpected Guest: How a Homeless Man from the Streets of Los Angeles Redefined Our Home* published by Diversion Books (2020).

Mary Kay Rummel's "A Pandemic Story: Sister Theresa Louise" and "The Spinning Universe: Konya, Turkey" appear in her newly published book, *Nocturnes: Between Flesh and Stone* from Blue Light Press.

Heather Tosteson's "The Air You Breathe" originally appeared in *Germs of Truth* (Wising Up Press, 2013).

Johnny Townsend's "What Would Anne Frank Do?" was previously published in a work of the same name at BookLocker.com (2020).

Andrena Zawinski's "It is Enough for Now, Villanelle for Morning" previously appeared in *California Quarterly* (45: 3).

Photographs by Heather Tosteson.

The Wising Up Writers Collective Editorial Board—Kerry Langan, Michele Markarian, and Murali Kamma—provided invaluable assistance in bringing this anthology to print. We can never thank them enough—we could never do what we do without them.

EDITORS/PUBLISHERS

CHARLES BROCKETT has a PhD from UNC-Chapel Hill and is a recipient of several Fulbright and National Endowment for the Humanities awards. A retired political science professor, he has written two well-received books on Central America and numerous social science journal articles and book chapters. With Heather Tosteson, he is co-founder of Universal Table and Wising Up Press and co-editor of the Wising Up Anthologies. They are also the co-authors of *Sharing the Burden of Repair: Reentry After Mass Incarceration* (2020), the result of a Wising Up listening project on reentry.

HEATHER TOSTESON is the author of seven books of fiction, poetry and non-fiction, including *Germs of Truth* and *The Philosophical Transactions of Maria van Leeuwenhoek, Antoni's Dochter.* She has worked in health communications with a focus on communication across disciplines, racism, social trust, and how belief systems develop and change. She has an MFA (UNC-Greensboro) and PhD in English and Creative Writing (Ohio University).

Visit our website and learn about our other publications,
our readers guides, and calls for submissions.

www.universaltable.org
wisingup@universaltable.org

P.O. Box 2122
Decatur, GA 30031-2122

www.ingramcontent.com/pod-product-compliance
Lightning Source LLC
Chambersburg PA
CBHW030647020726
47493CB00006B/1912

9781732451476